Bodies of Water

SUNY series in Latin American Cinema

Ignacio M. Sánchez Prado and Leslie L. Marsh, editors

Bodies of Water

Queer Aesthetics in
Contemporary Latin American Cinema

GEOFFREY MAGUIRE

Published by State University of New York Press, Albany

© 2024 State University of New York

All rights reserved

Printed in the United States of America

No part of this book may be used or reproduced in any manner whatsoever without written permission. No part of this book may be stored in a retrieval system or transmitted in any form or by any means including electronic, electrostatic, magnetic tape, mechanical, photocopying, recording, or otherwise without the prior permission in writing of the publisher.

Links to third-party websites are provided as a convenience and for informational purposes only. They do not constitute an endorsement or an approval of any of the products, services, or opinions of the organization, companies, or individuals. SUNY Press bears no responsibility for the accuracy, legality, or content of a URL, the external website, or for that of subsequent websites.

For information, contact State University of New York Press, Albany, NY
www.sunypress.edu

Library of Congress Cataloging-in-Publication Data

Name: Maguire, Geoffrey, author.
Title: Bodies of water : queer aesthetics in contemporary Latin American cinema / Geoffrey Maguire.
Description: Albany : State University of New York Press, 2024. | Series: SUNY series in Latin American cinema | Includes bibliographical references and index.
Identifiers: LCCN 2024000483 | ISBN 9781438499178 (hardcover : alk. paper) | ISBN 9781438499192 (ebook) | ISBN 9781438499185 (pbk. : alk. paper)
 Subjects: LCSH: Motion pictures—Latin America—History and criticism. | Bodies of water in motion pictures. | Sexual minorities in motion pictures. | Human body in motion pictures. | Queer theory. | LCGFT: Film criticism.
Classification: LCC PN1995.9.B617 M34 2024 | DDC 791.43/66—dc23/eng/20240411
LC record available at https://lccn.loc.gov/2024000483

For Jens,

who is always Certified Fresh

Theory (and, for that matter, seawater) is at once an abstraction as well as a *thing* in the world.

—Stefan Helmreich

Contents

LIST OF ILLUSTRATIONS ... ix

ACKNOWLEDGMENTS ... xi

INTRODUCTION
Beyond Fluidity ... 1

CHAPTER ONE
The Queer Art of Feeling: Fluid Futurities, *Fin de siglo*,
and New Queer Realism ... 35

CHAPTER TWO
On the Shores of Adulthood: Queer Adolescence and the Fallacy
of Fluidity in Contemporary Brazilian Film ... 59

CHAPTER THREE
The Coast Is Queer: Visibility and the Queer (Trans)National
in *Contracorriente* and *Praia do Futuro* ... 83

CHAPTER FOUR
Slow Waters: Marco Berger's *Taekwondo* and the Queer Erotics
of Boredom ... 109

CHAPTER FIVE
Postporn Flows: *Las hijas del fuego* and the Queer Poetics of
Sexual Pleasure ... 129

Coda
After *XXY*   153

Notes   161

Bibliography   187

Index   197

Illustrations

Figure I.1	Semen dissolving in the water of a swimming pool in *Y tu mamá también*.	10
Figure I.2	The Seine River turned crimson in *120 BPM*.	25
Figure 1.1	Obscured framing during a cruising sequence in a park in *Fin de siglo*.	37
Figure 1.2	Static camerawork during sex scenes in *Fin de siglo*.	42
Figure 1.3	Static camerawork during sex scenes in *Fin de siglo*.	43
Figure 1.4	Museal choreography and the queering of temporalities in *Fin de siglo*.	48
Figure 2.1	Sticky luminescent liquid bonds between bodies in *Tinta Bruta*.	60
Figure 2.2	Reflections of the teenagers through the prism of the beach in *Beira-Mar*.	70
Figure 2.3	Adolescent blemishes in *Beira-Mar*.	72
Figure 2.4	Searching for food scraps against the backdrop of water in *Sócrates*.	75
Figure 2.5	Embodied cinematography and gasping for breath in *Sócrates*.	76
Figure 2.6	Body parts and the elements in *Quebramar*.	78
Figure 2.7	Waves crashing against rocks in *Quebramar*.	80
Figure 3.1	Identity deconstructed in *Contracorriente*.	89

Figure 3.2	Heteronormative bliss and the queer threat in *Contracorriente*.	90
Figure 3.3	Tensions triangulated in *Contracorriente*.	91
Figure 3.4	Body and horizon in *Praia do Futuro*.	98
Figure 3.5	Donato singled out in *Praia do Futuro*.	99
Figure 3.6	Maritime trinkets and tropes in *Praia do Futuro*.	100
Figure 3.7	Maritime imagery on the walls in *Praia do Futuro*.	100
Figure 4.1	Slumbering bodies in *Taekwondo*.	113
Figure 4.2	Entangled, slumbering bodies in *Taekwondo*.	114
Figure 4.3	The voyeuristic gaze of *Taekwondo*.	117
Figure 4.4	Embodied tensions in the swimming pool in *Taekwondo*.	118
Figure 4.5	Haptic cinematography of sweat and skin in the sauna in *Taekwondo*.	120
Figure 4.6	Reflections on spectatorship in *Taekwondo*.	122
Figure 4.7	The "Berger shot" in *Taekwondo*.	124
Figure 5.1	A sexual tableau in *Las hijas del fuego*.	134
Figure 5.2	Neoprene pleasure in a religious setting in *Las hijas del fuego*.	135
Figure 5.3	A queer(ed) Ophelia in *Las hijas del fuego*.	136
Figure 5.4	Sex, sea creatures, and conceptual displacement in *Las hijas del fuego*.	140
Figure 5.5	Bondage in a religious pose in *Las hijas del fuego*.	148
Figure 5.6	Masturbation and the recalibration of hierarchies of spectatorship in *Las hijas del fuego*.	149
Figure C.1	Formal cuts to the body in *XXY*.	157

Acknowledgments

This book has been an immense pleasure to write, granting me the opportunity to pursue a field and a corpus significantly different from my previous research in cultural memory studies. The enjoyment I have felt comes largely as a result of discovering in queer theory a body of work that takes seriously what is often discarded as trivial, anomalous, or peripheral and that provides a way of critically understanding the personal attachments we nurture to the things we read and see. As any student or colleague in Cambridge will know from the spine-worn, sticky-noted copy of *Cruising Utopia* that sits upon my desk, I have found in many of the queer scholars I engage with in this book new ways of theorizing the world and of reflecting on academia's role within it. I am grateful to them, and to the directors included in this book, for their efforts in articulating and visibilizing these fundamentally queer structures of feeling.

It continues to be an enormous privilege to work with the undergraduate and postgraduate students at the University of Cambridge, whose critical insights, intellectual enthusiasm, and political drive prove to be a daily inspiration. The hours of supervision we have spent discussing the knots and urgencies of queer cinema and theory suffuse the pages that follow and the ideas within them. I am particularly thankful to students in IL1, SP13, and on the MPhils in Latin American studies and film and screen studies, whose perspectives on many of the films discussed in this book have regularly challenged my own; and to the PhDs in the Centre of Latin American Studies, whose intellectual ambition continues to be as impressive as it is inspiring.

I am grateful to the fellowships of Murray Edwards College, where this book began during an Early Career Research Fellowship, and of Gonville and Caius College, where the project entered its final stages. Many of the book's intellectual jagged edges and methodological infelicities were smoothed over during lunchtime discussions and coffee breaks, and I am deeply appreciative to work in an institution where so many colleagues show such curiosity for my work and the directions it takes. I am grateful in particular to Becca, Chris, Joe, Lila, Mike, and Victoria, a brigade who have offered their support, their encouragement, and their distraction, often in equal measure.

The broader Cambridge community has been a vibrant source of support in the development of this book. The Centre of Latin American Studies and the Section of Spanish and Portuguese have been intellectual homes for my work and for my teaching, offering me valuable opportunities to merge both through seminars, lectures, and workshops. I am particularly and forever indebted to Joanna Page and Geoffrey Kantaris, for their unswerving support and valued guidance since my arrival in Cambridge ten years ago, and to Brad Epps, for his intellectual engagement with this project and his generosity in funding and supporting the initiatives associated with it. The lgbtQ+@Cam program has played a special role in my time at Cambridge since its inception in 2018, introducing me to people, ideas, and ways of conducting research that have made this book go far beyond what it would have been without such inspiration. Outside Cambridge, the community of Hispanists that I count myself fortunate to be a part of continues to make research as meaningful as it is enjoyable. I am grateful to be able to consider a number of friends—Catherine, Dunja, Emily, Joey, Lucy, Natasha, Niall, Paul, and Rachel—as colleagues, too, and I look forward to many more conference reunions in the years to come.

An earlier version of chapter 1 was published in the *Journal of Cinema and Media Studies* as "The Queer Art of Feeling: Futurity, *Fin de siglo* and New Queer Realism," 63, no. 5 (June 2024). An earlier version of chapter 4 was published in *Screen* as "Slow Waters: Marco Berger's *Taekwondo* and the Queer Erotics of Boredom," 61, no. 2 (Summer 2020, doi: 10.1093/screen/hjaa015), published by the University of Oxford Press. The permission to reprint versions of these publications in *Bodies of Water* is greatly appreciated.

Finally, my thanks go to my family in Northern Ireland and to Jens, who are all ceaselessly generous and steadfast in their support. Just as the epigraph to this book suggests about the nature of seawater, their love is both an abstraction and a *thing* in this world.

Introduction

Beyond Fluidity

> A material element must provide its own substance, its particular rules and poetics.
>
> —Gaston Bachelard, *Water and Dreams*

> —Is the ocean a *queer* place?
>
> —How couldn't she be, with all those cross-currents and such a variety of life forms?
>
> —Elspeth Probyn

Rivers, swimming pools, lakes, beaches, and oceans: these watery spaces recur with remarkable frequency in recent queer world cinema, urging and enticing us to question the intimacies between queerness and the aquatic. Water's mark on the queer cinematic imaginary is due, at least in part, to its intrinsic mutability: currents and tides are as unpredictable as they are uncontrollable, reflecting a natural fluidity in our sexual desires and orientations; bodies of water are at once spaces of recreation and sites of potential danger, often demanding a nakedness that exposes bodies to both the elements and the gaze; and water itself is not simply a substance but also a space, one in which bodies surrender themselves to the force of natural flows, liberated from the terra firma of hegemonic constructions of gender, sexuality, and identity. Bodies of water are, in short, not simply narrative backdrops for contemporary queer cinema but potent formal and aesthetic devices through which queerness can be imag(in)ed, embodied, and *felt*.

Bodies of Water takes seriously the theoretical and political potential of queer cinematic waters; it thinks not only about water but also through it. The myriad formal and aesthetic strategies enabled by watery spaces—that is, the tactile, textural modes of spectatorship triggered by images of water on skin, or the camera's slow, haptic caressing of bodies submerged below the surface—demand a heightened critical sensitivity not only toward bodies *of* water but also toward bodies *in* water. The framework that this book adopts is therefore necessarily attuned to the physical and experiential distinctions in the form and composition of individual aquatic spaces, as well as to their respective sensory effects on the body. I move, in the chapters that follow, from exploring the saltiness of seawater to the chemical artificiality of the swimming pool, and from analyzing the damp, sandy coarseness of the beach to the slippery unknowability of the ocean's underwater creatures. Water's *queerness*—that is, its capacity to disorient the senses, attenuate our awareness of our place in the world, and offer a radically different environmental perspective—triggers, as Melody Jue writes in *Wild Blue Media*, "an epistemological check on human knowledge formation, presenting entirely different conditions for perception, sensation, and life than terrestrial environments."[1] Following Jue, I encourage readers throughout this book to think amphibiously about questions of sexuality, queerness, and cinema. I ask: What might be at stake for queer representation if we pay attention to the "milieux specificities" of distinct bodies of water?[2] What is to be gained, both theoretically and politically, when we divest our critical frameworks of exclusively land-based ontologies and forms of thinking?

In the pages that follow, I propose a comprehensive, overarching queer theorization of cinematic water and its aesthetic and political potentialities. In doing so, I position *Bodies of Water* at the intersections of several fields of academic enquiry: the blue humanities, queer theory, and studies of sexuality and cinematic embodiment.[3] I urge readers to move beyond the prevailing critical focus in cultural studies that has thus far restricted the potential of cinematic waters to their abstract narrative function as symbols of merely the fluidity of sexuality or gender identity. Instead, by moving *beyond* fluidity, I attempt to account for bodies of water as spaces that are historically, politically, socially, and cinematically constructed. By bringing the blue humanities, or the "blue turn," to bear on studies of queer cinema and filmic embodiment in this way, I hope to open up fresh theoretical and epistemological frameworks for grasping how film can engage queerly with a number of pressing political and theoretical concerns: issues, that is, centered on modes of (trans)national belonging, racial and sexual histories of colonialism, cinematic temporalities, and the environmental urgencies of the Anthropocene.

Taken as a whole, the chapters of *Bodies of Water* identify a pivotal moment in the dynamic history of queer world film, and they argue that the recent haptic, watery prominence of the body in contemporary Latin American cinema constitutes a significant formal and thematic evolution in the cultural representation of queerness more globally.[4] The primary corpus of films offers an evocative portrait of the most innovative contemporary queer directors from the region, including established directors such as Albertina Carri, Marco Berger, Karim Aïnouz, Lucía Puenzo, and Javier Fuentes-Léon, whose work has attracted significant international acclaim. I also focus on emerging directors such as Lucio Castro, Alexandre Moratto, and Cris Lyra, whose debut films gesture toward the future directions that queer cinema from Latin America is poised to take. Throughout these chapters, I remain compelled, to quote from Karl Schoonover and Rosalind Galt, by queer cinema's intrinsic capacity "to revise the flows and politics of world cinema and to forge dissident scales of affiliation, affection, affect and form."[5] In order to scrutinize this queer dissidence, I turn strategically to geographical and cultural contexts that have been chronically overlooked in—largely Anglophone—critical discussions of queerness and sexual politics. In doing so, *Bodies of Water* recenters Latin American cinemas within global debates over queer representation, through an interrogation of the radically queer epistemologies that emerge at the convergence of body, camera, and water. Ultimately, by remaining attentive to queer cinema's deterritorialized and often-decolonial ways of thinking about the persistence of hegemonic ontologies of sexuality and gender, the book poses a question that becomes one of both theoretical and sociopolitical concern: What's so *queer* about cinematic waters?

Of Flows and Currents

"Water is never simply water," write Lisa Blackmore and Liliana Gómez in *Liquid Ecologies in Latin American and Caribbean Art*. "Liquidity and flow are not straightforward concepts that merely describe physical phenomena but instead tropes and metaphors loaded with histories and ideologies whose usage is never innocent."[6] Water has indeed long played a privileged role in the cultural imaginary, celebrated both mythically and scientifically as the basis of all life, and, by way of floods, droughts, and torrential rains, also understood to harbor the potential to bring that life to an end, at times on a massive, geological scale. In *Water: A Biography*, Giulio Boccaletti notes that "the stories of deep antiquity reveal a *generative dialectic* between water and society."[7] His analysis moves from ancient Chinese myths that understood "how the world formed from the body of a giant, whose blood and veins turned into water and rivers," to the Lenape and Navajo peoples of North America, who "found in the story of water a powerful source of identity."[8] In Latin America's own story of water, Lúcia Nagib traces a similar generative dialectic, remarking that "the Bible is full of myths about large bodies of water," which have fused with indigenous mythologies to leave "traditions riddled with aquatic prophecies."[9] In their generative dissolving of contrasting myths and symbols, bodies of water have become sites endowed with significant representational potential across eras, cultures, regions, and disciplines. "Water," as Stefan Helmreich pithily observes, "is not one thing."[10]

The immense and dynamic cultural potential of water has led critics such as Gaston Bachelard to argue that "the material imagination of water is a special type of imagination," quite distinct from other elements and natural phenomena. In *Water and Dreams*, Bachelard defines water as "the truly transitory element," due to its "essential, ontological metamorphosis" and physical tendency toward "flux."[11] He endows water with many of the clichés that persist in its current treatment by cultural critics and political actors alike: bodies of water are, for Bachelard, "feminine," even "maternal," endowed with "a type of intimacy" and in need of human protection; they are capable of triggering a "profound reverie," in which "one drop of water suffices to create an [entire] world"; and they lay claim to "one of [the human mind's] highest values—that of purity."[12] In *Bodies of Water*, I take issue with the "complete poetic reality" that is so often ascribed to water, one that relies on a romantic interpretation of water's flows and power, and that remains largely within the realms of symbol and metaphor.[13] Even if we are to understand water as a "hyperobject," for instance, as contemporary environmental thought might compel us to do, the material specificities of bodies of water and their physical taxonomies often remain occluded and beyond our critical grasp.[14] Some of the bodies of water I examine in this book may indeed be "viscous," "nonlocal," and "involve profoundly different temporalities than the human-scale ones we are used to," which Timothy Morton suggests are archetypal features of the hyperobject, yet these cinematic bodies of water resist any such totalizing and abstract theorization through their proximate tangibility and experiential singularities.[15] *Bodies of Water*, in its attunement to what lies beyond these poetic regimes of fluidity, instead wrestles with what Adam O'Brien has referred to in his work on ecological cinema as "the unimaginably important [and] disconcerting complexity of water."[16]

Cinema's fascination with water is as long as the history of film itself. Louis Lumière's forty-six-second film *Boat Leaving the Port* (1895) is a recognizable and momentous part of early film history. In 1898, Affonso Segreto filmed the waters of the Guanabara Bay from the ship *Brésil*, in what is credited by Maite Conde "as the first movie made on Brazilian soil"; and the first Peruvian fiction film was Federico Blume's *Negocio al agua*, a 1913 comedy that has since been lost from the archives.[17] As access to cinema developed in these early decades, it is interesting to note how Ralph Steiner's cinepoem *H2O* and Joris Ivens's documentary short *Regen* (*Rain*), both released in 1929, emerge as milestones in the filmic relationship between water and the camera. In the former, Steiner offers "a meditative, visual ode to water in its many forms, focused on the liquid's various textures and shape-distorting reflective qualities."[18] In the latter, Ivens traces an "impressionistic arc through brief vignettes: rippling canals, seas of umbrellas, rising puddles, dripping windowsills."[19] In both short films, there is a striking visual emphasis on water's ability to refract and reflect, not merely literally in the case of drenched windowpanes and the surfaces of puddles, but also, particularly in Ivens's case, in a sociocultural sense: *Regen* explores the modernity of Amsterdam's new and developing urban space, a "city symphony" film in which, for Béla Balázs, "the wet pavement reflects the life of a city."[20] Measured in the nonhuman temporality of the rain shower, *Regen* is a film endowed with the capacity to reflect the disorienting, anonymizing force of modernity, with rain that "is not one particular rain which fell somewhere, some time" but a visual impression "unbound into unity by any conception of time and space."[21]

Directors remained captivated over the course of the early twentieth century not only with water and its accumulations, as in the examples above, but also with what lay beneath the surface, occasioning films such as Jean Painlevé's engrossing vision of the predatory techniques and life cycle of an octopus, *La Pieuvre* (*The Octopus*, 1928). Such films establish a desired visual and technological mastery over the ocean and its creatures. As Eva S. Hayward notes in relation to Painlevé's later films, *L'Hippocampe* (*The Seahorse*, 1934) and *Les Amours de la pieuvre* (*The Love Life of the Octopus*, 1965), both codirected with Geneviève Hamon, "The underwater camera enabled the presentation of a surreal technoscientific look, allowing wondrous but material visual extensions into the watery domain."[22] Nicole Starosielski, too, charts the development of the relationship between filmic media and the murky depths across the twentieth century. She moves from cinema's early tendency to view the subaquatic as the domain solely of the nonhuman and often-monstruous other, as in *Twenty Thousand Leagues Under the Sea* (1916), to the ocean "exploration" and "exploitation" of the 1950s, '60s, and '70s, in which cinema drew on space-age discourse to depict the ocean "as a place we could colonize with no opposition."[23] Starosielski writes:

> Diving into the ocean, whether via scuba or cinematic technologies, is seen as an escape from the social and cultural processes that characterize everyday life: the constraints of the nation, the progression of history, and racial and territorial conflict. [. . .] While there is significant potential in imagining the subaquatic as a subversive site where new discursive possibilities can be generated, this conceptualization of undersea environments as existing beyond the social, as a domain solely of nonhuman Others, has often masked the racial, cultural and gendered dynamics which have historically unfolded across the ocean.[24]

Starosielski does not dwell on the colonial undercurrents of water's social and political histories, which have been well documented by scholars such as Elizabeth DeLoughrey, who describes the Caribbean Sea in particular as "a living graveyard for the ancestors, a wound, an abyss," littered with "the submarine debris of human history."[25] Starosielski does, however, point to an important aspect of the relationship between the fluidity of water and its resultant aesthetic and formal filmic potential. She gestures toward the necessity to read oceanic images not as elementally separate from the land-based dynamics of history but as thoroughly and irretrievably marked by them.[26] "Clearly," writes Starosielski, "there is much at stake in how we visualize the ocean."[27]

In the case of queer cinema, directors have, in some fashion or another, continually embraced the representational possibilities of water on screen, even from its early stages. Barbara Hammer's "pioneering of the lesbian aesthetic" in the 1970s and '80s relied in several key works on the relationship between water and (the politics of) the woman's body.[28] In her discussion of Hammer's *Pools* (1981) and *Pond and Waterfall* (1982), Kathleen Hulser notes that "her camera eye is like an amphibian that [. . .] establishes a sense of intimacy and connection in a natural ecosystem."[29] She goes on to remark, however, that the body's movement between these two worlds disrupts any such symbiosis: "But this aimable underwaterscape acquires ominous overtones as the amphibian-camera surfaces. Splashes strike the lens, and the rock of the ocean surf is destabilizing and disorienting."[30] In Hammer's work, the connections between the body and water develop, as I suggest in chapter 5 of this book, according to a thoroughly feminist principle: just as with her earlier short film, *Dyketactics* (1974), in which a group of women have sex and swim in a river, Hammer works to correlate the woman's naked body with the naturalness of the environment, investing her films with a sexuality that is both a celebration of natural beauty and a provocation to the (hetero) normative filmic gaze.

The emergent connection between the body, water, and queer cinema is also present in Derek Jarman's *Sebastiane* (1976), in which the homoeroticism of a group of Roman soldiers provocatively plays out upon the shore and in the rock pools of a deserted coastline. Jarman's camerawork at times encourages a haptic relationship to the screen, as images of the men's buttocks and naked torsos are slowed down as they splash in the water, dissolving the distinction between the movement of play fighting and gestures of a more sexual register. Indeed, just as Gustave Flaubert described swimming in the Seine as "a thousand liquid nipples travelling over the body," and as Paul Valéry thought of swimming in the sea as "fornication avec l'onde" (fornication with the waves), Jarman here mobilizes—and *queers*—the long-held intimacy between water, waves, and sex.[31] There is an undeniable nod in Jarman's case toward the visual arts, particularly the maritime nudes of Henry Scott Tuke, exposing, as in the case of Hammer, the valuable semiotic links between the body and water that have been appropriated from the broader cultural imaginary and, in turn, queered via the cinematic apparatus.

The contemporary queer cinema I analyze in *Bodies of Water* retains this generative dialectic between the corporeal and the watery, relying on the rich history of combining queerness and the aquatic that has long endowed water with the dynamic capacity to reflect both emergent and veteran queer desires. While the New Queer Cinema of the 1990s and early 2000s turned to saunas and showers as metaphors for sexual deviance and contagion at the height of the HIV/AIDS epidemic, contemporary cinema is driven by distinct motivations, demonstrating how, over the course of the last half century, water on screen has been remarkably mutable in its ability to refract, through a queer lens, reigning cultural and sociopolitical concerns. We might venture with a degree of confidence that contemporary cinema's "liquidity and flows," to borrow again from Blackwell and Gómez, "are never innocent." By paying attention to the currents and trends of global queer film—in which, for instance, the precarity of labor in the work of Tsai Ming-Liang or the sexual latency in the films of Céline Sciamma exploit water's long-standing relationship to sexuality—*Bodies of Water* both identifies a pivotal moment in the contemporary history of queer world cinema and celebrates the richness of its elaboration and development in the contexts of Latin America. In moving beyond the symbolic regimes of fluidity, the chapters of this study account for water's formal, material, and sociopolitical complexities, examining how its cinematic ebbs and flows expose radical ways of visualizing the queer body and screening its genders, sexualities, and politics.

Bodies *of* Water

"Water's diversity," writes Veronica Strang, "is key to its meanings."[32] Owing to the multiplicity of its possible shapes and scales—materialized as ice, rain, steam, or stream, droplet, ocean, trickle, or flood—Strang argues that attention to water's "formal qualities and characteristics" becomes a crucial "basis for construction of meaning."[33] Following Strang's invitation to attend critically to "the form of water" and to "how humans experience these fluid qualities," I pay sustained attention in this book not only to the frequency of the contemporary cinematic waterscape but also to the dynamism of its matter and meanings.[34] Cinematic beaches, for instance, serve frequently as spaces in which the ebbs, flows, and rhythms of the tides symbolize a broader destabilization in the boundaries that police identity and belonging, while the chlorinated, contained water of swimming pools functions as a space of control that demands maximum corporeal visibility. Throughout its five chapters, *Bodies of Water* tackles a number of watery spaces—seas, oceans, beaches, swimming pools, and lakes—and pays extended attention to their composition, both physical and cinematic. In this section, I offer a preliminary taxonomy of their specificities and filmic histories, before moving on in the following section to engage theoretically with the notion of bodies *in* water; that is, how cinema captures the intimacy between water and skin, apprehending in formal and aesthetic terms the embodied experience of swimming, submerging, floating, drying, and diving.

PLEASE SHOWER BEFORE ENTERING THE POOL

Swimming pools are replete in contemporary world cinema: for Céline Sciamma, they are inherently "very cinematographic" sites; for Christopher Brown and Pam Hirsch, they are "dynamic and exciting cinematic spaces"; and for Peter Bradshaw they offer "an instant spectacle."[35] The filmic pool has a well-developed history as a site of sexual and psychological intrigue, such as in Jacques Deray's Hockney-inspired *La Piscine* (*The Swimming Pool*, 1969), François Ozon's *The Swimming Pool* (2003), and Luca Guadadigno's recent loose refashioning of Deray's film, *A Bigger Splash* (2015). Contemporary queer cinema, for its part, has both engaged with and extended the filmic potential of the swimming pool. In the work of Lucrecia Martel, from *La ciénaga* (*The Swamp*, 2001) to *La mujer sin cabeza* (*The Headless Woman*, 2008), backyard pools are emblems of economic privilege (or the decaying thereof), steeped in themes of adolescent sexuality and middle-class ennui, all the while focalizing the socioracial relations between bourgeois characters and their domestic staff. In *Naissance des pieuvres* (*Water Lilies,* 2007), Sciamma turns to the public swimming pool as a site of adolescent sexual discovery, both of others and of the self. And in his work, Marco Berger relentlessly exploits the space of the pool and its environs for their homoerotic potential, triggering, in the case of the secondary-school pool in *Ausente* (*Absent*, 2011), "a layer of spectatorship that is both haptically active and ethically problematic."[36]

In their status as either public or private, swimming pools exist on a spectrum of signification, from spaces of discipline, competition, and athleticism, to environments of recreation, relaxation, and at times, boredom. Private pools are, in particular, capable of visualizing economic privilege as much as financial ruin, through their presentation as either pristinely curated or stagnating, covered with dead insects and rotting foliage. "Empty pools," as Jack Halberstam writes in *The Queer Art of Failure*, "stand like ruins, abandoned and littered with leaves and other signs of disuse, and in this ruined state they represent a perversion of desire, the decay of the commodity, the queerness of disassociation of use from value."[37] Public swimming pools, too, are spaces of stratification, not only on the basis of economic wealth but of bodily ability, delineating physical capacity through speed lanes and allocated timeslots.[38] In many ways, the swimming pool of *Y tu mamá también* (2001) crystallizes the space's cinematic potency. Alfonso Cuarón presents a pool that straddles the public/private divide, a country-club perk that is accessible to the two protagonists only when closed to paying clientele. This necessarily out-of-hours setting provides the opportunity for the young men to swim naked and, in one scene, masturbate together on diving boards, ejaculating directly into the water. The submerged shot of the semen blending with the water explicitly foregrounds the relationship between fluidity and sexuality (figure I.1), just as the later image of the men swimming in a pool covered with leaves suggests the "covering up" of any potentially homoerotic sentiment. In this instance, the swimming pool is ultimately a space where contamination, either through bodily fluids or bodily desires, exposes the volatility of the divisions between the homosocial and the homosexual.

In physical terms, with its rigid edges, often-rectangular shape, and demarcated lanes, the swimming pool is a space, as Henning Eichberg notes, "dominated by the straight line; it is panoptical."[39] Along with the

Figure I.1. Film still. Semen dissolving in the water of a swimming pool in *Y tu mamá también*. *Source*: Dir. Alfonso Cuarón. Anhelo Producciones, Bésame Mucho Pictures (2001).

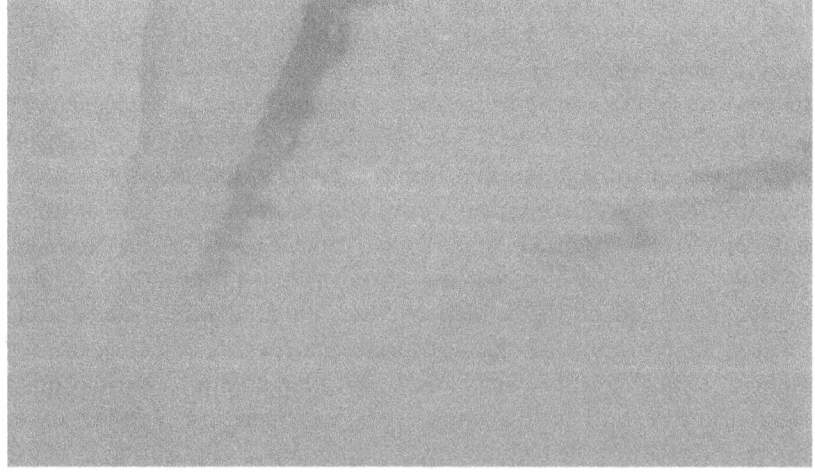

requirement that bodies be exposed, often in swimsuits that "show more than they hide," it is perhaps no surprise, then, that the filmic swimming pool is a common site for narrative and thematic queering.[40] Pools are, after all, often to an emphatic degree, environments of control: temperatures are regulated, pH levels are chemically maintained, and behavior is closely surveyed by lifeguards, all of which render the space an enticing cinematic location for deviance. Aluisio Abranche's *Do Começo ao Fim* (*From Beginning to End*, 2009) pushes this notion to its limits, depicting how the shared bathwater of childhood and the athleticism of swimming pools during adolescence lead to an incestuous relationship between two half-brothers. As professional swimmers, the men's relationship with one another is refracted through the space of the water. Against the rigidly controlled space of the pool, where their behavior and bodies are on display not only to each other but also to spectators (and, by extension, viewers), their private sexual relationship is figured as an overspilling of acceptable social boundaries, intimating the danger of desires taken too far.

As Miranda Ward notes, however, the atmosphere of control within the space of the swimming pool is more often an ideal than an actuality:

> Pool water, chemically purified, kept contained, seems on the surface to be untouched by what's outside—but indoor pools are places where "outside" forces are both carefully controlled and always-present, evident in the cracks; the outside spills in (mud tracked on changing room floors, mould in the tile grouting, plasters and hair ties stuck to the bottom of the pool). In this way, the composition of the pool is always different, always changing, always largely dependent on past and current inhabitants and liable to change, too, based on future inhabitants.[41]

Contamination is a significant and ever-present threat within the filmic swimming pool, as well as in its contingent spaces of the showers, the toilets, and the locker room. Crucially, the hazard of contamination is not simply physical, in the ways suggested by Ward, but also affective and sexual, via the "panoptical" potential described by Eichberg. As "an iconic site of sexual transgression" in a range of audio-visual media, from teen comedies to gay pornography, the changing room provides a space "in which same-sex nudity is considered legitimate" and, hence, where a scopic, sexually charged gaze is ever-imminent.[42] If, as Fernando Gabriel Pagnoni Berns points out, in professional sports settings "it is considered 'natural' for male spectators to watch male bodies sheathed in tiny swimsuits," the space of the locker room, however, promotes a sense of looking that can only ever be voyeuristic in nature.[43] Enhanced by its function and history as a site of gay male cruising, where the reception of a glance can spell the difference between violent rejection and sexual engagement, the locker room (as with the public bathroom) in contemporary queer cinema has a reigning optical paradigm of ambivalence and risk. "Furtiveness," writes Pagnoni Berns, "is a component of the queer gaze," an aspect demonstrated amply by the work of Marco Berger, in which queerness is always at risk of being exposed as a contaminant, of rupturing the homosocial through the voyeurism of the diegetic—and, by extension, the spectatorial—gaze.[44] More than merely spaces of fluidity, then, cinematic swimming pools and their environs are sites of risk and control (or the lack thereof), both literal and symbolic, as well as spaces that visibilize and stratify social relations on the economic, physical, and sexual planes.

ON THE WAVES THERE IS NOTHING BUT WAVES

As bodies of water, seas and oceans distinguish themselves from the artificial spaces of swimming pools, figured instead as "limitless, unfathomably deep, infinite," and comprised of waters that appear as "dark matter, borderless, and seemingly depthless."[45] For Roland Barthes, as for many others, the ocean is a space that resists interpretation: "In a single day, how many really non-signifying fields do we cross? Very few, sometimes none. Here I am, before the sea; it is true that it bears no message."[46] The cinematic ocean has, conversely, long been a source of considerable cultural potency, as much an emblem of intrepid exploration and extreme human endeavor as a poetic symbol of love, lust, and futurity. Though, as Hester Blum reminds us in her now-famous aphorism, "The sea is *not* a metaphor," and we must work to cut through the "ocean's abyss of representation."[47] Blum contends in her article that "the ready availability—and undeniable utility—of fluidity as an oceanic figure means that the actual sea has often been rendered immaterial," and she argues for "a practice of oceanic studies that is attentive to the material conditions and praxis of the maritime world."[48]

The recent documentary by Patricio Guzmán, *El botón de nácar* (*The Pearl Button*, 2015), exploits the poetic heritage of the ocean as a means of probing Chilean history, from indigenous worldviews, through the Spanish colonial project, to the tactics of political disappearance under the Pinochet dictatorship. The film is, as Alison Ribeiro de Menezes notes, a striking exploration of history through "the material entanglements of the human with the natural—geological and maritime, rocky and watery," which treats "the material world, whether in the form of rock, sand, or water, not just [as] a metaphor to convey the human story but a central—if often unacknowledged—force shaping that very story."[49] Similarly, Irene Depetris Chauvin observes in her work on oceanic imaginaries in artistic works from the Southern Cone that "[t]he uniqueness of the material is not simply poetic play or elemental physics: water is more than two atoms of hydrogen and one of oxygen, or three-quarters of the human body; it is a historical territory, a resource and a signifier in dispute."[50]

In *An Oceanic Feeling: Cinema and the Sea*, Erika Balsom offers a compelling history of the ocean on screen. She proposes a taxonomy of seas that have appeared in filmic media and charts their development and impact on cinema's oceanic imaginary: from the ocean of adventure to the rising sea levels of climate apocalypse, and from the sea of colonial exploration to the transnational ocean of globalized labor, among several others. Balsom's work is attuned to "how the deeply mythologised site of the ocean activates forms of relationality that prompt one to think beyond the individual, beyond a singular territory, and beyond the binary between nature and culture."[51] Read sociopolitically, the ocean is, for Balsom, "an archive of horror, wreckage, survival, and beauty, within which histories of capitalist accumulation and still-reverberating traumas flow alongside the captivating wonders of marine environments and *the romance of the waves*."[52]

Balsom gestures here toward the global histories of colonization that are often occluded by this untiring romance of the waves, an aspect that Steve Mentz counteracts in *Ocean* with the concept of "wet globalisation."[53] Mentz coins the term to refer to the early modern period of European colonization and argues that it "avoids canonizing individuals" (such as Christopher Columbus) in order instead to emphasize how it was "sea travel that connected humans, nations, empires, and religions—not to mention plants, animals, viruses, and ecosystems."[54] He notes, as does Balsom, the crucial importance of the slave ships of the Middle Passage in understanding the cultural history of the ocean, drawing on Édouard Glissant's assertion in *Poetics of Relation* that "the entire ocean, the entire sea gently collapsing in the end into the pleasures of sand, make one vast beginning, but a beginning whose time is marked by these balls and chains gone green."[55] While none of the queer films in the corpus of this book references, either explicitly or implicitly, these histories of slavery and the "womb abyss" that Glissant so insightfully traces, it has nevertheless been central, particularly in Caribbean cultural texts, to an understanding of the oceans and of their histories and entanglements.[56]

The epistemological capacity of the ocean to collapse the linearity of human-centered histories is, at least in part, due to the largely unknown, and perhaps unknowable, dynamics of underwater life. While the surface of the ocean is now thoroughly mapped, "the ocean's verticality," as Mentz puts it, "plunges down into hidden ways of thinking."[57] For Balsom, too, "radical alterity is to be found within the aquatic world, just as we find it within ourselves, in the unconscious."[58] Nowhere is such alterity clearer than in the sea's creatures, which are posited within cinema and other cultural media as thoroughly other. They are alien organisms that either pose an immediate threat to human life or fall stubbornly outside the realms of human cognition, from shark-infested seas and contaminated water reserves to the amorphous plasticity of the jellyfish and the octopus. Astrida Neimanis notes, in particular, the sea creature's queer relationship to land-based ontologies of sexuality and gender, writing:

> Oysters? Eva Hayward points out that they change sex up to four times per year. Sea squirts? Similarly queer. [. . .] Starfish exhibit a trans-speciation whereby we can understand regeneration as a kind of transsex. In other words, all of these animals are fascinatingly and "naturally" queer. [. . .] Most marine invertebrates are hermaphroditic, as are a large proportion of coral reef fish, including most species of wrasses, parrot fish, and large groupers, and some species of damselfish, angelfish, gobies, porgies, emperors, soapfishes, dottybacks, moray eels, and various deep-sea fish as well. Many of these fish oscillate between male and female, or they may be male and female simultaneously. [. . .] We can find such examples among terrestrial species too, but genderqueer lives are particularly abundant in the water.[59]

The sea's creatures, as well as its cultural and cinematic constructions as a space of danger, possibility, and mystery, in these ways lend well to filmic examinations of queerness. Against the demarcated regularity of the swimming pool, the ocean provides a discursively queer space that, in its vastness and in its alterity, defies human-centric ontologies of history, sex, and gender. Conceptually, these oceanic depths and their life forms decenter human subjectivities, while their formal presentation on the cinema screen emphasizes filmic embodiment and alternatively experiential modes of (aquatic) being.

No Nonswimmers beyond This Point

While Barthes deems the ocean to lie beyond representation, he is reluctant to restrict its shoreline to any comparable defiance of meaning: "But on the beach, what material for semiology! Flags, slogans, signals, signboards, clothes, suntan even, which are so many messages to me."[60] Along with its assault on the senses via the sensations of heat and sand on the skin, and through the sounds of birds and waves, the beach is critically understood as an interstitial space, "a place where dry land and the sea wrestle for control."[61] For Brady Hammond, this is an elemental struggle in which "the land is constantly inundated by the ebbing and flowing of the sea, creating a space that is neither land nor sea, but is caught between the two and the conceptual frameworks they represent."[62] Henri Lefevbre, too, gestures toward the epistemological potential of the "counter-space" of the beach in *The Production of Space*. While beaches "appear on first inspection to have escaped the control of the established order," he posits that any such freedom is "a complete illusion."[63] He continues: "Once a conquest of the working class, in the shape of paid days' off, holidays, weekends, and so on, leisure has been transformed into an industry, into a victory of neocapitalism and an extension of bourgeois hegemony to the whole of space. [. . .] [The beach] further reveals where the vulnerable areas and potential breaking-points are: everyday life, the urban sphere, the body, and the differences that emerge within the body."[64] Lefebvre's emphasis on the corporeal in this passage is striking, for despite his admission that the body may experience "total passivity on the beach, mere contemplation of the spectacle of sea and sun," he nevertheless emphasizes the beachscape as one "arranged at once functionally and hierarchically," both in its relationship to the body and to society.[65]

Similarly, for Jean-Didier Urbain, the beach "is a spectacular space, [. . .] a theatre in which society unveils itself, lays itself bare (both literally and metaphorically)."[66]

It is frequently the populated beach of seaside recreation that commands the attention of critics such as Lefebvre and Urbain, yet contemporary queer cinema has more often turned to the secluded beach, a space exempt from the gaze of society that offers a level of privacy unattainable elsewhere "in public." The narrative triggers of Barry Jenkin's *Moonlight* (2016) and Eliza Hittman's *Beach Rats* (2017), for instance, both transpire on the sands of a deserted beach: a moment of sexual adolescent experimentation in the former and the violence of a murder in the latter. The tension of Alain Guiraudie's *L'Inconnu du lac* (*Stranger by the Lake*, 2013) is anchored, too, in the space of the shore, not as the specific location of a murder (which takes place in the water) but as the site of witnessing said act of violence: in this instance, the risks of gay male cruising are merged into the existential threat of retaliation and death. Similarly, the beachscape of Lucía Puenzo's *XXY* (2007), discussed in more depth in the final section of this book, also understands the beach simultaneously as a site of escape and as a space of danger, one in which the gazes of characters and the spectator are exposed as (violently) intrusive when directed toward a body reluctant to be on display.

In a similar fashion to swimming pools, then, the beach encourages a sense of corporeal vulnerability, with (semi)naked bodies susceptible both to the elements and to the gaze. As Fiona Handyside remarks, it is a space "where corporeality and sensations of the body come to the fore"; and, for Jennifer Webb, it is a space the beachgoer leaves with a sense of the "pleasure in the freedom of the sea [as well as] the memory of its assault on [their] body, with every visit leaving [them] sunburnt, sandpapered, thirsty, headachy, grumpy, if still elated, and with a body reminding [them] across every centimetre of its need."[67] Far from sites of simply physical inbetweeness or social interstitiality, the cinematic beach is a space with its proper rules and regulations, encompassing a specific sense of exposure and risk through its own particular effects on the (cinematic) body.

Bodies of Water is not an exhaustive survey of the forms of watery and water-adjacent spaces that populate contemporary queer cinema, and there are other categories of bodies of water that are not given consideration within its pages. Estuaries and deltas, for instance, appear in several recent films, as spaces that complicate—in a less predictable and systematic fashion than the regularity of the tides on the beach—the divisions between land and water. They are spaces, after all, that are more susceptible in an existential sense to issues of climate change and ecological pollution. Papu Curotto's *Esteros* (2015) weaves its exploration of queer sexuality with environmental concerns in Argentina's agricultural north; the estuary in the film is, for Curotto, "sumamente determinante" (a significant factor), encoding the landscape with "esa cosa de latencia" (a degree of latency) that correlates its geophysical unpredictability with the sexual relationship between the two male protagonists.[68] Alongside a cinematography that affords a sense of protagonism to the natural environment, one of the men's jobs as an environmental biologist, working on transgenic crops for a local agricultural company, functions, according to Ben Bollig, to "ask the spectator to consider the *political* aspects of the landscape."[69] In their own fashion, estuaries, deltas, and swamps "all complicate the land-sea divide and thereby lead us to question assumed understandings wherein landmasses are the spaces of society and oceans are simply zones of exchange."[70] What they ultimately have in common with the bodies of water discussed in this book, however, is their cinematic capacity to emphasize corporeality—bodies, that is, that are free to swim among seaweed, fish, and flotsam, to enjoy the pristine waters of a private beach or swimming pool, or to find rest in water's vicinity and pleasure in its surroundings.

Bodies *in* Water

> A deep-sea fish has no means of apprehending the existence of water; it is too uniformly immersed in it.
>
> —Oliver Lodge, *Ether and Space*

Unlike the deep-sea fish, both submerged and oblivious, the human body does not *belong* in water. As Melody Jue writes in *Wild Blue Media*, "The practice of learning to dive has directed my attention to how our instinctive postures, embodied habits, and muscle memory are all adapted to the gravitational conditions of walking on land and breathing air."[71] Similarly, for Erika Balsom, "To leave *terra firma* and delve into the liquid flux of oceanic feeling is to undertake a radical reorientation of perspective."[72] Here, I understand Balsom's use of the term "perspective" to imply not simply an object and a spectator but, more crucially, a *way* of looking; as a concept, it raises questions about the forms and hierarchies of spectatorship as much as it opens up the politics of the gaze to a radical refashioning of epistemology. Indeed, it is precisely this reorientation of perspective that takes critical precedence in the chapters of *Bodies of Water*, which each think through water's uncanny liquid dynamics: how it disorients the senses, dampening sounds and refracting our vision, and how it feels on skin and limbs, as bodies immerse themselves in environments that, despite any human cartographic impulse, do not belong to us. These chapters interrogate cinema's capacity to screen acts of sensation and perception, questioning what a submerged vantage point may reveal about our "terrestrial habits" and about our intrinsically land-based paradigms of sexuality and gender.[73] How do bodies *in* water sense water's mystery and materiality? What do slipperiness, saltiness, breathlessness, and weightlessness look—and *feel*—like in the cinema?

Water's wetness has persistently been an inherently phenomenological challenge for cinema: its flows and textures have always had to reckon with the impasse of the filmic screen. For Adam O'Brien, in his essay on ecological complexity in cinema, "It is worth remarking at the very outset that water is, in every instance of creative evocation, description and visualisation, very difficult to deal with."[74] In the particular context of artistic creation, he writes: "When it comes to water and creative representation, formal and cognitive difficulties arise at the point of a work's conception and continue through to (and beyond) execution. And this is nowhere truer than in cinema, which in many ways can be thought of as a medium particularly ill-equipped to 'deal with' water."[75] While painting, sculpture, and, we might add, the performing arts can "literally include water within their own being," O'Brien posits that cinema, on the other hand, "proceeds in a manner which seems in many ways to work *against* water."[76] Quite apart from its optical deflections and refractions, the formal and cognitive difficulties that O'Brien associates with water lie as much with the technical complications of filming the subaquatic as they do with the figurative abstraction of bodies of water discussed earlier in this introduction. We might also speculate, however, that they arise from water's relentless sensory richness. The physical properties of the element—not least how movement and depth impact its transparency and translucency, and how it feels simultaneously present and absent on the skin when bodies are submerged—would seem in many ways to be counterintuitive to filmic representation. In other words, the synesthesia of being *in* and *around* watery spaces appears, at least in one sense, to fall beyond cinema's grasp.

For Ian Gordon and Simon Inglis, "Swimming pools are supremely tactile locations," transforming them into sites that are as much physical as they are experiential:

> We touch, we grab, we brush against a range of surfaces with our bare feet and hands. We hear sounds, muffled and echoing, soft and hard. We detect odours, natural and man-made. The quality of the light changes at each turn. Space and water, intimacy and anonymity we share with complete strangers; at once both part of a communal experience, yet locked within our own private worlds. [E]ach and every one of our senses is so powerfully assailed—whether we swim with vigour or simply splash for fun.[77]

These feelings of sensation, bodily exposure, and sociality are crucial aspects of how we might experience any of the watery spaces analyzed in this book, notwithstanding the particular sensory impressions of chlorine, currents, sand, or salt. For Veronica Strang, "One of the most compelling sensory experiences of water is that of immersion," and for Webb, it is at the beach, "where we are so obviously embodied, that we can experience *the relation of presence in the world,* of belonging to and *being possessed by the world*."[78] For Webb, immersion in water, however partial, triggers an intensely palpable mode of embodiment: "Even the weakest swimmer, when in the sea, experiences the sensation of being simultaneously dunked and supported by the water; but also the sensation of being enveloped by the water, and enveloping it."[79] Swimming pools, seas, and beaches all function as spaces that necessitate a heightened attunement both to our surroundings and to our body's place *within* them and experience *of* them. We are reduced—and I use this term deliberately, given how it betrays an inevitably terrestrial bias—to comprehending our bodies through immediately tactile, sensory, and embodied modes of perception.

In cinematic waters, then, we find ourselves adrift from conventional forms of spectatorship and ways of seeing, distanced from what Laura U. Marks and Vivian Sobchack respectively call the scopic regimes of "visual mastery" and vision's "overarching mastery and comprehension of its objects."[80] This brings me to one of the central theoretical arguments of the book. While O'Brien and others suggest a perceptual difficulty for cinema in apprehending water's complexity, I contend instead that filmic representation is poised, through a range of formal and aesthetic techniques, to represent the synesthesia of water in acutely creative and effective ways. Cinema's relationship to water is not one calibrated by sensory restriction or technical deficiency; it is, instead, one of significant formal and aesthetic potential. In *Carnal Thoughts*, Sobchack works from an understanding of cinematic spectatorship as *always-already* embodied: "Even at the movies, our vision and hearing are informed and given meaning by our other modes of sensory access to the world: our capacity not only to see and to hear but also to touch, to smell, to taste, and always proprioceptively to feel our weight, dimension, gravity, and movement in the world. In sum, the film experience is meaningful not to the side of our bodies *but because of our bodies*."[81] While "our received knowledge" about film prioritizes the faculties of sight and hearing, Sobchack argues that, while *literal* touch, taste, or smell are impossible, "if I am engaged by what I see, my intentionality streams towards the world on-screen, marking itself not merely in my conscious attention but always also in my bodily tension: the sometimes flagrant, sometimes subtle, but always dynamic investment, inclination, and arrangement of my material being."[82] Following Sobchack, then, I understand cinematic bodies of water—and, especially, bodies *in* water—not to pose intrinsic problems of aesthetic representation for cinema. On the contrary, these bodies often suggestively and intensively exploit water's proclivity for embodiment in ways that enhance the *always-already* embodied nature of filmic spectatorship itself.

In the chapters that follow, I engage with a number of significant theories of cinematic embodiment and, more precisely, queer phenomenology. These are approaches concerned primarily with accounting for how, in Jennifer Barker's terms, "embodied patterns and structures allow for a sensually formed (and informed) understanding of the ways that meaning and significance emerge in and are articulated through the fleshy, muscular, and visceral engagement that occurs between films' and viewers' bodies."[83] In *The Tactile Eye*, Barker builds on what Paul Stoller terms "sensuous scholarship" to offer an understanding of how cinematic "'touch' comes to mean not simply contact, but rather a profound manner of being, a mode through which the body—human or cinematic—presents and expresses itself to the world and through which it perceives that same world as *sensible*."[84] The ensuing relationship between the body of the film and the body of the spectator is, therefore, one in which "tactility contains the possibility for an infinite variety of particular themes or patterns: caressing, striking, startling, pummelling, grasping, embracing, pushing, pulling, palpation, immersion, and inspiration."[85] We might also, for the purposes of the present study, add the following to Barker's indicative, inexhaustive list: splashing, swimming, shivering, burning, diving, drowning, gasping, floating, and holding one's breath. In *Bodies of Water*, I understand cinematic touch not as merely a figurative connection between viewer and image, curtailed by the physical reality of the filmic screen, but as a *sensible* relationship of "intimacy and reciprocity" between bodies, be they of characters, of spectators, or of water.

I return at various stages throughout this book to Marks's theorization of "the ways cinema can appeal to senses that it cannot technically represent."[86] In *The Skin of the Film*, Marks identifies a range of specific filmic techniques—including, but not limited to, the close-up, the graininess of an image, depth of focus, and changes in distance—that function "by bringing vision close to the body and into contact with other sense perceptions; by making vision multisensory."[87] This notion of *haptic visuality*, as Marks terms it, contrasts with the conventional regimes of optical visuality in cinema, in which a spectator's "mastery" over the image aligns "visual information with knowledge and control."[88] Significantly, Marks describes the dynamics of haptic visuality "as a kind of visuality that is not organized around identification, [but] one that is labile, able to move between identification and *immersion*."[89] It is this immersive aspect of embodied spectatorship that I explore throughout this book, examining the "tactile epistemology" it promotes, through which spectators are encouraged to "think with [their] skin, giving as much significance to the physical presence of an other as to the mental operations of symbolization."[90] Water, in all its textural and tactile richness, augments and exacerbates this spectatorial immersion, heightening our attunement to senses other than sight and triggering "an acute awareness that the thing seen evades vision and must be approached through the other senses."[91]

While Marks is interested in how intercultural cinema communicates an embodied sense of memory, particularly the memory of minoritized diasporic communities, my interests in *Bodies of Water* are instead focused on queerness and all that such a term entails: a mode of *being* in the world, as well as a means of *resisting* the world. As Katherina Lindner remarks in *Film Bodies*, this is an aspect that has been conspicuously absent from theoretical debates surrounding embodiment and the haptic: "There appears to be a strange disjunction between the intense focus on the specific materiality of the body (skin, musculature, viscera, synapses) and a seeming disregard for how this materiality is lived."[92] She continues: "We might say that the 'neutral' body that appears in this work is a kind of reincarnation of the Merleau-Pontyan lived-body that has been identified by queer and feminist critics as being underpinned by very specific heteronormative, white, Western, able-bodied modes of embodiment. It tends to be based on assumptions of a very particular *kind* of lived experience that is so normative and 'habitual' as to be invisible and unfelt."[93] *Bodies of Water* foregrounds the material realities to which queer bodies are subject in recent Latin American film, focusing specifically on how cinema communicates their embodied experiences of gender, sexuality, race, and socioeconomic circumstance. For her part, Marks contends that haptic cinema "does not invite identification with a figure [. . .] so much as it encourages a bodily relationship between viewer and image."[94] Consequently, she argues, "it is not proper to speak of the *object* of a haptic look as to speak of a dynamic subjectivity between looker and image."[95] This is the immersive, corporeally calibrated relationship that takes priority in *Bodies of Water* and in its analyses of contemporary Latin American film. What does "queering" this relationship imply for cinematic spectatorship? What do haptic, tactile, textural images of naked limbs and water *mean* for the filmic spectator, whose gender, race, sexual orientation, and bodily ability may be calibrated along distinct axes from those bodies on screen? What does *immersive* spectatorship feel like, and what can it do, both aesthetically and politically?

To respond to these questions, I draw theories of embodiment into dialogue with the work of various queer theorists, including Elizabeth Freeman, Jack Halberstam, and Sara Ahmed. Attentive readers will note that one queer thinker in particular, José Esteban Muñoz, looms large throughout each of the chapters of this book, often explicitly but always implicitly. This is an intentional move, for reasons that are as political as they are intellectual. In *Cruising Utopia*, Muñoz offers a critical understanding of queerness that works against the antirelational and antisocial theses of Leo Bersani and Lee Edelman, who both, in their own ways, embrace a form of "radical presentism" as political strategy and reject the future-oriented optimism they diagnose in contemporary queer politics and culture. Under the banner of "No Future!" Edelman counteracts the "fatal embrace of a futurism" through a radical—and now well-known—rejection of society's "reproductive futurism."[96] He writes: "Fuck the social order and the Child in whose name we're collectively terrorized; [. . .] fuck the whole network of Symbolic relations and the future that serves as its prop."⁹⁷ In direct contrast, for Muñoz, "the future *is* queerness's domain."⁹⁸ "Queerness," he argues, "is a longing that propels us onward, beyond *romances of the negative* and toiling in the present"; it is "that thing that lets us feel that this world is not enough, that indeed something is missing."⁹⁹ *Bodies of Water* responds to Muñoz's invocation to counteract these romances of the negative—just as it attempts to shatter the "romance of the waves"—demonstrating a sensitivity to the critical optimism of queer representation that suffuses contemporary Latin American film.¹⁰⁰ It does so in a way that does not naively overlook the oppressive political and social realities faced by queer communities, but instead it embraces the pressing political need to "combat the force of political pessimism" through a framework of "hope, which is both a critical affect and a methodology."¹⁰¹

Significantly for the argument of this book and the critically optimistic nature of its analysis, Muñoz invests heavily in the notion of a queer aesthetic. He writes:

> Often we can glimpse the worlds proposed and promised by queerness in the realm of the aesthetic. The aesthetic, especially the queer aesthetic, frequently contains blueprints and schemata of a forward-dawning futurity. [. . .] Turning to the aesthetic in the case of queerness is nothing like an escape from the social realm, insofar as queer aesthetics map future social relations. Queerness is also a performative because it is not simply a being but a doing for and toward the future. Queerness is essentially about the rejection of a here and now and an insistence on potentiality or concrete possibility for another world.¹⁰²

It is for this reason that I have resisted the initial urge to use the term "queer Latin American cinema" in the subtitle of this book, despite its intellectual and practical currency. Instead, by opting for "queer aesthetics," I attempt to open up the notion of queerness in this corpus as "a doing for and toward the future," rather than "simply a being." In a manner that resonates with the thematic and theoretical concerns of *Bodies of Water*, Muñoz endows the queer aesthetic with a critical and political optimism that I see pervading contemporary queer narratives on screen: "What we need to know is that queerness is not yet here but it approaches like *a crashing wave of potentiality*. [. . .] Willingly we let ourselves feel queerness's pull, knowing it as something else that we can feel, that we must feel."[103]

Bodies of Water is, in these ways, indebted to Muñoz's theorization of queerness and the significance he places on both the queer aesthetic and its crashing wave of potentiality. In the chapters that follow, I take up his challenge that in order "to see queer visuality we may need to squint, or to strain our vision and force it to see *otherwise*, beyond the limited vista of the here and now."[104] If watery spaces, through their formal and aesthetic qualities on screen, emphasize the always-already embodied nature of filmic spectatorship, then they also point to the queer potential in disrupting that perspective and of "feeling queerness's pull" through the formal presentation of water's cross-currents and tides. Bodies *in* water, I argue, confront us with the possibilities inherent in straining our vision and forcing ourselves to see beyond the normative constraints of the present. In drawing the notion of queer optimism into contact—or, we might say, touch—with theories of filmic embodiment, it is ultimately this reorientation of perspective that I hope will trigger a queering of cinematic seeing and sensing that encourages us to transcend static regimes of gender and sexuality in order to see and feel *otherwise*.

Contemporary Queer Aesthetics

The panoramic shots of the blood-red River Seine in Robin Campillo's *120 BPM* (2017) are as poignant as they are unsettling (figure I.2). Against a soundtrack that layers flowing water over the heavy breathing of a young man on his death bed, the sight of the iconic river turned uncannily crimson draws to mind both those who lost their lives during the AIDS epidemic and the political activism of ACT UP at a time of governmental inaction and rampant societal misinformation. The oneiric quality of the sequence, which intersperses wide shots of the cityscape's bridges with close-ups of blood-red water lapping against the river's edges, realizes cinematically one of the group's unfulfilled ambitions. As Campillo himself suggests, having been an active member of the group in the late 1980s, "We had two big projects at ACT UP: one was to put a condom on the Obelisk, which we did, and the other was to colour the river, but that proved impossible."[105] Almost forty years after its first conception as an idea, the realization *on screen* of the plan to dye the Seine red underlines the power of the cinematic in the creative (re)envisioning of queer politics and identities. If the flow of the river can be read ambivalently as symbolizing the unstoppable force of both virus and activism, it also connotes in its redness the fear of contamination, infection, and death, all of which wind their way artery-like through the cinematic topography of the city itself.

We might read Campillo's strategy in this scene as revealing something of a paradox at play in the film's thematics and aesthetics more broadly: while *120 BPM* is often unrelenting in its treatment of death and suffering, lingering visually on bodily lesions and dying (or dead) bodies, there is however a sense of collective joy that flourishes in spite of such unflinching realism (and, at times, precisely because of it). The film's politics are ever present, yet the narrative focuses on the intimate relationships between the characters through a lens that dedramatizes both love and suffering. Bereavement and pain are treated with the same frankness as cleaning up semen after an act of masturbation on a hospital bed, imbuing such scenes with a mundane sense of (comic) relief.[106] While *120 BPM* might be understood to flirt with the provocative and politically charged cinematic tendencies of New Queer Cinema, it is decidedly contemporary: its formal and aesthetic qualities do not match the militancy of its characters, yet, crucially, its blood-red river is no less politically critical or emotionally affecting as a result. There is a defiance in the film, to be sure, not least through the incisive critiques of both the government and multinational pharmaceutical companies (and the nefarious connections between them), but the overwhelming focus is one of a microcosmic

Figure I.2. Film still. The Seine River turned crimson in *120 BPM*. *Source*: Dir. Robin Campillo. Les Films de Pierre, France 3 Cinéma (2017).

scale: just as with the film's sequences of HIV infecting cells under a microscope, the film zooms in to the personal consequences of living with AIDS and the quotidian experiences of life as an LGBTQ+ person during the epidemic.

In comparable ways, the films I analyze in *Bodies of Water* are deeply indebted to the "lack of respect for the governing codes of form or content, linearity or coherence" that characterizes New Queer Cinema and its "Homo-Pomo style," yet they, like *120 BPM*, are categorically distinct from the radical politics of such a movement.[107] Monica B. Pearl defines New Queer Cinema as being "made in the midst of the AIDS crisis" of the 1980s and 90s and forged "defiantly" within the ensuing "epistemic shift in gay culture."[108] José Arroyo presses this connection further, writing that "AIDS is why there is New Queer Cinema, and it is what New Queer Cinema is all about."[109] In that sense alone, it is to be expected that contemporary queer cinema has developed along distinct axes from those films of the 1980s and '90s: though access to preventive medicine is vastly unequal across the world, antiretroviral therapies mean that those living with HIV can achieve undetectable viral loads and live healthy lives. On a broader plane, queer communities have enjoyed increased rights over the past two decades; though, as is shamefully apparent, societal progress is always reversible. In Latin America, there has been a significant shift toward affording same-gender couples civil protections on the basis of sexual and gender identification and equal rights to institutions such as marriage.[110] These seismic societal shifts, discussed in further depth in the first chapter of this book, have prompted distinct emotional and political environments for contemporary cinema, which has largely moved away from New Queer Cinema's gritty focus on queerphobic violence and societal repression toward microcosmic, often-intersectional explorations of queer life in the twenty-first century. Contemporary queer films do not "eschew positive imagery," as Michele Aaron notes as a defining feature of new queer film, but instead they present narratives marked by a sustained emphasis on the quotidian and by emotionally fulfilling relationships, or at the very least the potential thereof.[111]

In focusing on the queer aesthetics of primarily Latin American cinemas, *Bodies of Water* attempts to remedy a gap in critical approaches to contemporary queer cinema, which have tended to focus on European and North American iterations of the genre and to leave non-Western cinemas largely to one side. In *New Queer Cinema: The Director's Cut*, published ten years after Aaron's foundational reference point, *New Queer*

Cinema: A Critical Reader, B. Ruby Rich addresses the initial omission of Latin America in critical discussions of New Queer Cinema, writing that, at the turn of the century, "a New Queer Cinema emerged within the resurgence of energy (and outside interest) in Latin American cinemas, and in fact has provided a crucial counterweight to the drift toward global movie industry norms in national cinemas which once had been the site of innovative, ground-breaking experiments in political and aesthetic oppositionality."[112] Disappointingly, Rich offers only several brief analyses of films that may fall under such a label, including Julián Hernández's *Mil nubes de paz cercan el cielo, amor* (*A Thousand Clouds of Peace*, 2003) and Lucrecia Martel's *La ciénaga* (*The Swamp*, 2001), concluding that, "eventually, against formidable odds, a new generation of Latin American filmmakers would come into its own."[113] There is something implicitly problematic—if illustrative, on a wider critical plane—about Rich's use of the terms "eventually" and "formidable," which suggest a relationship with North American and European cinemas that is marked by delay—*eventually*—and by a sensationalizing, othering view of Latin American societies—*formidable*. This embedded assumption of the belated development of Latin American cinemas is symptomatic more broadly of global perspectives toward the region's industries, which are often taken to be recipients and imitations of filmic trends elsewhere, with "elsewhere" typically understood as either Hollywood and/or European art-house cinemas.

Bodies of Water positions contemporary directors from Latin America at the forefront of this new global movement in queer cinema. Filmmakers such as Lucía Puenzo, Marco Berger, Lucrecia Martel, Daniel Ribeiro, Javier Fuentes-León, Lorenzo Vigas, Sebastián Lelio, Filipe Matzembacher, and Marcio Reolon have attracted weighty international prizes, *even* an Academy Award, and their work has received significant critical attention. In the academic sphere, Gus Subero's *Queer Masculinities in Latin American Cinema* (2013) offers an excellent study of machismo, *mariconería*, and male effeminacy in a robust corpus of Latin American film until the early 2000s; and Vinodh Venkatesh's *New Maricón Cinema: Outing Latin American Film* (2016) presents a comparative analysis of Latin American film from the 1980s and '90s with productions from the early 2000s onward. While the term *maricón* is somewhat restrictive in its approach to a corpus that includes a diverse range of gender and sexual identities, Venkatesh does nevertheless offer a solid preliminary theorization of the formal and aesthetic capacities of this contemporary wave of queer cinema, specifically from the Latin American context. He writes:

"New Maricón cinema features a preference for an affective schema, that is, a milieu of techniques, images, sounds, textures, and surfaces that engender a polysensorial, haptic interaction with the moving image."[114] By focusing exclusively on Latin America, these foundational studies from Subero and Venkatesh celebrate the diversity and political potency of the region's cinema, underscoring its queer film not simply as reflective of global filmic trends but also as a driver of formal and aesthetic innovation.

Yet *Bodies of Water* adopts a distinct methodological approach to the study of cinematic queerness than the frameworks proposed by Subero and Venkatesh, as well as than the earlier pioneering text to which both studies owe an intellectual debt, David William Foster's *Queer Issues in Contemporary Latin American Cinema* (2003). In his study, Foster performs a surgical cut on the notion of queerness, cleaving lesbian representation from a broader understanding of "queer issues" that concentrate for the most part on "male-centred narratives."[115] This is not, as he writes, "a consequence of [his] desire to privilege masculinist culture," but instead derives from his conviction that lesbianism poses its own "queer challenge to the heteronormative patriarchy" and that, "clearly, this filmmaking deserves its own study."[116] Nevertheless, the delimited scope of the study undermines the critical potency of its analyses, restricting queerness as primarily a marker of identity through its focus on male sexuality and effeminacy. In a similar fashion, Subero also mobilizes a narrowly understood conception of queerness in his work, seeking to "offer an initial insight into how the bodies of 'queer' male characters are (re)presented and how those (re)presentations influence, perpetuate or challenge the perceptions that different audience have of male 'queer' sexuality."[117] Subero's study focuses on a number of questions of vital importance to the representation of gay male sexualities, proposing, for instance, "new readings of queer male sexuality beyond the active versus passive paradigms," as well as an acknowledgment of the Western-centric nature of the term "queer" itself. His repeated positioning of the term in quotation marks, however, which he does to demonstrate its resistance to "any identifiable category of gender or sexuality within the Latin American socio-sexual system," belies a broader theoretical hesitation in its critical deployment, specifically in its overlapping with the term "gay."[118] Subero writes that "gay identity is formed on the basis that all subjects share the same sexual desires, surrounded by stigma, along with a history of sexual repression," and goes on to suggest that his "use of the term 'queer' [. . .] shows a political willingness to take the findings of this study beyond gay and transgender theory."[119] Like Foster, however, Subero harnesses "queer" to "gay" in a somewhat cautious fashion, resulting in an exploration of nonnormative gay male masculinities that stops short of interrogating the potential of queerness to develop politically or aesthetically beyond the confines of sexual identity.

While Foster and Subero, for their own theoretically informed reasons, define queerness primarily as a marker of (sexual) identity, Venkatesh offers a more fluid conception of the term, one that is not fixed "solely on narratological traits or plot turns [. . .] but preoccupied with the praxis and composition of representation and how these impact and shape our perception of gender and sexual difference."[120] His is, put simply, "an interrogation into how queerness is portrayed and to what collective effect."[121] Indeed, though Venkatesh proposes a number of discernible thematic features of New Maricón Cinema, including (but not limited to) "the minting of varying aural and visual affective intensities" and "the use of nonurban spaces, metaphors and movements," what emerges as most theoretically innovative in his study is the "critical understanding of the relationship between the camera and queerness."[122] By taking these cinematic structures of queerness seriously, Venkatesh proposes a methodological framework that presupposes the term "queer" not "as one of identity but as an affirmation of power based on heteronormativity"; one, he argues, that is "defined more by varying affective flows and perceptions than by any sustained thesis, [and that] surpass[es] any traditional 'reading' of the moving image."[123] *Bodies of Water* aligns itself with this phenomenologically informed approach to the queer moving image, one in which the stress never rests solely on *which* identities are visible but also on *how* queerness is visualized. It does so, building on Venkatesh's work, through a critical contemplation of the ways these structures of representation are "rooted in a viewership experience that is embodied," and of how they encourage us to "no longer simply *see* difference, [but] actively touch, caress, and participate in the sensuality of libidinal urges, bodily identifications and often-multidirectional orientations."[124]

In several crucial ways, I develop and extend Venkatesh's work, offering a contemporary corpus of filmic material that maps out a broader and more diverse range of sexual and gender identities, as well as rallying through the notion of the queer aesthetic a robust and precise theoretical framework for the study of these cinematic structures of queerness. As the chapters of *Bodies of Water* demonstrate, this expanded notion of the queerness of the cinematic image cuts across aspects of content, form, style, and spectatorship, all of which are intricately bound up in the notion of the queer aesthetic. While critical interventions into earlier cinematic movements in the region have argued for the political potential of certain key formal and aesthetic techniques that I explore in this book—take, for instance, narrative slowness and dispersion, which Gonzalo Aguilar distinguishes as key features of New Argentine Cinema; or the "minimalist, intimate styles" that Joanna Page identifies in the work of Martel and others—here I tether them in an essential fashion to a politics of queer representation, one that prioritizes issues of sexuality, sexual orientation, and gender.[125] More relevant to the argument of this book than these earlier Latin American movements, then, is the queer cinematic heritage with which these films engage, and I insist throughout this book on taking these connections and influences seriously, not least those of the New Queer Cinema of the 1990s and early 2000s. Thus, while the insistence on a queer aesthetic sets this study apart from the work of Foster and Subero, its simultaneous focus on water and forms of cinematic embodiment also builds on more recent work by scholars such as Venkatesh. The contemporary corpus of films I have curated in *Bodies of Water* foregrounds the body both as a site of phenomenological potential and, in its interaction with bodies of water, a potent cinematic device for the exploration of a range of pressing political issues, including those implicated in questions of gender, sexuality, race, and socioeconomics. In terms borrowed from Muñoz, these filmic bodies—of both flesh and water—serve as a means of glimpsing the "blueprints and schemata of a forward-dawning futurity," one that is attentive to the political exigencies of queerness and to the radical potential of their cinematic figurations.

Structure of the Book

In the first chapter of this book, I propose the term New Queer Realism to account for the stylistic, formal and aesthetic trends of contemporary queer cinema, as well as for its specific relationship to what we might understand as cinematic realism. Through a preliminary examination of the beachscape in Lucio Castro's *Fin de siglo*, I explore how the film is representative of broader formal and aesthetic shifts in queer world cinema, most notably toward narrative slowness, a lack of dramatic tension, and an intimate focus on the quotidian realities of queer characters. The chapter takes a necessary detour from an exclusive focus on bodies of water to lay the foundations for the book as a whole; and, by drawing the film into dialogue with Andrew Haigh's *Weekend*, I examine in more critical depth the contrasts between contemporary cinema and the formal and political radicality of New Queer Cinema. I argue that recent queer film's lack of engagement with broad sociopolitical issues, such as HIV/AIDS, queer-triggered violence, or the need for sexual discretion is not a refusal of politics but rather a recalibration of how we understand queerness *as* political in the contemporary period. Through its focus on the fleeting nature of Grindr hookups, the practicalities of gay sex, the confluence of same-gender marriage and parenthood, and the crucial liquid temporalities that it deploys, I take *Fin de siglo* as an example of how contemporary film represents in a more realistic and observational manner the lives of its protagonists.

Chapter 2 extends the focus on New Queer Realism and responds to the striking development of adolescent-focused queer cinema in Latin America, taking as its case studies the Brazilian films *Beira-Mar* (*Seashore*, 2015), by Filipe Matzembacher and Marcio Reolon; *Sócrates* (2018), by Alexandre Moratto; and *Quebramar* (*Breakwater*, 2019), by Cris Lyra. By challenging the prevailing focus in coming-of-age films that restricts the use of beaches and oceans to their symbolic value as spaces of interstitiality and (postmodern, poststructuralist) becoming, I argue that the formal and aesthetic strategies deployed by these directors in screening the adolescent body—which, in these films, is figured as gendered, racialized, and socially classed—demand a more sensitive recognition of the material and intersectional realities of queerness as *lived*. The chapter introduces one of the book's overarching concerns, namely, what I term "the fallacy of fluidity," whereby critics tend to confine the critical and theoretical value of cinematic waters to a sense of postmodern fluidity, without taking into account the material and haptic qualities of water's representational potency. The argument historicizes the development of "sea images" within Brazilian filmic history and builds on Brad Epps's theoretical caution regarding the "fetish of fluidity" in queer cultural texts, through which he argues that "the body is itself in trouble, rendered so discursive as to matter little or not at all."[126] In this way, the chapter examines the adolescent body not as an exclusive site of becoming but as one that is already both cinematically and politically a "desiring subject."[127] In keeping with the politics of New Queer Realism, the analysis of these films ruptures the utopian conception of fluidity as *always in flux* and instead argues that the material realities of bodies—not least their gender, race, and sexuality—must be accounted for if our contemporary approaches to the body in queer theory are to remain politically and theoretically effectual.

In the third chapter, "The Coast Is Queer," I analyze themes of visibility and (trans)national belonging in Javier Fuentes-León's *Contracorriente* (*Undertow*, 2009) and Karim Aïnouz's *Praia do Futuro* (*Futuro Beach*, 2014). The chapter understands the shorelines in these films to function as both "theme" and "method," serving not only as secluded retreats for moments of queer intimacy (theme) but also as sites for the formulation of alternative, queer forms of relationality (method).[128] These cinematic oceans are scrutinized not simply as allegorical or poetic spaces of marginality, but instead as sites endowed with the queer potential to challenge heteronormative notions of progress and futurity and render visible histories of queerness that have been obscured by the homogenizing forces of globalization and neoliberalism. Through a framework that responds to the recent call to "queer the transnational turn" and to challenge the transnational as "an unquestioned dominant framework within queer studies," the chapter argues that the protagonists' journeys—either from the urban to the rural, or from Latin America to Europe—challenge the simplistic interpretation of global mobility as "the movement from repression to freedom," instead offering a more dynamic, iterative notion of queer transnational belonging.[129] The chapter looks to the ocean in order to deterritorialize conservative, heteronormative notions of "home," arguing that these films visualize alternative modes of being and belonging in the global present that figure "home" for their queer characters as "a destination rather than an origin."[130]

Marco Berger's queer cinematic oeuvre over the last decade has consistently been set in and around watery spaces, from the voyeuristic inspection of the adolescent physique in the showers of *Ausente* (*Absent*, 2011) to the drawn-out contemplation of poolside bodies in *Hawaii* (2013). Chapter 4 chapter focuses primarily on *Taekwondo* (2018), attending to the film's sensual, haptic screening of the male body and arguing that its tendency toward narrative and formal slowness represents a crucial—and *queer*—iteration of the slow cinema genre. While recent critical approaches to slow queer film in Latin America have focused almost exclusively on the narrative depiction of nonnormative sexualities and desires, neglecting both the representational politics of cinematic slowness and the haptic potential of screening queer corporeality, this chapter bridges that critical gap through a theoretical framework that combines a phenomenological reading of the film with an examination of its "sexual politics of the slow and the boring."[131] Berger's consistent visual emphasis throughout his work on the (semi)naked male physique in the spaces of showers, swimming pools, and saunas demands a critical sensitivity toward the filmic nexuses of touch and sexuality and of slowness and queerness. As such, the chapter extends the discussions of queerness, temporality, and realism introduced in chapter 1 to argue that Berger's work represents a significant attempt to decenter queerness from conventional cinematic modes of narrative representation, instead reinvesting its nonnormative potential within filmic surface and texture. Through a triangulation of critical approaches to queer temporality, cinematic slowness, and the haptic, the chapter demonstrates how the film's treatment of bodies and boredom works to undermine normative structures of temporality and spectatorship, foregrounding a queer mode of seeing—and *feeling*—the cinematic image.

In final chapter, I return to discussions of sexuality and sexual pleasure, initially explored through the gay male body in chapters 1 and 3, to examine the provocative intersections of watery imagery and explicit lesbian sex in Albertina Carri's *Las hijas del fuego* (*Daughters of the Fire*, 2018). The chapter deploys the concept of "postpornography" to argue that *Las hijas* offers a critique not only of pornographic media itself but also of the broader sociopolitical and cultural structures of repression through which women's bodies have historically been policed.[132] By scrutinizing the "conceptual displacement" of the film's sexualized aquatic imagery of jellyfish, anemones, and sea urchins, and by moving beyond the "crude parameters of shock and sensation" to which studies of cinematic sex have conventionally been subject, this chapter focuses on the embodied dynamics of queer sexual pleasure that Carri deploys in order to recalibrate explicit sex as a mode of critical interrogation.[133] The argument situates the film's pornographic provocations within theoretical discussions from sexuality and porn studies, as well as within their artistic and cultural contexts, examining the resonances with Barbara Hammer's influential lesbian aesthetic of the 1970s. The chapter argues that Carri radically subverts dominant hierarchies of spectatorship to expose the normative taxonomies of pleasure that govern mainstream pornography, doing so through a queer poetics of sexual pleasure that not only necessitates a reconditioning of the gaze cast toward the female body but also demands cinematic visibility for the flows and impulses of queer sexual desire.

Taken as a whole, these chapters account for a dynamic and innovative wave of contemporary queer cinema from Latin America, which is linked inextricably, if in ways that are too-often critically overlooked, to queer cultural representation more globally. It is for this reason that *Bodies of Water* so insistently embeds the aesthetic and political significance of these films within broader cinematic and cultural histories, embracing—just as this introduction has done—the vital crosscurrents between regions, genres, disciplines, and eras. The aesthetic and formal features that each of the chapters explores—that is, the registers of queer realism, the material realities of bodies, modes of transnational belonging, and the mechanics of slowness and sexuality—are not prerequisites for contemporary queer film from Latin America, but they are overwhelmingly present to varying degrees and intensities in much recent cinematic work from the region. This is a corpus of films that turns to bodies of water not simply as narrative backdrops but as filmic devices in the representation of nonnormative sexual desires, genders, and bodies; and it is one that mobilizes bodies *in* water to suggest the alternative forms of being and belonging that lie beyond the normative restrictions of hegemonic societal and political structures. By immersing theories of cinematic embodiment and sexuality in the histories and materialities of watery spaces, *Bodies of Water* proposes a generative act of queering that thinks *with* and *through* the aquatic. In doing so, I hope, in the pages that follow, to open up new lines of flight for scrutinizing how bodies can act as sites of queer experience, be they of flesh, of film or, indeed, of water.

Chapter One

The Queer Art of Feeling

Fluid Futurities, *Fin de siglo*, and New Queer Realism

> Maybe it is stupid. But who fucking cares? Why does it bother you that maybe two people fucking love each other, and they want to get married, and they want a relationship, and they just want to be happy. They just want to be happy.
>
> —Russell, *Weekend* (dir. Andrew Haigh)

Lucio Castro's *Fin de siglo* (*End of the Century*, 2019) is a film concerned both thematically and structurally with the passing of time and its unrealized possibilities. The chance encounter of the film's two protagonists, Ocho and Javi, on a Barcelona beach in 2019 sets into motion the first of the film's three chapters, which ends abruptly and unexpectedly with the realization that the men have met—and shared a strikingly similar weekend of sex and sightseeing—before. The second chapter, which details their initial introduction in 1999, makes little attempt to account for the twenty-year gap in terms of costume, makeup, or mise-en-scène. Instead, this lack of visual shift imbues the scenes with an oneiric quality that gently unsettles linear chronologies, a strategy prioritized in the film's concluding chapter, in which the narrative flashes forward—or, perhaps, sidewards—to an alternative, fantasy-driven present in which the men did not part ways in 1999 but rather remained together in the intervening years to build a home and a family. This "dream logic" that pervades the narrative and formal structures of *Fin de siglo* progressively calls into question the normativity of the temporalities we conventionally associate with life and with love, that is, those expectations of "the good life" that Sara Ahmed contends orient us heteronormatively toward "happiness as a form of duty."[1] *Fin de siglo*, through its temporal twists and turns and via a lens attentive to the quotidian realities of queer lives, instead offers a vision of queer futurity that, as this chapter will argue, destabilizes (chrono)normative regimes and opens up a range of affective possibilities traditionally foreclosed to queer cinematic characters.

From the outset, *Fin de siglo* crafts an atmosphere of unhurried contemplation. The twelve-minute-long, dialogue-free opening sequence languidly documents one of the two protagonists' arrivals in Barcelona, through long sluggish takes that dispel any sense of narrative tension as they chart his touristic flânerie through the city's distinctive gothic and modernist architecture. When Ocho and Javi finally encounter one another on a beach, their meeting—though charged with a latent sense of sexual potential thanks to their furtive glances at each other's unclothed bodies—ends abruptly and anticlimactically: just as their gazes fail to meet, their paths cross but similarly fail to connect. The cinematic beach, which, as Fiona Handyside remarks, "like the cinema itself, [is] coded as a place of display," in this instance lays bare not only the toned and conventionally attractive bodies of the two men but also the "social organisation" of gay male cruising.[2] During the sequence, when Ocho follows Javi into the water, the sudden unsteadiness of the camerawork contrasts with the previous static shots of angular architecture and the rigid cityscape, reflecting the uncertainty of a gaze that is charged with intentionality yet uncertain of reciprocity. The water of the ocean accentuates the men's athleticism as they dive through the waves and against the tides, a formal strategy of exposure shared by many contemporary queer films, and the refraction of sunlight through the ocean's spray visually imitates this moment of missed connection between the pair.[3] As the men leave the water one after another, and then the beach separately, each surprised at the other's apparent disinterest, Castro crafts this first instance of dramatic potential into a moment of quiet frustration, both for the protagonists and for their spectators.

That this moment in the film's "present" of 2019 is juxtaposed indirectly with a more explicit example of gay male cruising in the second chapter of the film, set in 1999, is significant not only for how the film crafts its narrative arc but also for the argument of this chapter. While the example above on the beach is notable for its subdued narrative tension and lack of immediate sexual resolution, the chronologically earlier episode, by contrast, is more conventionally dramatic in both diegetic and formal terms. In a wooded area of the Parc del Laberint d'Horta, an unnoticeably younger Ocho has his first sexual encounter with a man, after following the stranger along a path and into some nearby bushes. The camerawork of the scene insists on a sense of voyeurism and danger, with impartial shots of the men obscured by branches and leaves (see figure 1.1), quite unlike the open horizons of the film's earlier beachscape. Moreover, not only does Ocho visibly have second thoughts about the sexual encounter and attempt to flee, but the entire experience leaves him physically ill and psychologically unsettled for days afterwards, able to leave bed only to search for information about oral HIV transmission on the internet. As this chapter will argue, these two moments of the film are not only representative in the most explicit sense of what Castro himself refers to as "el cambio drástico en la vida de los gais en los últimos veinte años, desde el miedo a VIH hasta Grindr" (the drastic change in the lives of gay men over the last twenty years, from the fear of HIV to Grindr).[4] They are also emblematic of a broader cinematic shift in queer-themed film, from the works of the New Queer Cinema in the 1990s, which were "radical, not just in their politics but also in their filmic form," and which "emerged out of the time of and the preoccupations with AIDS," to a more mundane, realist focus on the everyday experience of queerness in the present.[5]

Figure 1.1. Film still. Obscured framing during a cruising sequence in a park in *Fin de siglo*. *Source*: Dir. Lucio Castro. Alsina 427, JWProductions (2019).

The primary concern of *Fin de siglo* does not revolve around issues of HIV/AIDS, shame and rejection, homophobic violence, or the need for sexual discretion, which are all similarly absent from the films that comprise the corpus of *Bodies of Water* more broadly. Instead, the film focuses on certain aspects of contemporary queer lives that have understandably been absent from earlier cinematic explorations of queerness: the fleeting nature of Grindr hookups, the juncture of same-gender marriage and parenthood, and the practicalities and pitfalls of open relationships. *Fin de siglo*'s focus on the intimate dynamics and everyday experiences of queerness can therefore be read through the framework of New Queer Realism, a cinematic register that that embraces slowness over dramatic conflict, the microcosms of individual relationships over broader societal issues, and the realities and practicalities of queer sex over an emphasis on its deviance or overt political potential. New Queer Realism has become a defining feature of much contemporary queer film from Latin America and beyond, identifiable through a lack of dramatic narrative or a formal insistence on observational camerawork, as with the work of Marco Berger, Albertina Carri, Lucrecia Martel, and Karim Aïnouz, all of whom appear in subsequent chapters of this book.[6] As with queer world film more broadly, the representational power of these works lies not in their engagement with identity politics in the most immediate or explicit sense of the term but, instead, in their claim to represent in a more realistic and observational manner the lives of characters represented on screen.

As several critics have noted, *Fin de siglo* shares its narrative accent on the queer quotidian with the British director Andrew Haigh's *Weekend* (2011), along with an aesthetic emphasis on shots that depict characters against the imposing architectures of their urban environments. Andrew Moor remarks that "*Weekend* is intimate, disarmingly simple, coolly naturalistic and politically astute."[7] This relaxed embrace of the personal in *Weekend* and its interrogation of the intimate likewise pervade the narrative of *Fin de siglo*, leading several film critics to draw comparisons between the two specifically on the levels of plot and cinematography.[8] The narrative present of *Fin de siglo* unfurls over a similar timeframe to Haigh's film, with both productions featuring two men who meet and (re)develop a relationship over the space of a couple of days; both films also feature intimate discussions between their protagonists, which offer an insight not only into gay relationships in the age of social media and the hookup app but also into broader societal issues of gay parenting and same-gender marriage. These films approach the intimate, the ephemeral, and the familiar with a lens attentive to the affective dynamics that lie beneath their seemingly overt refusal to engage in broader social and political issues.

Castro's experimentation with temporality in *Fin de siglo*, however, stands out as an immediate marker of difference from *Weekend*, one that enables the director and his characters to explore in a more profound sense what José Esteban Muñoz has referred to in *Cruising Utopia* as "a queer temporality, a thing that is not the linearity that many of us have been calling straight time."[9] Mirroring the film's narrative focus on moments of transition, from the sunset backdrops of the pair's most intimate revelations to the setting of the second chapter at the eponymous end of the twentieth century, this playfulness with nonlinear dynamics and temporal porosity is pivotal, left as the characters and their environments are unconcealed by shifts in costume, visual effects, or mise-en-scène. Most suggestively, the fantasy sequence in the final moments of the film, which flashes sideward to an impossible alternative present, consolidates the film's preoccupation with time's junctures and its potentialities. The momentary glimpse of domestic complacency offered in this closing scene, with its contented-but-humdrum routine of childcare and household chores, is far from radical in the futurity that it pictures. As this chapter will argue, however, *Fin de siglo* defends itself from accusations of homonormativity through the very possibility of the future that it envisions, one in which "we can glimpse the worlds proposed and promised by queerness" and through which the film strikes one of its most affectively resonant chords.[10]

In his review of the film, Bilal Qureshi writes, "What these millennial queer masterpieces share is a new kind of creative freedom, a conscious and discernible break from past stories of loss, tragedy, and isolation."[11] He continues: "Even when such films do not explicitly address the question of civil rights, their politics are central to their deceptively universal story lines and constitute a sort of anthem for dignity and recognition."[12] *Fin de siglo*'s nostalgic glances backward, forward, and sideward constitute an interrogation of an affective realm formerly foreclosed to queer cinematic characters (and their audiences), one that harnesses the representational power of the everyday as a means of reinscribing queer experience within a broader collective—and sociopolitical—history. In this sense, and to a greater extent than Qureshi suggests in his review of the film, *Fin de siglo*'s matrix of New Queer Realism not only engages implicitly with the question of social and political equality, but it also interrogates the scope and substance of queer happiness, or what Sara Ahmed has referred to in *The Promise of Happiness* as the political potential of being "happily queer." Ahmed writes: "The queer who is happily queer still encounters the world that is unhappy with queer love but refuses to be made unhappy by that encounter. [. . .] To be happily queer is to explore the unhappiness of what gets counted as normal. To be happily queer can be to recognise the unhappiness that is concealed by the promotion of happy normativity."[13] In its interrogation of the resonances and realities of the contemporary queer experience and, crucially, of their affective range, *Fin de siglo* becomes not only an "anthem for dignity and recognition" but a much more complex questioning of what underpins, restricts, and facilitates queer happiness in the contemporary moment.

In this way, the film can also be understood to reflect a broader theoretical development within queer theory, from antisocial stances toward the heteronormative institutions of marriage, parenthood, and monogamy, à la Leo Bersani and Lee Edelman, to alternatively optimistic modes that recognize the importance of the lived realities of queerness *alongside* their political and theoretical abstraction.[14] In challenging the pervasive and normalizing nature of society's "happiness scripts," which orient us toward both traditional notions of success, fulfillment and, by proxy, heteronormativity, Ahmed suggests that "rather than reading unhappy endings as a sign of the withholding of moral approval for queer lives, we must consider how unhappiness circulates with and around this archive, and *what it allows us to do.*"[15] While the ending of *Fin de siglo* can certainly not be straightforwardly read as unhappy, not least given that the ambiguity of the film itself rejects any such facile interpretation, this chapter will nevertheless respond to Ahmed's encouragement to examine what notions of queer (un)happiness *allow us to do*. *Fin de siglo*'s treatment of Javi and Ocho's fleeting weekend reunion through the lens of New Queer Realism, with its sensitivity toward the affective intensities of the narrative and the observational dynamics of the camera's gaze, merges with the film's playful temporalities, figuring a queer domesticity that has both a past and, albeit imagined, a future. As such, in its realist embrace of feeling and through the rejection of any singular model of happiness, the film deals in the future-oriented "glimpses of queerness" that serve as alternatives to the "happiness scripts" imposed and policed by a heteronormative society.[16] In forgoing an explicitly antisocial stance toward the established institutions of marriage, career, and family, *Fin de siglo*'s optimistic exploration of the intimacies of the queer domestic experience thus becomes one of both representational and political significance. The film suggests that these "glimpses" of the happy queer home need not be *real* in order to affect us but, instead, exist simply as *realizable* possibilities among the many potential paths and futures that time may offer.

Sex and Sincerity

Following the unhurried opening sequence of *Fin de siglo* and its moment of missed connection, the two protagonists eventually interact when Ocho notices Javi walking on the street from his balcony and invites him upstairs. The pair's small talk quickly turns to their recently crossed paths on the beach, and each one reveals that he was indeed aware of the other's presence but was prevented from acting on any impulse by prevailing social codes: "Es muy difícil toda esa ajedrez" (All these chess games make it difficult), remarks Ocho. There is, in the slightly stilted dialogue about Airbnb rentals, Grindr, and reasons for visiting Barcelona, a distinct lack of tension: Javi appears equally as aware as Ocho of the purpose of his visit upstairs, yet the eventuality of sex between the men is rendered mundane both through the script and the cinematography, appearing as the default option rather than a dramatic one. The static nature of the medium full shot of the two men standing in the kitchen curtails a sense of intimacy, emphasized by the clinical hue of the stark lighting against the blue tiles of the kitchen wall. When the pair eventually kiss, Javi's jibe that Ocho temper the intensity of his passions suggests that this will not be a stereotypical foray into the cinematic sex scene, a tone quickly consolidated in the film's following moments. Despite Ocho's assurances that he is taking PrEP, Javi prefers to use protection, meaning that Ocho must leave the apartment—adjusting his noticeable bulge as he enters the street—to go in search of condoms. The realistic nature of both the script and the men's actions, from the discussion of protection and the adjustments of bulges to the time-consuming unwrapping and donning of the condom itself, offers a subdued, observational tenor to their—finally successful—moment of cruising.

The "measured ordinariness" that some critics have noted in the film's first chapter as a whole is here woven into the structures of the sex scene itself, which avoids any explicitly pornographic camerawork or full-frontal exposure of genitals, though, it should be said, it still maintains a sensual charge despite such narrative and formal discretion.[17] Ocho's jokes about awkwardly hiding the condoms among other items in his shopping basket at the local store, along with Javi's pretend dislike at the brand of lubricant that Ocho has bought, imbue the scene with a sense of comic levity. The time taken for Ocho to unwrap the condom and then initially penetrate Javi augments the scene's formal and narrative emphases on the practicalities of gay sex, rather than on its erotic potential: this shot lasts fifty seconds, in comparison to following shot of the pair having sex, which lasts only forty seconds (see figures 1.2 and 1.3). Though Ocho's facial expression is visible as he reaches climax, the filmic grammar of conventional pornographic sequences is notably absent; the intimate camerawork and explicit money shot so essential to the visuality of male sexuality elsewhere is here replaced by the conspicuously less visceral image of a used condom being wrapped in toilet paper and thrown into a bin.[18]

The camera does permit a sense of sensuality, to be sure, but refrains from what Cüneyt Çakırlar and Gary Needham refer to as either a "monogamous" or "promiscuous optic," refusing to offer any point-of-view shots and instead opting exclusively for two static medium takes, first from behind as the pair begin to have sex and then from the side as they reach climax.[19] While Richard Dyer and Linda Williams point respectively to the "importance of the visual" and the value of "maximum visibility" in representations of male sexuality, *Fin de siglo* instead chooses strategically to foment a sense of intimacy not through the sexual act itself but through its observational approach to the actions that surround it: jokes

Figure 1.2: Film still. Static camerawork during sex scenes in *Fin de siglo*. Source: Dir. Lucio Castro. Alsina 427, JWProductions (2019).

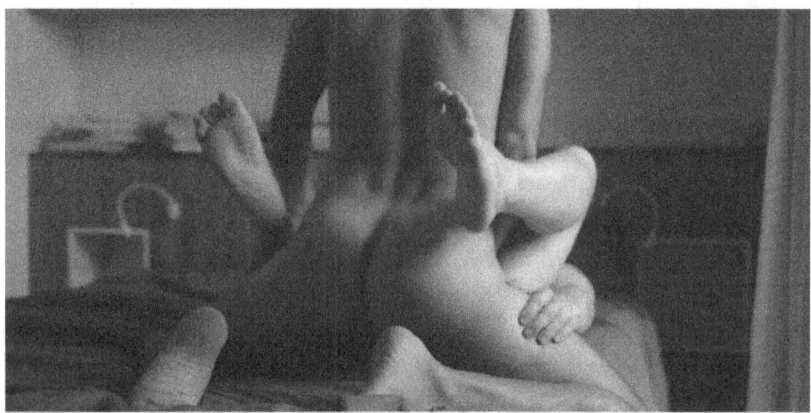

Figure 1.3: Film still. Static camerawork during sex scenes in *Fin de siglo*. *Source*: Dir. Lucio Castro. Alsina 427, JWProductions (2019).

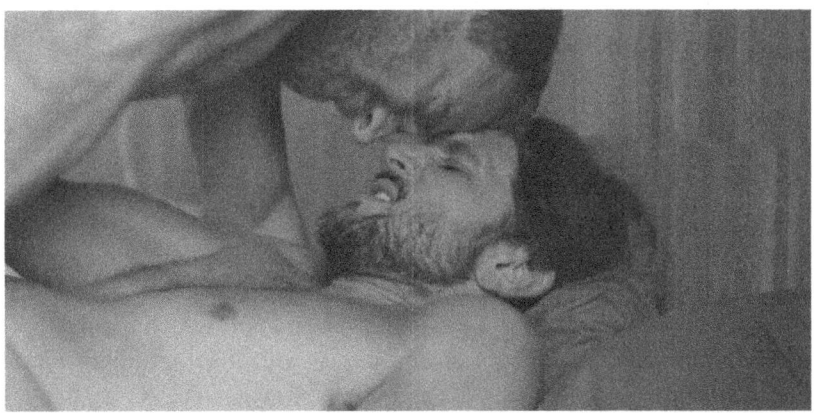

about Ocho's shopping spree, the clumsiness of unwrapping a condom, and the breathless discussion immediately afterwards of Perro Viejo, a cartoon character, and his inability to be adopted.[20] Though sex is of central importance to the pair's weekend relationship, these scenes do not exist in a social or narrative vacuum. In this way, Castro recalibrates the intimacy of the erotic by encouraging the spectator not to watch but to *observe* the relationship that develops, through a realist aesthetic that focalizes the mundane practicalities of sex over its outrightly erotic potential.

In his review of Ira Sach's *Keep the Lights On* (2011), Ben Walters positions the film at the beginning of what he labels a "new-wave queer cinema," in which "no one comes out or dies, and everything is shown with the same fluid energy."[21] He writes: "*Keep the Lights On* is at once very good and conspicuously ordinary. [. . .] It's a peculiarly powerful mode that represents a welcome shift in queer cinema—an embrace of the real."[22] Moor, for his part, astutely notes a sense of what he terms "New Gay Sincerity" in the representation of nonnormative sexualities in this recent wave of queer-focused independent film. For Moor, films such as *Keep the Lights On*, *Weekend*, and Travis Matthews's *I Want Your Love* (2012) all "choose a mode of frank, observational realism and seem to capture everyday lives in ways that "feel authentic."[23] Moor's incisive analysis of *Weekend* notes a number of discernible formal characteristics that could also be attributed to *Fin de siglo*, not least the exclusive use of diegetic sound and a "commit[ment], to a mathematically emphatic degree, to a mode of observational realism founded in the long-take."[24] Indeed, it is precisely *Weekend*'s "landscape of ordinariness" in its treatment of sex that can also be said to pervade the narrative and aesthetic registers of *Fin de siglo*.[25] Similarly, in a broader sense, from its long opening shots of Ocho wandering through Barcelona to the numerous sequences of the men against the Catalan sunset, the film tends toward an embrace of shot duration over narration, crafting an authenticity in the men's interactions that is unbound by conventional narrative pathways. In *Fin de siglo*, it is more often than not the act of conversing that emerges as meaningful and consequential, rather than the content of the conversations themselves.

There is, in this observational and realist approach to the relationship between Javi and Ocho, a stark contrast with the formal dissonance and aesthetic experimentation of contemporary queer cinema's most notable precedent, New Queer Cinema. *Fin de siglo*, as with *Weekend*, *Leave the Lights On*, and many other recent queer films from around the world, refrains from the "Homo Pomo style" that B. Ruby Rich identifies in films of the New Queer Cinema, a movement defined as much by its "traces of appropriation and pastiche, and irony" as by its "irreverent, energetic, alternately minimalist and excessive" engagement with identity politics.[26] Nor can these more recent films be said to "eschew positive imagery" or "give voice to the marginalised," which Michele Aaron sees as distinctive of New Queer Cinema's "defiance" and its inescapably critical attitude toward "cinematic convention in terms of form, content and genre."[27] As noted above, the conversations that take place between Javi and Ocho are intimate and often introspective, ranging from the emotional dynamics of fatherhood to the pleasures and pitfalls of loneliness, and at no point could their discussion of sexual preference or practice be considered deviant or subversive, or indeed *defiant*. *Fin de siglo*, in its commitment to New Queer Realism, is far from well versed in the radical visual and formal language of "the exigency and urgency and drama" of previous waves of queer cinema.[28] In this sense, there is a danger inherent to the film's candid realism, namely, one that sees in the characters' discussions of marriage, children, and careers an assimilatory value, even a homonormative embrace of what Lee Edelman would call the "reproductive futurity" of the child.[29] At one point in the film, Ocho flirts with such an idea when he talks about the "meaning" that comes from parenthood, though it must be noted that any such reflection is not naïve on the part of the director, inflected as it is with such intimate detail about Javi's daughter, a mosquito, and the desire to reproduce away the intolerance of the world. *Fin de siglo* serves as a paradigmatic example of a range of contemporary queer world film that contrasts unambiguously in formal and thematic terms with the defiant, radical nature of their queer cinematic precedents.

These are not, however, films that conservatively supplant the political with the poetic. Moor's discussion of "New Gay Sincerity" provides a productive means of approaching contemporary queer cinema's rejection of an outright sense of political defiance and its less tangible engagement with queer identity politics.[30] Taking his corpus of post-2012 films as prime examples of a new, less provocative wave of queer representation, he writes: "Rebellion is not within New Gay Sincerity's frame of reference. Its long takes, its neutral gaze, its avoidance of cliché and gay stereotypes, and its presentation of understated narratives might all sound worthily pious, but in navigating away from the artful provocations of queerness and the performativity of postmodernism, it is not culpably naïve. It risks seeming like it, though."[31] Indeed, the risk inherent in *Fin de siglo*'s movement away from the "Homo Pomo style" of the New Queer Cinema is one that not all critics have managed to navigate effectively, drawn as some of them are to reading in the film's closing sequence a simultaneous acceptance of homonormative domesticity and a rejection of the observational realism of the film as a whole. "But if *Weekend* progressively inches towards the real, *End of the Century* embraces only fantasy in the end," writes Ed Gonzalez. "It is a jarring endnote to an initially mysterious film, as the philosophical inquisitiveness of the first two parts is replaced by an indulgence of fiction as wish-fulfilment."[32] The indulgence that Gonzalez reads in this ending, which he argues "leaves us with the not-so-ambiguous impression that Castro believes that a gay man's contentment is only possible through the performance of domesticity," overlooks both the film's affective deconstruction of the strictures associated with such domesticity and, on a more profound level, its broader queering of temporal frameworks.[33] Read through the lens of New Queer Cinema's defiance, as implicitly suggested by critics such as Gonzalez, there is indeed a case for arguing that *Fin de siglo* offers a vision of a gay couple that embraces the homonormative institutions of parenthood and monogamy. Read, however, through the lens of New Queer Realism, a lens attentive to the queer potential of the film's distinct temporalities and aesthetic textures, *Fin de siglo* becomes a more complex interrogation of the "happiness scripts" imposed by a heteronormative society and of the affective politics of a domesticity traditionally foreclosed to queer cinematic characters.

There is, therefore, something distinctly less "sincere" in *Fin de siglo*'s playfulness with temporalities and in its aesthetic mobilization of the queer quotidian, rendering incongruous Moor's attribution of narrative authenticity. On the one hand, extended shots of Ocho in the shower, devoid of any narrative importance or erotic function, and those of him scrolling through Grindr or simply reading in bed, ensure that the registers of realism remain prominent throughout. The narrative tension that one might ordinarily attribute to acts of masturbation or sex scenes between the pair finds itself instead dissipated through static camerawork, extended takes, a mundanity of dialogue, and an excision of any canonically erotic content. On the other hand, however, the closing sequence purposefully deviates from this dose of quotidian realism, with its fantasy-driven scenario that precludes a sense of linearity or any discrete division between the imagined and the real. The latter is an important distinction: though Moor notes a tone of observational sincerity in the corpus of films he analyzes, in which "realistic imagery, where the emphasis is on the content matter and a supposed fidelity to the actual, dominates," the temporalities of *Fin de siglo* are calibrated precisely to undermine any absolute fidelity to the real or to the sincere.[34] Though the observational impulse of its filmic structures imbues the men's conversations and sex with a credible sense of intimacy, the temporal frameworks into which they fall, as the final section of this chapter will argue, demand a more open, future-oriented contemplation through the cinematic registers of New Queer Realism.

If Moor's theorization of "New Gay Sincerity" rests on a filmic commitment to an "aura of authenticity," *Fin de siglo* instead strategically ruptures any such spectatorial expectation through a reflexive, knowing gesture that confuses and confounds through its temporal *recalibration*.[35] Not only do we jump fluidly back and forth between distinct epochs, with no immediate or discernible difference in visual cues, but the film also ultimately refuses to demarcate the actual from the possible. Karl Schoonover and Rosalind Galt note in *Queer Cinema in the World* that "queer texts are often marked by a troubled temporality in which non-synchronous activity throws a wrench in the gears of heterosynchronics. If heterosynchrony manages dominant forms of narrative pleasure, then *queer structures of feeling* simmer in less synchronous texts."[36] *Fin de siglo*'s simultaneous embrace of the real in narrative terms and rejection of a linearity in structure and temporality thus offer a more complex regime of representation. In its refusal of the committed formal and narrative sincerity that Moor discerns in earlier queer filmic production from the decade,

Fin de siglo deploys its "troubled temporalities" alongside an observational realism in order to render its visions of the future both possible and, via its "queer structures of feeling," politically affective.

The Queer Art of Feeling

Fin de siglo's playful approach toward temporality is not restricted to its narrative structure but extends through the film's script and into its mise-en-scène. In a sequence at the Museu Nacional d'Art de Catalunya in the second chapter of the film, when Javi takes Ocho on a tour of the city, their interactions with various pieces from the museum's collections strike a playful note of irreverence toward history and its artistic mediation. "Me impresiona la cantidad de relatos necesarios para poder pintar algo así, ¿no?" (The number of stories you need to paint something like that is impressive, right?), remarks Ocho, as he and Javi face away from the camera and contemplate the busy landscape of a battle scene, whose image fills the entire screen.[37] He continues: "Porque en esa época no había otro registro. Alguien tuvo que haberle contado cómo era la batalla y él la pintó" (There wasn't any other way to do it back then. Someone must've told him what the battle was like, and then he painted it). The faceless figures on the canvas correspond with the spectator's parallel lack of access to the men's facial expressions in that moment, quietly reflecting the film's own mediation of the pair's developing relationship and, more broadly, the subjectivity and diversity of experience encapsulated within any representation of the past. In the following scene, the pair contrive a genealogy of characters and connections from a series of marble busts before making their way through a room of full-body sculptures, enacting a deliberate choreography that visually likens their own poses to those of the statues they observe (see figure 1.4).

While these scenes may be interpreted as evocations of the vitality of the men's evolving relationship against the static pastness of the historical artifacts before them, or even as markers of institutional subversion through the tongue-in-cheek invention of alternative familial histories, any such reading would fail to appreciate the textures of the film's broader treatment of temporality. As the men wander through the distinctly demarcated historical periods of the museum's exhibition rooms, from classical sculptures to Dalí's modernist Schiaparelli perfume bottles, their frivolity gently mocks the methodical delineation of past and present.

Figure 1.4. Film still. Museal choreography and the queering of temporalities in *Fin de siglo*. *Source*: Dir. Lucio Castro. Alsina 427, JWProductions (2019).

Their alternative interpretations of these historical artifacts imitate the film's broader structural "out-of-timeness," through which there exists a porosity not simply between 1999 and 2019, but also, via the closing sequence, between reality and fantasy.[38] There is, in other words, both a queer vitality to their interactions with the marble busts and sculptures, and a counterhegemonic subversion of the linearity of the history they represent. This "out-of-timeness," which Manuel Betancourt explains in his review of the film as a "shuffling of time [that] feels not so much disorienting as dreamlike" (Betancourt 2019), foregrounds the "conexión mágica, no racional" (magic, nonrational connection) that Javi sees in the subject matter of one of his favorite paintings in the museum. Just as the camera allows time for the men to contemplate the pieces of art, so too does Castro weave, for us as spectators, an affective resonance across the film's timeframes that displaces linearity and prioritizes the value of subjective interpretation and experience.

In the scene that follows their trip to the museum, as Javi and Ocho share a carton of Don García wine against the backdrop of a Catalan sunset and discuss Javi's documentary in progress about the imminent turn of the millennium, their conversation again implicitly insists on the affective importance of individual experience. Ocho contends that the relevance of Javi's documentary lies not in its capturing of a specific historical moment but instead as a marker of his own personal perspective toward living through it. "Siempre va a ser una impresión de tu experiencia,

¿no?" (It's always going to be a snapshot of your experience, isn't it?), he says, in defense of Javi's concerns about releasing the film too long after the turn of the century, once society's collective anxieties about "el fin del mundo" (the end of the world) have subsided. Ocho's insistence on the artistic value of subjective experience chimes with his earlier remarks in the museum that it is "mejor ver el cuadro, ver lo que [le] pasa a [él]" (better to see the painting for himself), rather than to have "la mirada condicionada" (his gaze conditioned) by another's interpretation of it.[39] Significantly, in the same sunset scene, Ocho reveals his intentions to switch his studies from business administration to literature, in order to be a writer or, rather, as he suggests, "tener una vida de escritor" (to have the life of a writer), one that he connects with flexibility, creativity and personal freedom. That he then describes his incipient drunkenness moments later as "un equilibrio químico justo, *puro presente*, perfecto" (just the right chemical balance, *pure presentness*, perfection) encapsulates the film's emphasis on the *presentness* of the men's experience over the course of the weekend that they share.

The visual and narrative parallels that Castro sets up between the sunset conversations in 1999 and 2019, all of which involve wine, intimate exchanges, and a backdrop of Barcelona at dusk, embed *Fin de siglo*'s affective investment in the intimate realities of the men's lives within the structure of the film itself. The conversations act, too, not only as moments of revelation but also as turning points that demonstrate how desires and emotions change over time: Ocho's reflection in 2019 that he no longer wants children contrasts with his earlier aspirations to have a house full of them, perhaps even *ocho*, eight of them; similarly, their candid discussions of relationships, sex lives (or lack thereof), and feelings of loneliness offer a sense of depth and complexity to the years that have passed in between. Here, the intimate nature of the conversations, the fluid, quasi-improvised tone of the dialogue, and the presentation of the men's desires as neither linear nor always fulfilled refuse to instill their respective experiences with a sense of universality or stereotype. Instead, what develops from these interactions is an inherent recognition of the many ways that queer identities can transform, adapt, and exist over time.

In *The Queer Art of Failure*, Jack Halberstam argues that "failing is something queers do and have always done exceptionally well," noting that "under certain circumstances failing, losing, forgetting, unmaking, undoing, unbecoming, not knowing may in fact offer more creative, more cooperative, more surprising ways of being in the world."[40] There are indeed traces of failure to be found in the film's sunset exchanges: Ocho's twenty-year relationship has come to an end, and he describes his desire to be alone with a distinct sense of disillusionment; Javi's relationship with his husband is no longer a sexual one, despite tangible demonstrations of his erotic appetite over the course of the weekend with Ocho; and both men discuss loneliness, lost friendships, and missed opportunities, with Javi admitting that he had tried to find Ocho on Facebook after their initial hookup but had not succeeded in doing so. Their remarks, moreover, are set into relief by the transience of the dusk scenes behind them, offering a visual and symbolic parallel to their unrealized aspirations of becoming (in Ocho's case) a writer and a father or (in Javi's case) a film director. Failure, in this sense, haunts the narrative in a quiet but sustained way, punctuating the pair's conversations with realistic observations of the complexities of the lives they have both lived and not (yet) lived.

We might unravel the significance of such scenes via Halberstam, who argues that while "failure comes accompanied by a host of negative affects, such as disappointment, disillusionment, and despair, it also provides the opportunity to use these negative affects to poke holes in the toxic positivity of contemporary life."[41] *Fin de siglo* cannot, of course, be understood to mobilize failure as an explicitly political or anti-normative strategy, as discussed previously in relation to the radical defiance of the New Queer Cinema, which did indeed challenge the "punishing norms that discipline behaviour and manage human development with the goal of delivering us from unruly childhoods to orderly and predictable adulthoods."[42] Instead, there is in the film's realist impulses—that is, in its acknowledgment of the inherent unruliness and complexity of lives, in its refusal to dwell melodramatically or melancholically on any single moment, and in its honest confrontation of dashed hopes and failed ambitions—a discreet sense of acceptance that plans do not always go to plan. Instead, as Halberstam goes on to suggest, "The queer art of failure turns on the impossible, the improbable, the unlikely, and the unremarkable; it quietly loses, and in losing it imagines other goals for life, for love, for art, and for being."[43] It is in this way that *Fin de siglo* recalibrates the queer art of failure into one of *feeling*, prioritizing the affective resonances of the men's relationships and their potential to offer a politics of representation that acknowledges the diverse and changing dynamics of queer lives.

For her part, Sara Ahmed tackles the emotions conventionally associated with failure and their queer potential in *The Promise of Happiness*. Ahmed argues that the political imperative to *be* happy necessitates the rigorous policing of certain social norms related to the "good life"; that is, those expectations, or "happiness scripts," of love, careers, marriage, and the future that mediate and condition our relationship to the world and those around us.[44] For Elizabeth Freeman, these "chrononormative" aspects of societal expectations demand that a life be "narrated in a novelistic framework: as event-centred, goal-oriented, intentional, and culminating in epiphanies of major transformations."[45] There is, correspondingly, a political imperative in Ahmed's work to "embrace the unhappy queer" as a means of liberating queer subjects from hetero- and chrononormative notions of what constitutes success and fulfillment. She writes:

> The freedom to be unhappy is not about being wretched or sad, although it might involve freedom to express such feelings. [. . .] The freedom to be unhappy would be the freedom to live a life that deviates from the paths of happiness, wherever that deviation takes us. It would thus mean the freedom to cause unhappiness by acts of deviation. [. . .] To share what deviates from happiness is to open up to possibility, to be alive to possibility.[46]

Fin de siglo carves out a space for the quiet, even speculative, contemplation of contemporary society's "paths of happiness," attending to the realities of the queer experience and, through the film's sustained sense of New Queer Realism, laying bare an entire spectrum of affective associations within which the two characters' lives are positioned. The film refuses to pathologize the failures of its characters as essentially connected to their sexual orientations or identities. Instead, it dwells in the realm of the affective, moving our focus toward the feelings that drive the men's discussions of their fears and regrets and of their pasts and futures. The film's final fantasy sequence, discussed in more depth in the following section, can be read as a candid example of the openness "to chance, to chance arrivals, to the perhaps of a happening" that Ahmed sees as requisite for the relinquishing of normative scripts of happiness.[47] But these sunset sequences also exude a nostalgic and aspirational tenor through which a sense of the "happily queer" emerges, a recognition of the "unhappiness that is concealed by the promotion of happy normativity."[48] In the twists and turns of the men's lives during the twenty years between their two chance encounters, Javi and Ocho's intimate discussions gesture toward the fragility of normative conceptions of domesticity, as well as the potential of deviating from these established expectations for life, love, and the pursuit of happiness.

(Un)happy Encounters

In the final fifteen minutes of *Fin de siglo*, the characters and their storyline slip into an alternative reality, exchanging the weekend-long romance between Javi and Ocho for a glimpse of what their lives could have been had they spent the previous twenty years together. At the beginning of the sequence, when Javi leaves the apartment for the final time in the film's "present," making it clear that to stay would flaunt the ground rules that he and his husband have established for their open relationship, Ocho goes to the balcony to watch Javi exit the apartment block. When Javi fails to leave the building, Ocho returns inside and steps on a rubber duck, an index of childhood whose sudden and unexplained presence both literally trips Ocho up and figuratively announces a rupture in the narrative. As Ocho moves across the threshold between the balcony and the apartment, he enters an alternate, fantasy-driven configuration of reality, which, with the exception of a now fully stocked fridge and a rubber duck, remains visibly unchanged, in keeping with the film's broader reluctance to signal any jump in temporality through costume or mise-en-scène. Despite the wistful goodbye between the men some moments earlier, Javi is then to be found sleeping in the Airbnb's bedroom, leaving a noticeably confused Ocho with no other option than to go to sleep beside him, waking up the following morning to the perplexing sight of Javi feeding their daughter breakfast, followed by her playing with the rubber duck.

This is a sequence shot through with temporal dislocation. Not only does it stage an alternative present for the two men, which sits parallel—or, as Elizabeth Freeman might say, "aslant"—to the reality of the weekend they spent together, but Ocho also insists that he ever-so-faintly remembers the life he did actually lead, the twenty-year life in New York that we are told about in an earlier chapter of the film.[49] "Pasábamos veinte años juntos, vivíamos en Nueva York," Ocho says to Javi, while the pair stands on the balcony, "Lo único de que estoy seguro es que no eras vos. Estoy seguro de eso: no eras vos" (I spent twenty years with someone, and we lived in New York. The only thing I'm sure of is that it wasn't you. I'm sure about that: it wasn't you). Moreover, Javi's ex-girlfriend, Sonia, who we learn had passed away in a road traffic accident, appears singing in a secluded Barcelona *plaça*, materialized into a spectral presence that both troubles the film's linearity and calls into question how our choices come to affect the lives of others. Castro again refuses to offer any explicit narrative marker of rupture to the sequence, over and above a rubber duck, submerging Ocho—and us—into the uncanniness of a reality-turned-dream or, perhaps, a dream-turned-reality.

The momentary glimpse of domestic complacency offered in this closing scene is far from radical in the futurity that it pictures. Javi, for instance, insists on clearing out the men's wardrobe, injecting the sequence with the hum-drum reality of lives that are twenty years entwined. His suggestion that they get rid of the Kiss T-shirt that played such a pivotal role in their relationship also gestures toward how our connections to objects and people shift as time marches on. A thirty-second sex scene between the pair, filmed through a single static shot as earlier in the film, is directly bookended by discussions that dissipate any of its erotic charge, with Javi first offering to "hacer el esfuerzo" (make the effort) despite not being in the mood to have sex and then followed by Ocho's vague memories of leading a life in New York that resolutely did not include Javi. That this latter discussion takes place on the balcony is significant. It is a space that initially serves as the vantage point that facilitates the men's first verbal interaction, but here it also functions as a space in the margins of the domestic sphere where the boundaries between reality and fiction blur. Moments later, when Ocho stands alone on the balcony and the film returns—again unprompted and with no discernible cut—to the present, Javi can be seen leaving the apartment block wearing the Kiss T-shirt, an emblem now recalibrated as a testament both to the serendipity of their chance encounters in 1999 and 2019 and, thanks to this closing scene, to the possibilities of paths not taken and of lives unlived.

In the contemplative, ten-second shots of Barcelona that herald the close of the film, temporalities also visibly collide via the images of old *plaças*, modernist architecture, palm trees, and lampposts, with the twilight setting evocatively acting as a coda to the film's sustained investment in moments of transition and change. That Castro intersperses two twenty-second images of the sea within this closing montage is crucial: the beach the space where the men's weekend (re)encounter began, after all, and the water reflects the fluidity of the film's approach to temporality, matched as these two shots are by the minor key of a soundtrack that tonally implies a sense of the unresolved. The fireworks in the closing shot, which appear alongside the film's title, suggest that the impending millennium of the film's second chapter has arrived, condensing and compressing the film's timeframes in an uncanny manner befitting of the film's broader treatment of time's divisions and deviations.

In *The Promise of Happiness*, Ahmed discusses the challenges posed by queer temporalities to the linear logics of heteronormativity, locating in their destabilizing thrust the potential for a happiness based not on the present but on "the future of the perhaps."[50] She writes: "Such a happiness would be alive to chance, to chance arrivals, to the perhaps of a happening. [. . .] A happening is an encounter, the chance of an encounter, or even a chance encounter. Such encounters recreate the ground on which things do happen. To recreate a ground is to deviate from a past that has not been given up. When things go astray, other things can happen. We have a future, perhaps."[51] Just as the entire narrative of *Fin de siglo* revolves around the chance reencounter of Javi and Ocho on a Barcelona beach twenty years after their first meeting, the temporal disjuncture of this closing sequence can also be read as another "chance encounter," as an overt rendering of Ahmed's "future of the perhaps." The routine complacency of a twenty-year-old relationship may not immediately resemble an explicitly happy future; nor may the matter-of-factness of the pair's lackluster sex drives offer a positive image of their relationship, especially when contrasted with their more energetic carnal desires in the film's "present." If we read this final sequence through Ahmed's lens of the happy queer, however, it is the very possibility of visualizing such domestic complacency that surfaces as a counter to the hegemonic scripts traditionally attributed to queer characters. "In imagining what is possible, in imagining what does not yet exist, we say yes to the future," writes Ahmed. "It is not that the future is imagined as the overcoming of misery; nor is the future imagined as being happy. The future is kept open as the possibility of things not staying as they are, or being as they stay."[52]

Fin de siglo's final flash sideward to an alternative present is steeped in the optimism of queer futurity, offering a reconciliation—though specifically *not* a conclusion—of the intimate details that Javi and Ocho have shared with one another over the course of their weekend together: their desires (or not) to have children, the development (or not) of their respective relationships, and their aspirations for their own lives, careers, and futures. Indeed, in what could serve as a critical summary of the film itself, Ahmed concludes in her discussion of futurity and queer happiness: "Possibilities have to be recognised as possibilities to become possible.

[. . .] Embracing possibility involves returning to the past, recognizing what one has, as well as what one has lost, what one has given, as well as what one has given up. To learn about possibility is to do genealogy, to wonder about the present by wondering about the how of its arrival. To learn about possibility thus involves a certain estrangement from the present."[53] In the cinematic excavation of the genealogy of Ocho and Javi's relationships, whether between themselves or with others, *Fin de siglo* carves out a space for its queer characters in which there presides "a certain kind of openness to the possibility of an encounter."[54] It is a film of wandering and wondering, of returning to the past and arriving in the present, and of embodying possibilities. Castro explores the conventional routes of happiness and, by estranging the men from their present, imag(in)es how they inhabit—or, at least, might be permitted to inhabit—such scripts. *Fin de siglo* locates happiness not in domestic bliss or in heteronormative notions of success and fulfillment but, instead, through the film's temporal twists and turns, in the possibilities thereof.

In a way that might, again, be attributed directly to the film itself, Elizabeth Freeman considers in *Time Binds* how artistic representations of queer temporalities often "invent possibilities for moving through and with time, encountering pasts, speculating futures, and interpenetrating the two in ways that counter the common sense of the present tense."[55] Though *Fin de siglo* does not, it must be noted, explicitly correspond with the radical potential Freeman sees in "living aslant to dominant forms of object-choice, coupledom, family, marriage, sociability, and self-presentation," there is a crucial and critical significance to the film's momentary engagement with the affective politics of the conventional domestic unit.[56] While Gonzalez perceives in the film's ending an acquiescence to "the performance of domesticity" on the part of Javi and Ocho, this chapter has instead argued that the ambiguous location of this domestic vision in the future, or rather in an alternative present, belies a more complex queering of the film's temporal structures, which works to expose the affective and political significance of its cinematic interrogation of queer (un)happiness.[57] The film actualizes the plane on which its politics of representation unfold, allowing the space—and *time*—for an exploration of a queer domesticity that breaks free from the "common sense of the present tense."[58]

In her discussion of homonormativity and Haigh's *Weekend*, Stephanie Deborah Clare argues that critiques of homonormativity often "posit overly strategic subjects who make decisions about how to navigate the social world" and, thus, overlook "homonormativity's affective and emotional pull."[59] I have argued here that *Fin de siglo* sidesteps an endorsement of the homonormative politics associated with domesticity through both its parallel interrogation of the affective dynamics associated with any such eventuality for the men and its setting of this eventuality in the realm of the ephemeral and the oneiric. Clare's discussion is, however, imperative, not least in terms of how she argues that "homonormativity's allures lie in sensibilities, affect, desire and sentiments such as love, happiness and hope, and queer studies cannot imagine a viable otherwise unless we attend to these feelings."[60] Far from the radical rejection of family, monogamy, children, and success that we might associate with the New Queer Cinema and with certain strands of antisocial queer thought, *Fin de siglo* instead focalizes the emotional pull of these "happiness scripts," locating them within an ambiguous temporality that mobilizes a sense of optimism for its queer characters. As Michael Snediker argues: "Queer optimism doesn't ask that some future time make good on its own hopes. Rather, queer optimism asks that optimism, embedded in its own immanent present, be *interesting*."[61] *Fin de siglo*'s alternative visions of the future through the lens of New Queer Realism lay bare the imaginative inhabiting of certain aspirations and desires, as well as the more complex interrogation of their affective implications. The film asks not that Ocho and Javi get their happy ending but, rather, that they be allowed to envision the possibility of sharing one together, and that such an "openness to an encounter" be possible more broadly for both queer characters and their cinematic spectators.

Futury, Perhaps

Both at the beginning and at the end of *Fin de siglo*, Ocho is to be found in his Airbnb apartment alone. The film avoids a conventionally happy ending, yet it also represents a broader, revitalizing shift in contemporary queer cinema away from spectacles of tragedy, homophobic violence, or the melodrama of coming out. *Fin de siglo* delves instead into the microdynamics of queer relationships and into the aesthetic and affective textures of queerness in the contemporary moment. It moves away, as this chapter has demonstrated, from the radical offensive of antisocial failure and defiance associated with previous waves of queer cinema and theory to one that embraces the optimism and political potential of feeling. In doing so, the film offers a countercritique to allegations of homonormativity; it deconstructs the happiness scripts that regulate contemporary society, laying bare their fictions but refusing to deny their affective draw. *Fin de siglo* allows Ocho and Javi to revel in the realms of fantasy and uncertainty and to experiment with time and space as dimensions replete with queer potential.

In a scene during the second chapter of the film, when Ocho leaves Javi the morning after their first sexual encounter in 1999, the words from a passage of David Wojnarowicz's *Close to the Knives: A Memoir of Disintegration* scroll across the screen: "I'm getting closer to the coast and realise how much I hate arriving at a destination. Transition is always a relief. Destination means death to me. If I could figure out a way to remain forever in transition, in the disconnected and unfamiliar, I could remain in a state of perpetual freedom."[62] While, admittedly, this superimposed text announces a pivotal turning point of the film in a way that feels somewhat heavy-handed, its testimonial construction of freedom is one that chimes with the theoretical concerns of queer futurity, as explored in this chapter through theorists such as Ahmed, Freeman, and Muñoz. For the latter, "Queerness is a longing that propels us forward, [. . .] that thing that lets us feel that this world is not enough, that indeed something is missing. [. . .] Queerness is not simply a being but a doing for and toward the future."[63] *Fin de siglo*'s deploys its temporal playfulness and observational realism to explore the nature of open relationships, queer parenthood, Grindr hookups, chance encounters, and the affective registers of gay life in the twenty-first century; but there also exists a future-oriented impulse that asks us to imagine the realm of possibility available for its queer cinematic characters. Unlike Moor's New Gay Sincerity, the New Queer Realism of *Fin de siglo* circulates not through narrative linearity or via a sense of documentary realism, but instead through a fluid futurity that emphasizes the lived realities *and* imagined possibilities of the queer experience. It offers us the affective politics of a domesticity routinely foreclosed to queer cinematic characters and, in doing so, offers glimpses of "an anticipatory illumination of a queer world, a sign of an actually existing queer reality, a kernel of political possibility within a stultifying heterosexual present."[64] From the reflexive knowingness of its art gallery scenes to the authenticity of its sunset discussions of parenthood and marriage, *Fin de siglo* locates happiness not in inhabiting the normative strictures of the traditional domestic unit but, through its temporal dislocations and affective realism, in the potential to imagine futures in which this might be possible. Ultimately, the film permits us—and indeed affectively *urges* us—to glimpse queer (un)happiness in the futurity of the perhaps.

Chapter Two

On the Shores of Adulthood

Queer Adolescence and the Fallacy of Fluidity in Contemporary Brazilian Film

> Water is the truly transitory element. [. . .] A being dedicated to water is a being in flux.[1]
>
> —Gaston Bachelard, *Water and Dreams*

The cinematic merging of fluidity, sexuality, and queerness in Filipe Matzembacher and Marcio Reolon's *Tinta Bruta* (*Hard Paint*, 2018) represents one of the most recent examples of a growing trend in Brazilian film that combines narrative explorations of queer identities with thematic and formal emphases on the aquatic. NeonBoy, as the adolescent protagonist of *Tinta Bruta* is known to his online followers, carves out a niche on the internet through his erotic webcam performances that involve neon paint smothered over his seminaked body and illuminated by a blacklight. His eventual collaboration with Boy25, a rival online performer, who transforms NeonBoy's solo show into a double act, provokes questions surrounding not only the exploitative and predatory nature of online camming but also the adolescent mutability of sexuality and sexual orientation. As their followers demand more explicit material from the duo, each of the teenage men struggles to reconcile the homoeroticism of their online performances with the performance of a heteronormative masculinity in the broader—*offline*—public sphere. The formal qualities of these webcam scenes in *Tinta Bruta* focus haptically on the toned bodies of the men, both of whom are in their late teens, indulging visually in the stickiness of the luminescent threads of paint that connect their chests, limbs and mouths, at once metaphorically intimating the fluidity of the teenagers' sexual desires and synecdochally alluding to the bodily fluids shared between them that the camera does not screen (figure 2.1).

The script and soundtrack of *Tinta Bruta*, moreover, embellish the eroticism of these acts of fluidity, such as when one performance is accompanied by a soundtrack that describes "molhando seu corpo na água" (soaking his body in water) or when the men dance in the open air by the coastline to the following lyrics: "Boca grande, braços firmes, olhos fixos / mãos, dedos duros / entrando por dentro do roupa / Escorro, afogada em líquidos / que saem do corpo do meu amigo / Derreto" (Large mouth, firm arms, fixed eyes / hands, hard fingers / reaching inside his clothes / I'm dripping, drowning in liquids / that come from his body / I'm melting). The explicit materiality of the adolescent bodies in *Tinta Bruta*—from their "dedos duros," engaged in a series of on-screen sexual acts, to the recurrently haptic screening of their bare torsos—in this way contrasts with the liquid mutability of the identities and orientations that are ascribed to them. At once, these scenes both expose the arbitrary nature of certain normative categories of sexuality through the teenagers' online (and offline) experimentation and draw our attention, as spectators, to the erotic potential of cinema's capacity to screen the body. Indeed, while the grainy footage of the cam shows initially distinguishes them from the polished cinematic gaze of the rest of the film, the subsequent

Figure 2.1. Film still. Sticky luminescent liquid bonds between bodies in *Tinta Bruta*. *Source*: Dir. Marcio Reolon and Filipe Matzembacher. Avante Filmes, Besouro Filmes (2019).

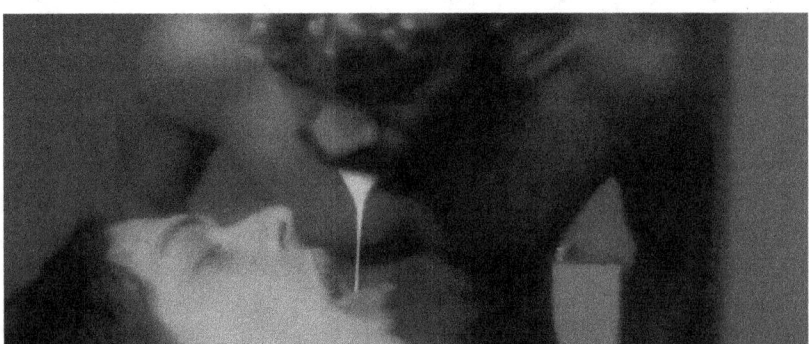

collapsing of these two modes into one another draws attention to the artifice of both, conflating the filmic spectator with the online follower in suggestively aesthetic and ethical terms. Fluidity, in *Tinta Bruta*, is therefore fashioned not only thematically but also in formal and conceptual terms, mobilizing and molding gazes via the film's queer aesthetic and bringing into focus the sexuality and desires of the adolescent body.

Tinta Bruta's idiosyncratic exploration of online camming is one of a number of evolutions in contemporary Brazilian queer cinema that turn to liquids and watery spaces as aesthetic strategies in the screening of queerness. As this chapter will argue, this is a trend that attends at once to the theoretical and political potential of sexuality's *fluid* nature, particularly as it intersects with the adolescent experience, as well as to the concrete material realities of race, economic privilege, bodily ability, and social class to which bodies are subject. In Aluisio Abranches's *Do Começo ao Fim* (*From Beginning to End*, 2009), baths and swimming pools provide the homoerotic backdrops for the development of an incestuous relationship between two adolescent half-brothers, with the uncontainable volatility of water in this case symbolizing the dangers of desires taken too far. In Marcos Prado's *Paraísos Artificiais* (*Artificial Paradises*, 2012), the time and space of a coastal festival in Praia do Paiva, Recife, act as the setting for a drama of drug-fueled desires, against images of waves and the horizon that connote both the escape from the normative confines of the city and the naturalness of adolescent sexual experimentation. Karim Aïnouz's *Praia do Futuro* (*Futuro Beach*, 2014), for its part, calibrates the narration of a transnational homosexual relationship through the space of the beach and the ocean, both of which serve to complicate any straightforward notion of (national) belonging for the film's Brazilian lifeguard protagonist and his German partner. In these films, as well as in those analyzed in this chapter, fluids—most often water, in its various natural presentations—are invested at once with a metaphorical quality that capitalizes on liquid's capacity to rupture static, hegemonic identities and discourses, as well as with a formal capacity that emphasizes the materiality of bodies. Moreover, it is often via a haptic cinematography that these images "bring vision closer to the body," a cinematography that dwells sensually on sweat and skin, rendering "vision multisensory" and thereby filmically invoking the synesthesia of the erotic.[2]

Critics have, however, tended in their discussions of the above films to gloss over the significance of this formal potential of water, restricting their analyses to the levels of symbol and metaphor by interpreting fluidity primarily—or, indeed, exclusively, in certain cases—as a mirror for the volatility of sexuality against the fixity of societally imposed heteronormative and *heteronormalizing* strictures. In his discussion of *Do Começo ao Fim*, for instance, Fernando G. Pagnoni Berns writes that "in the act of sharing water, the brothers reach a space where cultural and societal boundaries loosen up and they can express, to some extent, their feelings for each other openly."[3] Likewise, in the same chapter, he notes in his discussion of *Praia do Futuro* that "perhaps only queer subjects, those who must hide their sexual identity can truly appreciate this space [of water] as a liberating one."[4] While there is no doubt that many of the films discussed in this chapter do indeed rely, at times in a superficial manner, on this symbolic capacity of water, the language that binds fluidity to freedom—the language, that is, of "loosening up," of "openness," and of "liberation"—belies a more complex dynamic between fluidity and identity, comprehensible only when due attention is paid to the materiality of bodies and the textural modes of spectatorship that are employed to screen them. As this chapter will argue, contemporary queer Brazilian cinema, in its simultaneous invocation to the aquatic and to the corporeal, challenges any exclusionary focus on the abstract poetics of watery spaces. It exposes unbridled fluidity as a political and identitarian fallacy. Instead, we witness an emphasis on the material realities of the bodies that move within and through these spaces, bodies, that is, that can be (mis)gendered or differently abled, socially and economically marginalized, and, importantly for the Brazilian context, visibly—and often violently—racialized.

    Discourses of fluidity have, of course, been a longstanding framework within studies of sexuality and adolescence, both of which have been theoretically inflected through the lens of a postmodern, poststructuralist mutability for several decades. Sexuality and sexual orientation are now understood to exist dynamically on a spectrum, refuting any tendency toward fixity in a way bolstered by the acknowledgment of the performativity of gender and gender identities.[5] Likewise, studies of childhood and adolescence are notable for their recent embrace of flux and experimentation, rejecting any coherent or stable boundaries in the development of identity and instead promoting a dynamic approach to how adolescent identities are acted upon continually and irreducibly by societal and cultural forces.[6] As Kathryn Bond Stockton reminds us in *The Queer Child, or Growing Sideways*, such turbulence is only to be expected from a period of time in one's life that is, in itself, "queerly" mutable.[7] Both sexuality and adolescence, therefore, particularly in their queerer iterations and developments outlined above, espouse fluidity as the necessary means for counteracting the solidifying and stultifying heterononormative, heterocapitalistic parameters of contemporary societies.

It is important to note, however, several significant challenges to these prevailing paradigms with which the present chapter aligns itself. Brad Epps, in "The Fetish of Fluidity," argues that "by insistently setting its sights on fluidity, by taking it as that which at once denies and affirms disciplinary power, queer theory performs a little magic of its own: to put it provocatively, even perversely, it makes fluidity a fetish."[8] For Epps, the theoretical and conceptual embrace of an *essential* mutability serves to obscure the material realities faced by queer people, undermining certain valuable categories and structures of identity through the relentless prioritization of (queer) instability. "As with many other things," writes Epps, "the body is itself in trouble, rendered so discursive as to matter little, if at all."[9] Within studies of children and young adults, numerous scholars have also begun to take cinematic representations of adolescence more seriously, cutting through reductive ideas of adolescence as merely a prospective period of becoming, defined essentially by a sense of free-flowing—and as-yet-unfulfilled—development. Geoffrey Maguire and Rachel Randall, in their work on adolescent visuality in Latin American cinema, shun the idea of the adolescent as merely a symbolic category of transition to point out that "that young people are themselves [already] desiring subjects."[10] Maguire and Randall argue that in the prevailing rush to read adolescence allegorically as a site of futurity (often in terms of the nation), we obscure, and even suppress, the ways in which teenagers experience race, class, gender, and sexuality in the present. Their approach parallels a more general cleaving of studies of adolescence from those of childhood,[11] one that recognizes, primarily through the lens of sexuality and gender, the distinct postpubescent experiences faced by adolescents and the inherent potential they possess to "complicate the dichotomy between the 'innocence' of childhood and the 'rigidity' of adulthood."[12]

As such, this chapter takes seriously the critical potential of both fluidity and adolescence, arguing that the prominence of their merging in contemporary queer Brazilian film points to innovative theoretical and political expressions of queerness.[13] While cultural studies critics have, for some time, focused on the poetics of water and its potential to reflect and refract a sense of flux or utopian potential, not least in the way that Gaston Bachelard does in the epigraph to this chapter, I argue instead how the present corpus of films draws our attention to the materiality of both bodies *and* bodies of water. These films expose how a critical overinvestment in fluidity may obscure how subjects—particularly, for this study, *adolescent* subjects—experience the intersections of sexuality, gender, social class, ability, and race. In other words, these cinematic depictions of adolescence articulate what I take to be the *fallacy of fluidity* in contemporary cultural media, which, in its most profound etymological sense, works to embed a deceptively or artificially simplistic understanding of fluidity and its utopian relationship to identity. In order to counter this fallacy, the first section of the chapter begins by charting the symbolic heritage of what Lúcia Nagib terms "sea images" in Brazilian film, noting how the utopian capacity of the ocean and its horizon have, categorically, excluded progressive representations of queer identities.[14] The second and third sections offer close analyses of the sea and the coastline in a range of contemporary adolescent-focused films from Brazil—namely, Filipe Matzembacher and Marcio Reolon's *Beira-Mar* (*Seashore*, 2015), Alexandre Moratto's *Sócrates* (2018), and Cris Lyra's *Quebramar* (*Breakwater*, 2019)—to demonstrate how the recent imbrication of fluidity, adolescent sexuality, and queerness constructs alternative epistemologies that both transcend any exclusively national focus and, yet, draw attention to the realities of racial, social, and gender oppression in Brazilian society. Indeed, just as José Esteban Muñoz argues in *Cruising Utopia* that "we can often glimpse the worlds proposed and promised by queerness in the realm of the aesthetic," this chapter ultimately turns to the formal representation of the ocean and the adolescent body as a means of registering an embodied, intersectional understanding of the queer experience in contemporary Brazil.[15]

Queer Bodies in Brazilian Cinema

In her seminal publication, *Brazil on Screen: Cinema Novo, New Cinema, Utopia*, Lúcia Nagib notes in her discussion of visions of the ocean, "From its beginnings, Brazilian cinema has abounded in sea images."[16] Similarly, in *Foundational Films: Early Cinema and Modernity in Brazil*, Maite Conde examines how seascapes recurred in the earliest Brazilian film, including in "what is credited as the first movie made on Brazilian soil," Affonso Segreto's recordings of Rio's Guanabara Bay from the ship *Brésil*.[17] Although Brazilian cinema, as Conde writes, became increasingly focused on the modernity of the urban in the ensuing early decades of the twentieth century, an epoch in which "tropical visions gave way to urban locations as filmmakers pointed their camera's towards the city's new boulevards," Nagib pinpoints a notable return to the oceanic in the films of the Cinema Novo in the 1960s and '70s.[18] These films exhibited a desire to reinvest cinema, in Nagib's words, with the "inaugural myths and impulses attached to Brazil's formation and national identity, favouring the return of utopian thought."[19] Through her analysis of *Deus e o Diabo na terra do sol* (*Black God, White Devil*, 1964) and *Terra em Transe* (*Entranced Earth*, 1967) by Glauber Rocha—a filmmaker unrivaled in instilling images of the sea "with such symbolic power"—Nagib goes on to analyze how cinematic figurations of the ocean during this period became inscribed with the tensions of modernity and socioeconomic prosperity, cyphered through the politics of the *sertão*-coast divide.[20] Ivana Bentes, too, discerns a similar dichotomy, writing in her discussion of Cinema Novo aesthetics, "The *sertão*, the barren and unruly land, with its exploited and destitute characters who have nothing to lose, is ready to undergo radical changes, moving from extreme aridity to extreme exuberance as it becomes the sea, a utopian and mythical place."[21] For both Nagib and Bentes, then, the ocean is figured in these films as "a paradise" against the "poverty and drought" of the *sertão*'s "failed modernity," transforming the famous dictum from *Deus e o Diabo*—"O sertão vai virar mar, e o mar vai virar sertão" (The *sertão* will become sea, and the sea will become *sertão*)[22]—into a utopian-orientated prophesy of socioeconomic possibility and political revolution.[23]

While the *sertão* does not figure prominently in the queer corpus of films discussed in this chapter, the seascape does however maintain a symbolic and aesthetic potential, as well as an affinity to the idea of the nation and its construction(s). Nagib stresses throughout her work how "maritime imagery became [after *Cinema Novo*] the main source of utopian motifs available to recent Brazilian cinema," as well as how "the sea returns in current films so insistently that it could suggest a utopia come true."[24] She also consistently makes the case for reading such sea images through the framework of the national, arguing how "recent cinema's reinterpretation of the maritime utopia" and the sheer prevalence of "monumental sea images" have rendered the space of the ocean as one endowed with the capacity to navigate the tensions and contradictions of Brazilian identity.[25] Such tensions in the Brazilian context predate the advent of cinema, of course, with Marilena Chaui pointing out how in her work on Brazil's "foundational myth" that "Brazil's natural division between the coast and the backlands gives rise to a theory that has long persisted, that of 'two Brazils,'" a theory that emerges at the beginning of the colonial period and "refers not to social divisions, but to divisions of and in nature itself: the New World is divided between the coast and the backlands."[26] While the spaces of the coast and the *sertão* have in these ways been of significant political and cultural import, what is vital for the contemporary context, however, is that "images of the sea have become," in Nagib's terms, not only historically resonant symbols but also "a privileged *cinematic* representation of the Brazilian Utopia."[27]

There is no doubt, therefore, that the queer films discussed in this chapter are indebted to the cinematic heritage that Nagib so insightfully traces in her work, imbued as they are with the utopian potentiality of the ocean and its connection, à la Muñoz, to the futurity of the horizon. "Queerness is always on the horizon," writes Muñoz. "We must strive, in the face of the here and now's totalizing rendering of reality, to think and feel a *then and there*."[28] However, the correlation between the ocean, the utopic, and this future-oriented *then and there* belies a considerably more fractious relationship in the case of queer subjects, not least given the difficult and often-violent histories that LGBTQ+ identities have had with the very idea of a national project. On the one hand, queer subjects have traditionally been excluded from the idea of the nation, figured as threats to the integrity of family and society; while on the other, as Jasbir K. Puar points out, the more recent neoliberal incorporation of queers into a "homonational" collective identity is precisely "contingent upon the segregation and disqualification of racial and sexual others from the national imaginary."[29] Within the localized history of Brazilian film, queer bodies and their subjectivities have been notably excised from the discursive construction of any collective identity, a point that a cursory glance at the scant history of on-screen representation serves to corroborate.

As Simone Cavalcante da Silva notes, popular cinema in the early decades of the 20th century engaged in a merely caricature fashion with queerness, initiating a damaging tendency through the "presence of cross-dressers, *bichas*, and *travestis* [. . .] that has been a recurring motif since the 1920s."[30] Stephanie Dennison and Lisa Shaw, in their discussion of the *(porno)chanchadas* of the 1960s, '70s, and '80s, write that homosexual themes "spoke to aspects of the Brazilian male psyche at the time, such as machismo and fear of castration."[31] They continue: "Hence the presence of the homosexual character in these films: laughing at these modern-day court jesters proved the audience's masculinity and exorcised their sexual insecurity and fear of impotence."[32] João Nemi Neto concurs in his analysis of the history of transvestitism in Brazilian cinema, writing, "[The *pornochancada's*] play on gender bending seems revealing of misogyny rather than illuminating an interest in or affinity with queer representation."[33] Likewise, in Antonio Moreno's sweeping, seminal study of LGBTQ+ cinema across the twentieth century in Brazil, O Personagem Homossexual do Cinema, he points out that in the decades that followed the filmic production of the 1970s, there emerged a stark divide between the homosexual character on screen and the development and diversity of actual queer subcultures within Brazilian society, listing an exhaustive array of films in which homosexual men, stereotyped in their presentation as *bichas* and *veados*, were typecast as objects of ridicule, derision, and comic relief.[34]

In a significant moment for Brazilian cinema, Karim Aïnouz—the director of one of the most sensitive and mature recent depictions of homosexuality via his film *Praia do Futuro*—prompted a pivotal juncture in the screening of queerness with his 2002 portrayal of the drag performer João Francisco dos Santos, better known as Madame Satã. Released at the tail end of the *cinema da retomada*, Aïnouz's eponymous portrait of Madame Satã's life and work binds the fluidity of sexuality and gender expression to the realities of violence in the context of the racial oppression of 1930s Rio de Janeiro. In this queerly revisionist, backward-looking glance at Brazilian history, Aïnouz rejects the disavowal that would have made such a figure at the time invisible both on screen and in mainstream society. As B. Ruby Rich points out in *New Queer Cinema: The Director's Cut*, the film serves as a "time capsule of what was as well as what might have been," affording the viewer "a glimpse, however brief, of new categories of personhood suggested by the trail-blazing, powerful, and tragic figure of João Francisco dos Santos."[35] Crucially, Rich points to the intersectional innovation of Aïnouz's portrayal of dos Santos, writing: "Race and class are often too incidental to queer narratives. In this tale of Brazil's unlikely hero-heroine, such omissions were impossible, for they are the core of Madame Satã's life narrative. In *Madame Satã*, João's twists and turns of gender reveal a filmmaker's commitments to inhabiting all the spaces of marginalization to which he, and the viewer, have access."[36] In Marcus Welsh's more recent analysis, which draws on Rich's reading of the film, he argues for an appreciation of the politics of embodiment at play in *Madame Satã*, noting astutely how the queer body functions as "a space of intersection with the social discourses of gender, race, and class," as well as how it becomes a site for exploring how "the performance of gender can be used as a *fluid*, dynamic, and purposeful means for contesting heteronormative standards."[37] Both Welsh and Rich emphasize the formal and aesthetic significance of the on-screen body, not least because it functions the vehicle of Madame Satã's performances, but also because it acts, in Welsh's terms, as the "nexus" through which the intersectional implications of queerness and the mutability of gender and sexuality may be grasped. "In the end," writes Welsh, "while dos Santos is able to express his fluid gender identity through performance, he is unable to manipulate or escape his social position as regulated by other factors."[38]

It is precisely this same impasse, embryonically present in *Madame Satã*, that I argue pervades many recent filmic explorations of queerness in Brazil. These are films that suggest a more explicit connection between the political and identitarian potential of fluidity (through the literal screening of seas, oceans, lakes, and pools) but that also ultimately expose, as Aïnouz does, the rigidity of certain socially and historically enforced structures of sexuality, gender, race, ability, and social class. While Rich claims in relation to *Madame Satã* that "these questions [of queerness, race and class] are not commonly operative in what has become, over time, a much more normative queer cinema in Brazil," this chapter recognizes a notable and growing number of films that refuse any such reductive treatment of queer bodies and their identities and that instead accentuate the material realities of the sociopolitical norms that regulate them.[39] As Cavalcante da Silva contends, "while outdated assumptions about the representation of non-heteronormative identities still prevail in the mainstream media," there has however been a tendency within recent film to "present queer protagonists who question their personal, political, and social subjectivities."[40] To be sure, these are not films endowed with the rampant iconoclasm of those of the New Queer Cinema in the 1990s and early 2000s, which were "radical, not just in their politics but also in their filmic form," but they are nevertheless attentive—as the following sections of this chapter will show—to the aspects of racial discrimination and socio-political marginality that have become fundamental to contemporary discussions of queerness.[41] Through their narrative counteraction of the offensive and often-misogynistic stereotypes of previous iterations of queer characters in Brazilian cinema, and via a formal investment in the queer body as a site marked by the violence of normative societal structures, recent queer cinema, I argue, recalibrates any utopian notion of fluidity through the cinematic reimag(in)ing of other modes of being and belonging in contemporary Brazil.

Beira-Mar, Affect, and the Adolescent Turn

In his analysis of the shores and coastlines in Javier Fuentes-León's *Contracorriente* (*Undertow*, 2009) and Alain Guiraudie's *L'Inconnu du lac* (*Stranger by the Lake*, 2013), Christopher Pullen remarks that "the queer male within the beach setting offers a representational nexus of pleasure, vulnerability and possible fulfilment."[42] Pullen contends that his chosen corpus of films—all of which infuse their watery spaces with both queer sexualities and the violence to which they are so often subject—counteracts Hollywood's historical ignorance toward gay men and their reduction to stereotype and victim, arguing that "the representation of the sensory nature of queer skin [in these beach settings] challenges histories of subjugation."[43] For Pullen, this formal emphasis on the queer body signifies, in turn, a crucial politics of representation: "There is a resistance to the notion of a fixed terrain, establishing a different way of viewing the queer body as not fixed to a place or an identity, but rather, as grounded in a sensory, emotive and affective state."[44] It is precisely these aspects of pleasure, vulnerability, and fulfillment, explored through the lens of the affective, that are present in Matzembacher and Reolon's *Beira-Mar*, a film that narrates a weekend trip two friends, Martin and Tomaz, take to a seaside town in southern Brazil. The symbolic capacity of the ocean is invoked from the outset of the film: as the two adolescent protagonists drive along the coastline toward the beach house, the diegetic music that accompanies their journey—which repeats the lyrics, "I know that there's no place left to hide, [. . .] my life is starting over again, over again, over again"—parallels the image of the sea behind them and its horizon in the distance. This combination of lyric and image connotes the possibilities of their weekend escape, far from the adult supervision of Porto Alegre, as well as how their friendship will develop unexpectedly over the few days that they spend with one another. As Martin attempts to repair a strained relationship with his extended family members and navigate this new connection that he fosters with Tomaz, the ocean becomes both a backdrop and a barometer for his sense of belonging in the world, all the while "grounded," to borrow Pullen's words, "in a sensory, emotive and affective state."[45]

The maritime landscape of *Beira-Mar*, which appears on several occasions refracted through windowpanes and merging with the teenagers' own reflections (figure 2.2), is endowed throughout the film with the formal potential to mirror the dynamics and flows of the young men's desires, both for one another and for the characters around them. The

Figure 2.2. Film still. Reflections of the teenagers through the prism of the beach in *Beira-Mar*. *Source*: Dir. Marcio Reolon and Filipe Matzembacher. Avante Filmes (2015).

isolated setting of the house, moreover, located on the beach itself and only a stone's throw away from the water, emphasizes a sense of marginality and functions as a quasiheterotopic space that allows the adolescents to indulge and experiment—with alcohol, with creative pursuits, and with their sexual drives—away from the policing eyes of their parents and, by extension, of society. The beach is thus figured in *Beira-Mar* as an interstitial space of potential, one that permits the young men the time and space to explore their homosexual desires for one another and, significantly, one whose marginality in both physical and conceptual terms mirrors the nature of the adolescent experience as one of potential and change. Importantly, the cinematography within the beach house lingers on the protagonists' faces and bodies, through unsteady camerawork and relatively lengthy shots that foreground their often-tacit engagement with the environment around them. An early, fifty-second shot of Tomaz staring out a window toward the ocean, for instance, is screened directly before the film's title appears and focuses exclusively on the teenager's face, as the accompanying sounds of waves, birds, and wind chimes slowly reach a mild crescendo. As Tomaz stares, the spectator is explicitly refused access to the seascape he contemplates; instead, the camera focuses unremittingly and unsteadily on the young man's silent act of observation. The formal and thematic embedding of Tomaz's perspective in this initial sequence and, obliquely, of the beachscape itself, at once evokes the space (and sounds) of the coast as a site of potentiality and prioritizes the significance to the narrative of the teenager's own affective response.

In many regards, not least through the aesthetic connections suggested between the coast and the emotions of its protagonists, *Beira-Mar* is representative of a broader tendency in recent adolescent-focused cinema in Brazil (and Latin America more generally), which relies, in the words of Laura Podalsky, "on a particular affective play [. . .] to explore the subjectivities of young adults who feel alienated from family and society."[46] For Podalsky, these are films that "share a common discursive tactic; they inscribe contemporary affective disjunction in terms of depth perception and, in so doing, register structures of feeling that question (and at times disrupt) dominant discursive formations."[47] Similarly, Maguire and Randall note how the affective impulse in these recent films is often registered through the body of the adolescent, noting "the strong association between adolescence, puberty and experimentation" and suggesting that "it is unsurprising that films about youth also draw on haptic techniques and focus on the evocation of bodily sensations in their explorations of adolescent sexuality and sensuality."[48] As discussed above, the camera in *Beira-Mar* regularly mobilizes an intimacy with its protagonists, underscored by a restrained script and a cinematography that relies frequently both on close-ups of the adolescents' faces and on extended shots of them doing relatively little: drawing or reading alone, contemplating the sea view, or slowly waking up in the morning. These are moments that urge a more sensitive, sensory grasp of the complexities of teenagers' emotional states, allowing time for the characters to process their experiences, whether it be the tensions between the pair the morning after a nightclub tiff or the sexual connection between them at the close of the film. That these moments are registered through the adolescent body is significant because they gesture not only toward the established link between coming of age and a phenomenological experience of the world but also toward the connection between queerness and adolescence as both potentially experiences of alienation and marginalization.

The mobilization of filmic depth, the haptic, and the sensorial in *Beira-Mar* speaks, in a manner similar to how Podalsky describes the work of the Argentine director Lucrecia Martel, to "the pregnant emotions percolating below the surface of everyday life as they strain against their representational containment."[49] The distinctive unsteadiness of Matzembacher and Reolon's handheld camera coincides with the film's focus on the inherent mutability of the adolescents' identities and sexualities, accentuating, at times, the exploratory nature and hesitation of the moments of experimentation mentioned above. The textural quality of the cinematography, which is enhanced within the space of the beach by the interaction of body, sand, wind, and water, implies that much of the affective charge of Tomaz and Martin's experiences does indeed lie beyond the reach of the regimes of the scopic. When the pair engage in sexual intercourse during the closing sequence of the film, the camera's intimate caressing of the young men's limbs and skin is complemented by a shallow depth of field and rack focus that emphasize their teenage blemishes and visible pores (figure 2.3). At the same time, the camera works to preclude a sense of the dramatic, through a slowness that avoids the spectacle or narrative shock of a conventional coming-out narrative; we are given to understand, after all, that this is Martin's first homosexual experience, even if Tomaz is comparatively much more experienced for his age in having sex with men. The gradual return of the diegetic sounds of wind and waves as the pair have sex, along with a final cut to the image of the horizon the next morning, which pans down slowly onto Martin's naked body lying in bed, imbues the sexualities of the men with a quiet sense of naturalness. Matzembacher and Reolon's sustained formal attentiveness to the affective experience of the protagonists and the refusal of the melodramatic through the slow and observational tenor of their camera combine in *Beira-Mar* to afford an insight into the dynamics of teenage sexuality that avoids stereotype or dramatic scenes of disclosure and rejects an overinvestment in adolescence as merely a time of emotional immaturity, becoming, or transition.

The alignment in *Beira-Mar* of these affective cinematic modes with the adolescent perspective is a defining feature throughout the queer cor-

Figure 2.3. Film still. Adolescent blemishes in *Beira-Mar*. *Source*: Dir. Marcio Reolon and Filipe Matzembacher. Avante Filmes (2015).

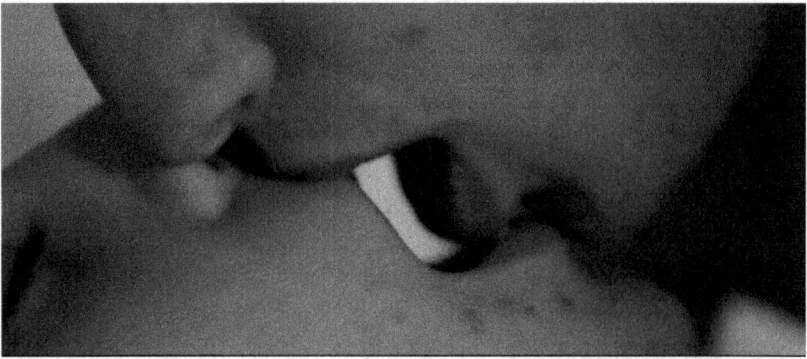

pus of films discussed in this chapter. In Deborah Martin's work on Martel, she describes how the director's aesthetics "produce not so much a child's gaze as a child's sensorium," going on to note that "the experiments with touch and sound [. . .] are a means of constantly gesturing to what is beyond straight, white, adult, bourgeois subjectivity."[50] Though Martin concentrates on the now-ubiquitous figure of the child, her analysis nevertheless applies in a fundamental sense to these films, not least through the connections she draws between "water and desire: that which can be contained and controlled but which also transgresses the boundaries that attempt to contain it."[51] More than this, however, Martin argues for an appreciation of the connection of "water and its sensual qualities on the skin to desire, and especially, to the depiction of marginal sexualities and desires which are often beyond representation: the desire of the young and non-normative desires."[52] Though the older age and relative maturity of Martin and Tomaz mean that their late-adolescent expressions of sexuality are not considered shocking in the way that Martin suggests in the case of the child, what nevertheless lies "beyond representation" is the(ir) experience of nonnormative desire and its break from the heteronormalizing structures of contemporary Brazilian society. As a result, the affective weight afforded to the adolescent body and its haptic prominence throughout the narrative of *Beira-Mar* works to normalize the desires shared between the teenage protagonists. The slow, observational screening of their relationship refuses to dramatize the nonnormative and instead invests its tension within the experiences of social marginality and adolescence more broadly.

In that sense, *Beira-Mar* gently challenges what Nagib understands to be the national project inherent in Brazilian cinema's recent rediscovery of its "monumental sea images."[53] The film relies formally and aesthetically on depictions of the ocean and its coastline to suggest, in Martin's terms, "that which can be contained and controlled," but which ultimately "transgresses its boundaries" to expose the restrictively normative confines of the nation and the fissures in its utopian construction. The ocean is figured at once in *Beira-Mar* as both erratic and erotic, connecting the unpredictability of teenage sociality with the conventionally ascribed adolescent capacity for sexual exploration. More than this, however, the "common discursive tactic" that sees "contemporary affective disjunction" inscribed with the depth of the image and in its cinematographic form is, here, mobilized by Matzembacher and Reolon to support a broader discursive positioning of their protagonists as complex and dynamic characters that resist any artificially static or traditional idea of society or the nation. As Nemi Neto writes, "[Contemporary] Brazilian queer cinema, [. . .] without losing track of its own national identities, [. . .] has opened space for a mesh of possibilities in regard to representation and visibility."[54] It is indeed this "mesh of possibilities," crisscrossed by the epistemological potential of both adolescence and queerness, that draws the realities of nonnormative sexualities, practices, and orientations into contact with collective societal values. As this chapter will continue to argue, if the beach and its liminal spaces serve as the loci for an adolescent questioning of desires and their social implications, then the maritime imagery also works on a broader level to focalize what lies "beyond representation," that is, those aspects of identity that have traditionally been ignored—or indeed violently expelled—by the heteronormalizing force that calibrates notions of (un)belonging for queer subjects in contemporary Brazil.

Sócrates, *Quebramar*, and the Coastal Utopia

Alexandre Moratto's 2018 film, *Sócrates*, narrates the story of a fifteen-year-old boy in a coastal city of São Paulo state, as he navigates the death of his mother, an abusive relationship with his father, extreme poverty, and rampant homophobia.[55] As one critic writes, the film's "style, locations and characters give a true sense of the lives of those on the margins of São Paulo's coast, [. . .] people surviving on the edges, in economic insecurity."[56] In terms of style, the film's cinematography recalls that of *Beira-Mar*, with handheld camerawork and close-up shots of the teenager's face and body as he comes to terms with his grief and the impact of his socioeconomic marginality. Likewise, the marginal space of the beach plays a recurringly symbolic role in *Sócrates*, functioning as a space that is at once connected to the urban yet—at least superficially—detached from the claustrophobia of its economic and social prejudices. In one sequence, when Sócrates and his relatively older love interest, Maicon, travel to the beach and share a kiss under a pier, the homophobic abuse to which they are instantly subject serves as a reminder of the imbrication of homophobia and violence that pervades all parts of society. In a manner quite different from other recent films, the beach in *Sócrates* functions not as a middle-class escape from the hustle and bustle of city life, or as the locus for experimentation with nonnormative desires: such poetics are invoked by the film but immediately undercut by the adolescent's unremitting experience of violence, prejudice, and exploitation. While, as one critic notes, "Much of the film emphasizes the beige, muted colors of the urban space, in contrast to the evocative images of the sea," this contrast does not serve to imbue the oceanscape with a utopian aesthetic of possibility or escape; on the contrary, it highlights how the beach acts as merely an extension of the oppression and hardship that the teenager suffers in his daily, urban life.[57]

Sócrates' admission of his fear of water in the scene immediately prior to the pier sequence described above is important thematically for the film's denouement, in which we see the teenager wade into the water clasping a box containing his late mother's ashes. The erratic close-ups and suffocating camerawork accentuate the danger of the situation and stress the sheer desperation he is experiencing, coming as the scene does at the end of a tense sequence in which he argues with a worker at the crematorium, assaults his father, steals his mother's ashes, and flees. The coast is consolidated as a space of desperation for Sócrates: it is there, after all, where earlier in the film he comes to drink alcohol by himself and to excess and where he searches for discarded food scraps in trash cans, with the image of the water directly in the background (figure 2.4). In

Figure 2.4. Film still. Searching for food scraps against the backdrop of water in *Sócrates*. *Source*: Dir. Alexandre Moratto. 02 Films (2018).

the closing sequence, as he submerges himself in the water, being drawn under the surface and flailing against the tides, the parallel submerging of the camera itself draws the spectator haptically into the turmoil of the young man's situation (figure 2.5). If, throughout the film, the camera's "shallow focus reflects the way in which Sócrates is trapped by his social condition," then here the cinematography evacuates any sense of possibility or utopian potential from the ocean and the vastness of the horizon.[58] This shattering of the symbol of the beach as refuge, invoked briefly at the beginning of the film, heightens the desperation of the adolescent's situation, underlined by the vulnerability of his own fear of water and inability to swim, as well as by his unremittingly hopeless attempts to find employment, to seek shelter with his extended family, or to cultivate a relationship with Maicon.

That *Sócrates* relies on the use of real-life actors, location shooting, and a collaboration with the Instituto Querô, an organization that works with at-risk teenagers in São Paulo from low-income backgrounds, affords the film a sense of "authenticity," as many critics have been quick to concur.[59] This socially realist impulse is heightened by the film's narrative and aesthetic emphases on the relentlessness of the prejudice that

Figure 2.5. Film still. Embodied cinematography and gasping for breath in *Sócrates*. *Source*: Dir. Alexandre Moratto. 02 Films (2018).

Sócrates faces, an aspect that is representative of a growing trend in the contemporary queer Brazilian cinema discussed in this chapter. The formal fixation on the teenager's affective responses to his environment stands in contrast, for instance, with earlier youth-focused films, such as Héctor Babenco's *Pixote* (1981) or Fernando Meirelles and Kátia Lund's *Cidade de Deus* (*City of God*, 2002), in which the intersections of adolescence and socioeconomic precarity are treated through the societal frameworks of crime and violence rather than the microcosmic lens of the individual. The inescapability of Sócrates's situation, in this regard, plays out through an intimate lens that is attentive to the affective and the sensory reactions of its protagonist. Moreover, as any potential for refuge or respite for Sócrates diminishes irretrievably over the course of the film, first through the loss of the only family member that he could rely on, followed by his apartment, and finally Maicon, the "authenticity" of both the film's production and its cinematography underwrites the narrative with a strong sense of the socioeconomic implications of the teenager's situation. In short, neither the ocean nor adolescence is employed for its symbolic qualities of potential or change; instead, respectively, they too become a space and a time infected by a sense of vulnerability and exposure.

This authenticity in *Sócrates* vis-à-vis the contemporary dynamics of racial discrimination is also discernible in Cris Lyra's short film, *Quebramar*, which tells the story of a group of (primarily lesbian) teenagers, who retreat to a remote house on the coast to write music, dance, and drink together to celebrate the New Year. The film foregrounds an intersectional approach to gender presentation, sexuality, and race through its dialogue, while also aesthetically relying on a range of techniques that connect the filmic body with diegetic bodies of water: for example, through extreme long shots of its protagonists engulfed within seascapes, recurring shots of waves washing over sandy hands and feet, or sequences in which water gently laps against the rocky shoreline while discussions of identity take place in the background (figure 2.6). Through the film's "jogo de dimensões" (playfulness with scale), as Alessandra Brandão and Ramayana Lira de Souza note, "Na areia do mar, no quintal da casa, sobre as pedras que cercam a praia, elas conversam e abrem seus corpos para a paisagem" (On the sand, in the backyard of the house, and on the rocks that surround the beach, the women talk with one another and open their bodies to the landscape).[60] The documentary nature of the short film combines with this sensual cinematography to prioritize, in ways similar to the two films discussed above, the affective and sensory subjectivities of its adolescent

Figure 2.6. Film still. Body parts and the elements in *Quebramar*. *Source*: Dir. Cris Lyra. Travessia Filmes (2019).

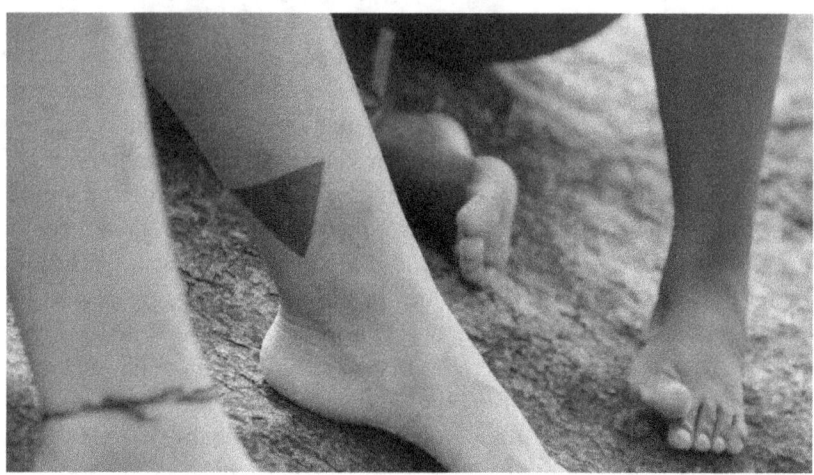

actors, who at times appear seminaked and whose images are texturally enhanced by the camera's persistent dwelling on sand, skin, body hair, and the shared act of touch.

There is, in the prominence of the haptic in *Quebramar*, a political strategy of representation, as regimes of sexuality and gender presentation are—quite literally—*exposed* as arbitrary and artificial, via a cinematic dissection of bodies and limbs that revels in difference and refuses to categorize. It is also a representational strategy unconfined to the realm of the aesthetic, with the film's subjects openly discussing their gender nonconformity, their lack of fixed sexual identity, and, in the film's most politically resonant moments, their own relationships to their racialized bodies. "Quando eu trabalhava, eu fiquei-me morrendo de medo de começar a trabalhar por causa do meu cabelo . . . porque sempre tive cabelo *black*," says one friend to another: "Tem gente branca que associa cabelo preto com sujeira, sabes, e eu lavava compulsivamente o meu cabelo, sempre, todos os dias; e passava perfume no couro cabeludo" (When I had a job, I used to be scared to death of going to work because of my hair . . . because I've always had *Black* hair. There are white people who associate Black hair with dirt, you know, and I used to wash my hair compulsively, all the time, every day; and I used to put perfume on my scalp). When the young woman then becomes upset and breaks down into tears, Lyra links her pain visually with the water of ocean, through an immediate cut that allows the spectator to ponder the friends' ongoing conversation about their experiences of racism against the images of waves crashing against the rocky coastline. While there is no doubt that the film mobilizes water as a metaphor for the young adults' own gender identities and sexualities, the affinity that is suggested in these poignant, often politically aware scenes between the dynamic force of the ocean and the desire to rupture oppressive categories of race and gender is rendered powerfully through a cinematography that places the materiality of the adolescent body at the forefront. As the lyrics that the group collaboratively write suggest, "Ela vem do mar, ela vem da dor / Resistência é uma menina, flor / Quebra-mar, quebra a maré / Quebra a maré, mulher" (She comes from the sea, she comes from pain / Resistance is a girl, flower / Breakwater, break the tide / Break the tide, woman).

Both *Sócrates* and *Quebramar*, despite their distinctions in mode and genre, turn to the beach, in Fiona Handyside's terms, as "a site where the body is on display [and] the place where corporeality and the sensations of the body come to the fore."[61] Through the shared strategies of shallow focus and the close-up, and via a haptic treatment of the adolescent body and a ubiquitous sensitivity toward the affective states of their protagonists, the films demonstrate how "the inevitable engagement with the elements forces us to concentrate on the body *as lived* rather than observed."[62] Similarly, as Jennifer Webb suggests in "Beaches, Bodies, and Being in the World," the combination between the human and the elemental on screen means that "it is places like the beach, where we are so obviously embodied, that we can experience the relation of presence in the world, of belonging to and being possessed by the world, and of being attenuated as a consequence of this."[63] While *Sócrates* focuses primarily on socioeconomic marginality and homophobic violence, and *Quebramar* on discrimination related to gender expression and race, the two films share this narrative and aesthetic strategy of focusing on the adolescent body as *lived*. That all of these moments take place on the coastline, often visually flanked by waves and the tides, is significant; not only is there an invocation to the fluidity of adolescent sexual orientation and identity, and a bid to the naturalness of nonnormative desires, but the space of the beach permits a more profound formal interrogation of how specific bodies are marginalized by hegemonic structures of gender, sexual orientation, social class, and race.

Far from an exclusively symbolic space of potential, then, as Nagib tends toward reading "sea images" more broadly in Brazilian cinema, the ocean serves as both metaphor *and* material in these contemporary queer, adolescent-focused films. They work to temper the abstract political potential of fluidity through a recognition, in Webb's words, of the "attenuation" of adolescent bodies in their "relation of presence in the world, of belonging to and being possessed by the world." In an oblique but crucial fashion, Webb's perspective echoes that of Epps, whose caution surrounding the tensions between the *body as lived* and an abstract theoretical fluidity opened the discussion at the beginning of this chapter. "Fluidity presumably flows beyond established channels, [. . .] and washes away essence entirely," writes Epps: "What also goes with this flow is gender, race, age, class, and so on, all restyled as so many moving parts in a generalized performance of the 'human' and the 'livable.' "[64] If, as Lisa Downing similarly remarks in her work on queer theory, "Privileging the ideal of fluidity leads to a concomitant stigmatization of the idea of fixity, establishing an unhelpful binary (fluidity or fixity) in a body of thought that usually attempts to deconstruct such dualities," then these films underscore the irresolvable "fixity" of their characters' sensory, haptic, and affective experiences of prejudices and politics, while still prioritizing an artistic and theoretical claim to the liberatory mutability of identity.[65] The recurring image in *Quebramar* of the ocean's waves crashing against the rocks of the coastline figures a resolution to such an opposition (figure 2.7): in its visual and aural play with both fluidity and fixity, the image at once gestures toward the potential of queer cinema to deconstruct rigid heteronormative boundaries

Figure 2.7. Film still. Waves crashing against rocks in *Quebramar*. Source: Dir. Cris Lyra. Travessia Filmes (2019).

through specific strategies of representation, while also ultimately exposing the inescapability of the racialized, gendered, and socioeconomic realities that govern queer bodies and their position within contemporary society.

Adolescent Flows

In *Liquid Ecologies in Latin American and Caribbean Art*, Lisa Blackmore and Liliana Gómez write: "Liquidity and flow are not straightforward concepts that merely describe physical phenomena but instead tropes and metaphors loaded with histories and ideologies whose usage is never innocent."[66] As this chapter has shown, the histories and ideologies of the ocean in Brazilian cinema have been reconditioned in recent years by contemporary queer filmmakers who look to water and fluidity not only as metaphors for the mutability of gender and sexuality but also as a material substance that accentuates bodies and the *embodied realities* of gender, sexuality, race, socioeconomic privilege and ability. That these directors merge such explorations of watery spaces with the adolescent body is vital: if water has been theorized for much of the last century as a symbol of flux and potentiality, so, too, has adolescence been reductively understood as exclusively a period of becoming, one in which *the idea of flux* has prohibited any substantive appreciation of political and identitarian realities. These films challenge any such narrow interpretations and expose them as fallacies, prioritizing the affective complexities and libidinal drives of their teenage protagonists and foregrounding their discrimination by and subjection to hegemonic social, racial and gender norms.

That the final scenes of *Beira-Mar*, *Sócrates*, and *Quebramar* all depict one of their teenage protagonists submerging themselves in the ocean is not incidental. Just as Hester Blum reminds us in her seminal study of oceanic literature that "the sea is not a metaphor," so too do these films preclude any representation that is not "attentive to the material realities of the maritime world" or that avoids "what is literal in the face of the sea's abyss of representation."[67] The water of the ocean and its textural environment of sand and wind accentuate the embodied experiences of the adolescent protagonists, concluding with the images of their submerging as a means of drawing attention as much to the fluidity of their identities as to the material realities of their bodies. If, as Epps' cautionary claim about queer theory's overinvestment in fluidity suggests, "the body is itself in trouble, rendered so discursive as to matter little, if at all," then this chapter has demonstrated how a range of recent film works to disrupt any such theoretical decontextualization through a formal and aesthetic sensitivity toward the intimacy and immediacy of the adolescent body as *lived*.[68] In this way, by avoiding the "totalizing, allegorical meaning" that Nagib reads in earlier filmic representations of the sea in Brazilian cinema, this new wave of directors cuts through the utopian potential of the ocean and its waters with the embodied realities of contemporary adolescent life. This is a materiality whose ebbs and flows expose the prejudices to which the queer (adolescent) body finds itself subject in contemporary Brazil.[69]

Chapter Three

The Coast Is Queer

Visibility and the Queer (Trans)National in *Contracorriente* and *Praia do Futuro*

In *Water: Nature and Culture*, Veronica Strang reflects on the cultural potential of water as an element intricately bound up with global histories of selfhood, movement, and time. "[T]he shoreline is an ambiguous and liminal space, between being and nothingness," she notes, considering the specific symbolic value of the seashore. She then poses the question: "How do people think with [shores]: with places where water loses its forward momentum?"[1] In contemporary Latin American film, the critical and epistemological capacities of the coastline have rendered it a site of significant discursive possibility, from its potential to reflect political or social marginality, such as in Paula Markovitch's *El premio* (*The Prize*, 2011) or Pablo Larraín's *El club* (*The Club*, 2015), or as the site of childhood and adolescent discovery, as is the case with Lucía Puenzo's *XXY* (2007) and Filipe Matzembacher and Marcio Reolon's *Beira-Mar* (*Seashore*, 2015). In the two films discussed in this chapter, Javier Fuentes-León's *Contracorriente* (*Undertow*, 2009) and Karim Aïnouz's *Praia do Futuro* (*Futuro Beach*, 2014), the shore serves not only as the setting for the films' diegetic action but also as a framework for understanding the protagonists' homosexual desires for one another, as well as the development of these desires within a heteronormative—and at times violently homophobic—society. As the protagonists carry out their daily activities against the backdrop of the ocean or retreat to isolated spots of the beach for secluded moments of intimacy, the space of the coast, and particularly the water in which they swim, becomes, to borrow terms from Erika Balsom, at once a "theme" and a "method," both a tool of narrative development and a lens for interpreting the significance of these diegetic acts.[2] As Balsom continues in *An Oceanic Feeling: Cinema and the Sea*, "The deeply mythologized site of the ocean activates forms of relationality that prompt one to think beyond the individual, beyond a singular territory, and beyond the binary between nature and culture."[3] In *Contracorriente* and *Praia do Futuro*, the protagonists' interactions with the peripheral site of the shoreline, either physically or from afar, call into question the dynamics between the queer individual and society, invoking water's capacity to challenge concepts of "time, memory, movement and flow" and drawing on the liminality of the coast to suggest alternative forms of queer being and (trans)national belonging.[4]

On the surface, *Contracorriente* and *Praia do Futuro* share a similar narrative impetus: the tragic drowning of a man triggers a period of turmoil, which, in turn, draws two men together emotionally and sexually. Each film also invests the beachscape with the potential to spatialize individual and collective tensions, whether these emerge between the lovers themselves during moments of disagreement or between individual queer characters and the familial and societal structures that attempt to constrain them. In the case of *Contracorriente*, the central romantic arc between a married fisherman, Miguel, and an out-of-town artist, Santiago, not only exposes the religious conservatism of Miguel's seaside hometown, but it also reveals the character's own internalized, heteronormalizing configurations of family and community. Following Santiago's death by drowning, his indeterminate presence as a ghost for the majority of the narrative, seen and heard only by Miguel, allows the film to toy with notions of visibility and secrecy, presenting the artist as a spectral threat both to the diegetic integrity of Miguel's family unit and, as this chapter will argue, to more abstract notions of reproductive futurity and social and national cohesion.

While the narrative of *Contracorriente* unfolds firmly within the national context of Peru, in which Santiago follows a trajectory of internal urban-to-rural migration, the geographical reach of *Praia do Futuro* extends considerably further. As their relationship develops, Donato, a Brazilian lifeguard, travels to Berlin with Konrad, his German partner, sketching out a transnational cartography that, at first glance, corresponds to the well-worn, Western-centric narrative of global mobility to Europe as "the movement from repression to freedom."[5] However, *Praia do Futuro*'s more complex treatment of this act of queer migration ultimately suggests alternative, transnational articulations of belonging and family that lie outside normative figuration, complicating any traditional or linear narrative of "coming out" as the escape from or the loss of a discrete sense of "home." As such, though both films share certain narrative and thematic traits, particularly in terms of the allegorical and sociopolitical charge of their maritime settings, each mobilizes its own politics of visibility via a distinct plane of reference.

As with many of the films discussed in *Bodies of Water*, the narratives of both *Contracorriente* and *Praia do Futuro* regularly return to a sensual focus on the bodies of their male protagonists, often naked or seminaked, during scenes in which they swim in the ocean or embrace one another on the damp sand. In this regard, there are striking resonances with earlier works of queer film, such as Derek Jarman's *Sebastiane* (1976), in which a distinctly homoerotic hue pervades the relationships between a group of young and athletic Roman soldiers. Posted to a remote part of the coast, the soldiers engage in various sexual acts both in and beside the ocean, encouraging a formal vocabulary through which "scintillating light on water provides the *mise-en-scène* for a depiction of male homoerotic desire."[6] However, while Jarman's distinctive direction ensures that male nudes in various states of ecstasy litter the screen and, as a result, that "the element of water aligns itself with flesh and sensuousness," the narrative and formal potential of screening bodies within these watery spaces lies, for Jarman, primarily in its poetic or allegorical function.[7] As this chapter will argue, the emphasis on the body in *Contracorriente* and *Praia do Futuro*, and indeed throughout much contemporary queer film more generally, at once capitalizes on the potential of the ocean to reflect the fluid unpredictability of the protagonists' sexualities, while at the same time going further to reconfigure the politics of screening corporeality.

As Jennifer Webb writes in "Beaches, Bodies and Being in the World":

> Being on the beach with the necessary connection to rock and sand and moving water demachines the body, and de-envelopes it. The inevitable engagement with the elements forces us to concentrate on *the body as lived rather than observed*, because all the while the burning of the sun and water and

wind textures the skin itself, the ingestion of saltwater affects the interior, and in every way the self turns out to become and to be experienced more as body, less as soul.[8]

Fiona Handyside, too, notes in her work on contemporary French film that the coast is not only "a place that is right at the edge—politically, socially, and culturally," but also one where "corporeality and the sensations of the body come to the fore."[9] Taking a cue from these studies and via a critical focus on the representation of the protagonists' bodies in these films as material rather than exclusively visual, this chapter will read the coastal spaces of *Contracorriente* and *Praia do Futuro* as both the mise-en-scène of cinematic queerness and the framework through which nonnormative conceptions of masculinity and sexuality find their embodiment. The shorelines of these films are, I argue, not simply allegorical or poetic spaces of marginality, but instead sites endowed with the queer potential to challenge heteronormative notions of progress and futurity, as well as with the capacity to visibilize alternative modes of being and belonging in the global present.

Contracorriente and the Specter of Queerness

The beachscape of *Contracorriente* provides the locus for the majority of the film's narrative, functioning as the site of Miguel's and Santiago's work (as fisherman and artist, respectively) and as the backdrop for the coastal community's daily activities, perched as the town is on the Peruvian littoral. In an early scene of the film, the camera documents the separate journeys of the two protagonists along this coast toward a secluded spot on the beach, the former travelling by boat and the latter traversing the rocky coastline. The textural quality of the ensuing scenes, during which water splashes against rocks, sand blows across the camera lens, and Miguel's head bumps against a cave wall, preempts the haptic nature of the men's subsequent, secretive act of sexual intercourse. As a hand stretches across the damp sand, metonymically suggesting a moment of sexual ecstasy, the textural quality of the sequence, with limbs dissected from torsos and a shallow focus on sand, skin, and body hair, invokes the beach's capacity to both "reimage" and "reimagine" corporeality.[10] The discrete images of the men's bodies—buttocks, shoulders, hands, and arms—and the shadowy composition of the image encourage the spectator to become part of this queer idyll, "to relinquish," in Laura Marks's terms, "her own sense of separateness from the image."[11] The camera focuses on the corporeal sensuality of the men's sexual union while, at the same time, visually and chronologically denying access to the act as a whole. In this sequence, then, not only do the panoramic landscapes connect the vast open expanses of water with the freedom the protagonists feel in expressing their mutual attraction to one another, but the beach also functions as the synesthetic context for an interpellative appeal to the spectator, refusing to let the viewer "distinguish form so much as to discern texture."[12] The apparent fluidity in their sexual desires is matched by the rolling waves and blowing sand, imbuing a natural hue to the homoeroticism of the sequence and disrupting the representation of the men's bodies as identifiably distinct. In a later scene of the film, discussed in more depth below, this particular part of the shoreline provides the backdrop for a second sexual encounter between the pair, when their muscular bodies are lapped by the waves while they embrace in shallow waters. In both scenes, *Contracorriente* offers a direct invocation to the embodied potential of water and to its contingent power to act as a site, as Fernando G. Pagnoni Berns suggests, in which there exists "flexibility in the regulation of the borders that control desire and the politics of (homo)eroticism."[13]

The symbolic capacity of the beachscape to reflect the fluidity of Miguel's sexuality—considered in the film to be both socially and religiously transgressive—and to serve as a space that permits such an embodied form of filmmaking are recurring elements in much queer film that is anchored in the space of the coast.[14] In her work on the queer potential of the beach space in the films of the French director François Ozon, Handyside comments: "Oscillating between being a place of pleasure and freedom or a place of pain, dissolution and death, with these differing states imbricated in its very figuration (the beach constantly shifts in its appearance through the action of the wind and waves), the beach reimag(in)es corporeality."[15] Handyside's analysis undoubtedly holds true for the beachscape of *Contracorriente*, as well as for the bodies that populate it: the reconfiguration of cinematic embodiment is here seen not only through the protagonists' sexual activities in the sand, but also, for instance, via the bodily strains of Miguel as he mends fishing nets or through the community's religious traditions that see dead bodies "returned" to the ocean during the rite of burial. Paradoxically, then, the beach functions in *Contracorriente* as both a place of desire and a place of death, a landscape that offers the protagonists privacy just as it acts as a site of revelation and confession.

In this way, the space of the coast not only becomes a means of exploring the affective and sexual potential of bodies, but it also works to expose the hierarchical power dynamics and societal structures that would attempt to police them. Following Jean-Didier Urbain, Handyside contends that "the beach is a spectacle, laying bare rituals and relationships. Like the cinema itself, the beach is coded as a place of display—both of the body, and more generally of social organisation."[16] It is precisely through this lens of corporeal and societal visibility that a study of *Contracorriente*'s queer politics is rendered more complex. The unexpected death of Santiago at an early stage of the film, drowned as a result of the film's eponymous undertow, followed by his subsequent return as a ghost visible only to Miguel, exploits cinema's intrinsic capacity for visuality—in both the literal and symbolic senses—and serves to challenge binaries both of absence and presence, and of openness and secrecy. As such, *Contracorriente* mobilizes a politics of visibility that is, at once, both revelatory in its exposure of the conservative prejudices of the seaside community and, as this analysis of the film will argue, problematically restricted by its own diegetic invisibilization of the protagonists' queer desires.

Santiago's indeterminate presence in *Contracorriente*, both as a secret lover in the first part of the film and then as a ghost for the majority of the narrative, problematizes Miguel's position as a patriarch of his community by exposing the normative religious and national traditions at play in the film's conception of family and community. As a photographer, Santiago's camera metaleptically captures the oppositional facets of Miguel's character: those that are visible to the community, such as his role in the religious rites of burial, and those that remain hidden behind the closed doors of Santiago's studio and their secluded beach hideaway. On several occasions, the tensions between these contradictory aspects of Miguel's character are brought more explicitly to the fore through the film's script, such as during an introductory argument in which he accuses Santiago of thinking "que todos son como [él]" (that everyone is like him), that is, that everyone is relatively comfortable with their own sexuality. Santiago's response, namely, that he thinks everyone is, in fact, like Miguel, explicitly acknowledges the latter's repressed sexual desires, obscured behind the weight of traditional family values and the expectations placed on him by the demands of a conservative, heteronormative society. That this argument takes place in an abandoned building on the shore, itself a place of temporal instability, with both men internally framed by unfinished structures of doors and walls, is significant for its emphases on liminality and transition (figure 3.1).

Similarly, Santiago's unpoliced intrusions into the domestic space of Miguel's house, again often framed by the building's thresholds, accentuates the potentiality of the threat he poses to the latter's understanding of his own sexuality and toward the status quo of heteronormative domesticity. In an explicit visualization of this threat, Santiago appears on several occasions juxtaposed against a clichéd image of heteronormative bliss—and, more abstractly, of reproductive futurity—in the form of Miguel and Mariela's wedding photograph (figure 3.2). As a ghostly figure caught between life and death, simultaneously present and absent, visible and invisible, Santiago commands both a queer presence (as a homosexual man) and a *queered* presence (as a ghost): as such, his existence not only poses a threat to normative institutions of family and community, but his return from death also works to challenge the film's linear conceptions of time and space. Handyside remarks, "In their timelessness, beaches become queer sites, undoing heteronormativity's insistence on a linear march towards the future and queering affective relations by insisting on the coexistence of differing experiences of time."[17] In this sense, the character of Santiago replicates the queer liminality of the coastal space,

Figure 3.1. Film still. Identity deconstructed in *Contracorriente*. *Source*: Dir. Javier Fuentes-León. Elcalvo Films, Dynamo, La Cinéfacture (2009).

Figure 3.2. Film still. Heteronormative bliss and the queer threat in *Contracorriente*. *Source*: Dir. Javier Fuentes-León. Elcalvo Films, Dynamo, La Cinéfacture (2009).

just as the space itself mirrors the peripheral threat of the character. In *Contracorriente*, therefore, both beach and body serve as sites of antinormative potential that threaten to disrupt, in temporal and ontological terms, the established and hegemonic discourses of family and futurity.

Following the second of the sex scenes discussed briefly above, during which the intimacy between the two men is enhanced by the sight and sound of lapping water, Miguel wakes up naked on the beach sometime later, with the image of Santiago's face transformed, via a shot-reverse-shot, into that of the town's religious leader. "Hace tiempo que no confiesas" (It's been a while since you've come to confession), the older man accuses Miguel, before reminding him of the expectations placed on him as a role model for the younger members of the community. The immediate cross-cut to a close-up of Miguel with his ear pressed against his wife's pregnant stomach stresses the padre's warning; the visual triangulation in this sequence between Miguel's face, his wife's stomach, and the cross hanging around his neck accentuates the symbolic weight of heteronormative expectation (figure 3.3), as well as intimating its potential subversion when Miguel subsequently displays his disinterest in having sex with Mariela. That this scene is preceded by images of Miguel and Santiago on the shoreline playing football and having sex is significant

Figure 3.3. Film still. Tensions triangulated in *Contracorriente*. *Source*: Dir. Javier Fuentes-León. Elcalvo Films, Dynamo, La Cinéfacture (2009).

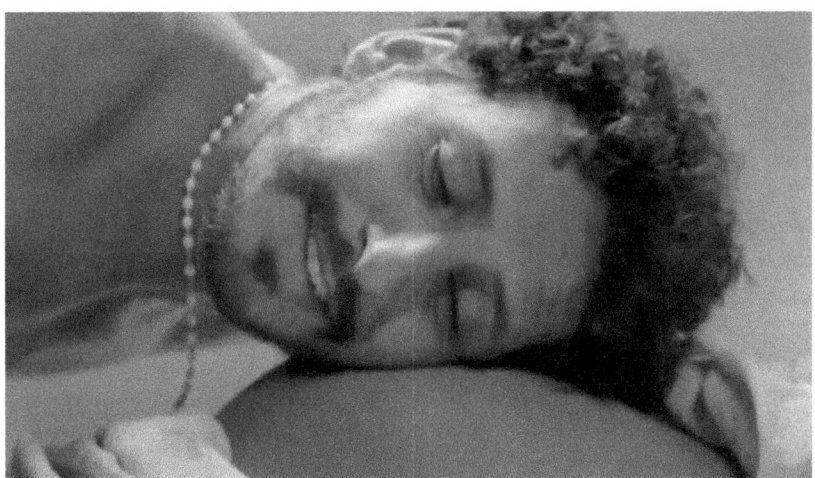

not only for the danger such actions pose to the traditionally engrained family values of town and church, but also because they work to legitimize alternative formations of masculinity, doing so from within the symbolically charged space of the beach. The ocean and shore serve, after all, as the source of the men's livelihoods and as a homosocial space for the fishermen's recreational activities, just as they function as the spaces where Miguel and Santiago express most freely (and physically) their homosexual desires for one another. The recurring emphases on the men's uncovered, toned torsos in the many sequences shot on the beach and underwater at once tend toward a reaffirmation of conventional tropes of masculinity, aligning strength, physicality, and virility, while at the same time queering the relationships that exist between these bodies. Moreover, given that the film's narrative is structured episodically by the loss, discovery, and eventual burial of Santiago's body, the emphasis on the corporeal in *Contracorriente* is thus mobilized on both the thematic and formal levels. Not only is the coast a space in which the spectator might consume exposed bodies in a visual as well as a haptic sense, but it also functions as a site through which normative conceptions of the masculine are laid bare, scrutinized, and at times, delegitimized.

As suggested in the introduction to *Bodies of Water*, one of the recurring fascinations in recent queer film from Latin America is the positioning of the uncovered male body as the object of the camera's gaze, renegotiating Laura Mulvey's assertions surrounding the "visual pleasure" of women's status as spectacle in mainstream narrative cinema.[18] In *Contracorriente*, the toned physiques of Santiago and Miguel are displayed as a means of queering such visual pleasure, rejecting any premise—at least on a superficial level—that would see the "male figure [as unable to] bear the burden of sexual objectification."[19] In *Ghost Faces: Hollywood and Post-Millennial Masculinity*, David Greven writes that "the post-millennial era [demonstrates] mutually reinforcing fascinations with male bodies and male faces, which emerge as allegorical zones as well as literal sites of cinematic interest for the depiction of male subjectivity, sexuality, and physicality in a post-queer moment."[20] Though Greven's selected corpus of films is taken from the North American context and focuses primarily (following Linda Williams) on the "body genres" of horror, comedy, and pornography, his discussion of the significance of the on-screen "dismantling" of the male body holds true for both *Contracorriente* and *Praia do Futuro*. He writes: "A project of physical and emotional disassembly occurs in the representation of males at the level of film content, e.g., the level of narrative and plot. This violence gets replicated, at times, at the level of form, e.g., editing and/or cinematography. [. . .] What remains continuous is the emphasis on male sexuality as a battleground for the fate of the nation and a testing ground for its current state of health."[21] There are numerous scenes in *Contracorriente* that illustrate such a tension between the deconstruction of masculinity and its necessary function as an icon of political and societal stability: a recurring image of Miguel in the front pew of the church, for instance, distinguishes his character from the other worshippers, reflecting through mise-en-scène a rupture already clearly visible through the emotion on his face. In another sequence, which takes place shortly after his relationship with Santiago is exposed, a high-angle shot of his body slumped in the corner of his kitchen reinforces in formal terms a sense of vulnerability, underscored when he adopts a passive position to weep in the arms of the spectral Santiago. Cinematography and narrative combine in these instances through a process of dismantling that, as Greven theorizes, demands the "cutting up and opening up of masculinity," in which "assaults on the body and psyche suggest [. . .] the desire to see masculinity laid open, *laid bare*."[22]

In this way, while Santiago acts as the film's literal ghost, the continued emphasis on Miguel's face as the synecdochic battleground of the film's broader challenges to heteronormative values means that he becomes, in Greven's terms, the "ghost face" of the narrative. The sustained formal interest in his expressions establishes faciality as "a key to the male self, index of its conflicts, map of its overlaps with various others, code to its breaking point."[23] The tender images of Miguel's head resting on Santiago's chest postcoitally thus strike an implicit parallel with the aforementioned scenes in which a close-up shot focuses on him listening to his unborn child by placing an ear on his wife's stomach. In a similar fashion, the sternness of expression we see accentuated during the initial funeral procession (an image whose significance is reiterated by its later appearance on one of Santiago's canvasses) is contrasted with the obvious joy in repeated images of his face on the beach with Santiago. Crucially, moreover, once Santiago returns as a ghost, it is the recognition on Miguel's face that can potentially expose his presence, imbuing his reactions with an added sense of gravity as the pair walk hand-in-hand down the street and in full view of passers-by. "Nadie me ve," Santiago repeatedly assures a clearly anxious Miguel, before adding: "¿Mejor así, no, todo afuera?" (No one can see me. Isn't it better this way, with everything out in the open?). By accentuating the focus on Miguel's face in this way, the film allows the spectator, again in the words of Greven, "to address a potent dimension of representation, a split between a normative understanding of masculinity as stable, coherent, and rigidly contained, and a queer understanding of masculinity as porous, fluid, open to interpretation, and always already destabilized."[24]

However, this filmic disassembly of the male body belies a more conservative politics of representation in *Contracorriente*; that is, despite Santiago's assurances that everything is better "afuera" (out in the open), their relationship is, conversely, only visible in the most delineated and restricted of senses. Greven notes in *Ghost Faces* how, though recent Hollywood film has explicitly foregrounded both homosexual desire and a drive to dismantle hegemonic iterations of masculinity, such processes of visibilization are ultimately contained by a more embedded impulse "to put the queer genie back in the bottle of straight masculinity."[25] In *Contracorriente*, this tension is evident in the at-times melodramatic narrative, which dilutes the radical potential of queer visibility embodied in the character of Santiago by affording much greater formal and thematic concern for the emotional turmoil and ensuing "crisis" of masculinity experienced by Miguel. When Santiago asks Miguel to find his missing body so that he might finally be laid to rest, the latter initially agrees to do so but later withholds the fact that he has found Santiago's lifeless body underwater, lodged between rocks on the ocean floor. This act of selfishness on the diegetic level replicates in a broader sense the film's more implicit impulse to keep the material evidence of queerness concealed. "¿Por qué no te quedas? [. . .] Me encantaría que te quedaras conmigo" (Why don't you stay? I'd love you to stay with me), Miguel says in the following scene, unable to comprehend the existential anguish of Santiago's position, who replies: "Me pasé un culo de tiempo esperando que me dijeras esto. Y mira cuándo me lo vienes a decir" (I've waited fucking ages for you to say that to me. And look when you finally decide to say it). In this way, as Pierre Losson remarks in his reading of the film, "El fantasma no amenaza las apariencias. [. . .] Los mecanismos de control social a través de la hipocresía están en marcha: Miguel vive su amor bajo la condición de que éste no amenace el equilibrio social de su familia y de su comunidad" (The ghost does not threaten the status quo. Hypocrisy fuels the mechanisms of social control: Miguel is able to embrace his love, just as long as it does not pose a threat to the social balance of his family and his community).[26] Just as Santiago's very presence for the majority of the narrative is entirely dependent on Miguel's desires toward him—"es una mierda cuando no estás, no hay nada" (it's shit when you're not here, there's nothing), Santiago explains tearfully to Miguel in one scene—the formal and narrative "dismantling" of Miguel's masculinity that takes place in *Contracorriente* thus remain at the service of containing queerness rather than embracing it.

In his article for *The Guardian* in 2013, film critic James Rawson commented on the vast difference in mortality rates between heterosexual and queer characters in the narratives of mainstream cinema, as well as offering a tongue-in-check analysis of the overwhelming tendency to deny sexually nonnormative characters a positive resolution. "Presumably overwhelmed by sheer homosexuality, his heart can no longer keep beating," wrote Rawson about Tom Ford's *A Single Man*: "Beware, non-heterosexuals: Sudden Gay Death Syndrome can strike anywhere."[27] In *Contracorriente*, while Santiago's sexual deviance does not "ultimately result in death by suicide, murder or AIDS," as Rawson notes is true for much Hollywood cinema, there is nevertheless a heavily repressive aspect to his death that belies the film's cautious engagement with a politics of visibility.[28] On one hand, as discussed above, Santiago's postmortem presence in the film creates a temporal and ontological sense of disruption, destabilizing the film's drive toward the reproductive futurity and heteronormative domesticity of Miguel and Mariela. On the other hand, despite the film's reflexive sensitivity toward Santiago's marginality through mise-en-scène and formal framing, the queer potential of the character is continually restricted, reduced to a prism through which Miguel's sexuality and masculinity are first challenged, then ultimately restored. In one sequence, the tension that exists between the pair is vocalized: "Eres un cobarde de mierda quien piensa ser hombre es tener mujer, hijos," accuses Santiago, before the pair ends up wrestling one another on the sand (You're a fucking coward who thinks being a man is having a wife and kids). "Hay mil maneras de ser hombre," Santiago continues, "y eres ninguna de ellas" (There are a thousand ways to be a man, and you're not any of them). That this sequence takes place immediately before the birth of Miguel's child is indicative: though the director presents Santiago as a vehicle for challenging normative discourse, not least given the visual parallels that are drawn between the men's fighting and fornicating in the same part of the beach, this ultimate reversion to heteronormativity reiterates the film's refusal to embrace the radical potential of the queer outsider.

In their reading of the film, Karl Schoonover and Rosalind Galt write: "In this retrograde fantasy of queer publicity, holding hands in public is contingent on violently expelling the actual queer. [. . .] This is a space that fully allows [Miguel and Santiago] to be 'here' and queer, as long as that here and queer remain a non-national space."[29] The culmination of such a "retrograde" act of queer expulsion is to be found in the closing scenes of the film, in which—supported by an apparent change of heart on the part of some villagers—Miguel buries Santiago's body at sea. While such a scene may gesture toward a utopia of queer kinship, in which the desire of Santiago's family to bury him in the family grave are eclipsed by Miguel's wish to "return" his body to the ocean, the burial is nevertheless presented almost exclusively as a moment of closure for Miguel, who *returns* Santiago to rest at sea so that he, paradoxically, may *return* to life with his family. Moreover, as Schoonover and Galt point out, "Not only [Santiago's] queerness but his atheism is punished by a narrative that teaches him a lesson by subjecting his body to both violent death and traditional religious rites."[30] In this sense, then, where the ocean once served as a symbol of the fluidity and potency of the men's sexualities, it is ultimately cast as a means of curtailing any such desire. While the shoreline acts as the haptic site for the embodied expression of their homosexual desires for one another, at the end of the film, it becomes the mise-en-scène and the medium for the repressive erasure of the queer body and the resultant restoral of societally endorsed, heteronormative family values.

In one of the final sequences of the film, Miguel cradles his newborn child on the shoreline and stares into the horizon, while Santiago's memory, in the form of the candle he gifted to Mariela, burns and is then extinguished. This generational image of reproductive futurity rests metonymically on the extinction of the queer threat, curtailing both the possibilities of the diegetic relationship between Miguel and Santiago and the capacity of the shoreline to function as the means of challenging the normative dynamics of the seaside society. As Greven asserts in his analysis of the threat posed by nonnormative sexualities: "Nearly taken to a level of total structural collapse, masculinity is then, even in the eleventh hour, reassembled and restored."[31] He continues: "Queerness may be registered, even positively affirmed, but it exists as a simultaneously irresistible and frightening netherworld that must be avoided or escaped after tentative entry."[32] Though, as several critics have claimed, Santiago plays an integral role in the film's questioning of normative figurations of family and sexuality, any challenge posed by his character is restricted to the thresholds of doorways, unfinished buildings, and secluded spots on a deserted beach: spaces, that is, where the queer threat he poses can ultimately be controlled and contained. As a liminal space on the periphery of a homophobic society, the beach of *Contracorriente* exercises its representational potential through a screening of queer desire and an emphasis on the male body. In the end, however, the coast serves as a restorative agent in the film's conservative impulse toward family and nation, reestablishing a locally acceptable sense of masculinity by crudely exorcising the specter of cinematic queerness.

Queer Migrations: *Praia do Futuro* and the Queer Transnational

Shot against the panoramic backdrop of the Brazilian coastline, the opening moments of Karim Aïnouz's *Praia do Futuro* establish the film's overarching critical concerns: on one hand, as the two protagonists speed through sand dunes on motorbikes, the film gestures toward its central thematics of movement and masculinity; on the other hand, when the men struggle in the water in the subsequent scene and have to be rescued, the confused underwater images of limbs and torsos signal the film's recurrently haptic approach to the filming of its protagonists. Indeed, if the men's bodies are presented formally as spectacular within the space of the coast, with frequent emphases on their strength and athleticism, they are also shown to be vulnerable to its natural forces, a point often accentuated by extreme long shots of lone bodies entering the water. Though the echoes here with the narrative of *Contracorriente* are unmistakable, not least through the homosexual relationship that develops between the protagonists as a result of a tragedy by drowning, there are significant distinctions in how *Praia do Futuro* mobilizes its politics of queer visibility. Crucially, it is not a queer body that is here excised from the narrative through disappearance but that of a heterosexual man, whose body is lost at sea and whose friend Konrad is rescued, in a physical as well as perhaps an emotional sense, by the Brazilian lifeguard, Donato. Nor does *Praia do Futuro* deal with ghosts in a literal sense but instead with specters on the figurative level, in the form of a family member who reappears toward the end of the narrative as an unexpected reminder of home, intent on troubling the film's figurations of transnational queer belonging.

The film's initial setting in the coastal city of Fortaleza, which provides the backdrop for the first third of the narrative, also shares certain characteristics with *Contracorriente*'s Cabo Blanco. Donato's job as a military lifeguard means that his and his colleagues' bodies are often on display, particularly when they train on the shore and are filmed exercising in such a way as to parallel the sensual images of intertwined bodies during the later sex scenes between Donato and Konrad.[33] In an early scene, both beach and body are linked not only by narrative location but also through a formal insistence on the spectacular quality of both the naked male figure and the seascape in which it is to be found: framed diegetically by the window of Donato's apartment, the muscular body of Konrad carves out a sensuous image against the horizon of the coastline, connecting the unknowability of the ocean with the seeming inscrutability of his character (figure 3.4). In *An Oceanic Feeling*, Balsom discusses the "radical alterity" that "is to be found within the aquatic world, just as we find it within ourselves," and she reflects on the inherent potential of the ocean to facilitate new forms of interconnectedness: "No matter their attitude towards class struggle, modernity, or mythic value, films that capture littoral labour tend to have something in common: they depend on the allure of otherness."[34] Such alterity is mobilized on various levels throughout the tripartite structure of *Praia do Futuro*, with the ocean functioning as a marker of both distance and connection. In the first of

Figure 3.4. Film still. Body and horizon in *Praia do Futuro*. Source: Dir. Karim Aïnouz. Coração da Selva, Hank Levine Film, Watchmen Productions (2014).

the film's parts, "O abração do afogado" (The Drowned Man's Embrace), the initial stages of Konrad and Donato's relationship sees both characters distinguished either physically or socially from their surroundings, the former far from his native country, and the latter out of sync with his conservative coastal hometown. In the two parts that follow, "Um herói partido ai meio" (A Hero Cut in Half) and "Um fantasma que fala alemão" (A German-Speaking Ghost), the setting of Berlin allows the film to interrogate notions of alterity in a more explicit manner, challenging normative conceptions of home by offering a transnational understanding of queer belonging that embraces mobility as a productive means of identity formation.

The town of Praia do Futuro, itself built on reclaimed land on the outskirts of Fortaleza, is presented in the film as a space of liminality, a feature accentuated by the recurring images of construction sites and the assertion that unidentified bodies regularly wash up on its shores. "Essa mar ia até ali, quase onde está a pista," says Donato, as the two men sit on the beach at night and watch the waves ebb against the sand: "É como se a gente estivesse no meio do mar. Agora" (The sea used to almost reach the street. It's as if we're in the middle of the sea. Right now). This prevailing focus on liminality implicitly parallels *Praia do Futuro*'s broader move beyond a restrictive focus on the nation, with the sea functioning throughout the film as a means of destabilizing rigid conceptions of origin. As both "theme" and "method," that is, the ocean not only reflects the potency of the protagonists' sexuality, but it also acts as a barometer of belonging. In the initial stages of the narrative, the film emphasizes

Donato's own peripherality within the space of Praia do Futuro: in recurring scenes with his younger brother, for instance, he plays the role of Aquaman, a superhero from the sea who protects his sibling from his fear of water. "Como é que o Aquaman vai sumir no mar?" asks Ayrton, "Se ele já é do mar!" (How could Aquaman disappear in the sea? He's from the sea!). Likewise, in the closing moments of the first part of the film, Donato is distinguished from the other lifeguards as he pauses on the shore and is then filmed swimming underwater alone for the final thirty seconds of the sequence (figure 3.5). Through these strong thematic and formal emphases on Donato's connection with water, his character embodies the peripherality of the coastal town, prefiguring the film's later interrogation of the idea of belonging. As this reading of the film will argue, *Praia do Futuro* offers both a realistic portrayal of being *away from home* and, at the same time, a problematization of the very notion of what it means to be *at home*.

The migration of the protagonists from Brazil to Germany is marked not only in narrative terms but also prominently through mise-en-scène: the bright and open expanses of the beachside town in Brazil are contrasted with the dull color palette of urban Berlin, with the horizontality of the ocean replaced by the verticality of the cityscape. Shortly after their arrival, Donato and Konrad stand on Berlin's Oberbaum Bridge and are filmed through an extreme long shot against the dismal city skyline. In a suggestion of the nostalgia he harbors for his hometown, Donato says that he would love to "pular nessa água" (jump into the water), just as a train passes by overhead and emphasizes a sense of urban claustrophobia.[35] In

Figure 3.5. Film still. Donato singled out in *Praia do Futuro*. *Source*: Dir. Karim Aïnouz. Coração da Selva, Hank Levine Film, Watchmen Productions (2014).

the city, water continues to play a significant role for the lifeguard, either through his work in an aquarium or when he escapes to swim in a local pool, most notably following arguments with Konrad or, later, his younger brother. Indeed, if the scenes in *Praia do Futuro* were notable for their panoramic vistas, then the images of Donato alone in the artificial space of the swimming pool and enclosed behind glass in the aquarium appear as both visually and affectively arresting. Moreover, Donato's apartment is dotted with visual reminders of the coastline, in the form of seashells, ceramic turtles, pictures of waves, and nautical windows, which serve to emphasize geographic displacement through a distinctly nostalgic key (figures 3.6 and 3.7).

Figure 3.6. Film still. Maritime trinkets and tropes in *Praia do Futuro*. *Source*: Dir. Karim Aïnouz. Coração da Selva, Hank Levine Film, Watchmen Productions (2014).

Figure 3.7. Film still. Maritime imagery on the walls in *Praia do Futuro*. *Source*: Dir. Karim Aïnouz. Coração da Selva, Hank Levine Film, Watchmen Productions (2014).

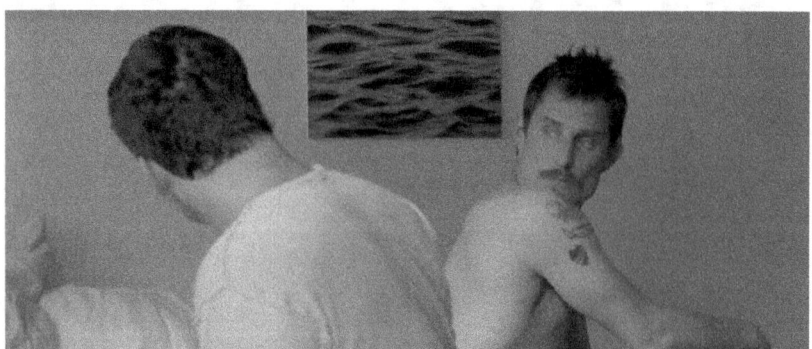

These visual and formal aspects of the film have, somewhat unsurprisingly, given way to reductive critical analyses of Donato's character, which superficially turn to water as primarily a marker of absence or secrecy. In "Water and Queer Intimacy," Fernando Pagnoni Berns writes of Donato's move to Berlin in the following terms:

> To embrace his queer identity, a new part on [sic] his life, Donato has left another part of himself behind. Thus, *he remains incomplete*. [. . .] As a newly displaced man with no nation, no sea and no water to hide in, he must accept the consequences of his decision and face his family; this fear being the only obstacle preventing him from *feeling complete*. [. . .] Donato utilizes water as a hiding place, a subjective space where he can escape from *fully accepting himself*.[36]

This restrictive tendency to read water as the thematic remnant of a life left behind relies on several problematic assumptions: first, there is an attempt here to question Donato's identity in terms of the nation, conflating a nostalgia for the Brazilian coastline with an apparent inability to embrace his queerness outside national boundaries; second, throughout his analysis, Pagnoni Berns wields a pathologizing force on queerness, reading Donato's queer identity in the film as chronically in need of completion; and finally, the suggestion that Donato's homosexuality may be read as a "new part" of his life depends on a problematic view of queerness, which invokes limiting notions of "coming out" as the rejection of origin or the loss of a conventional notion of home. In other words, Pagnoni Berns solidifies identity in his reading of the film, even as its oceanic images asks us to account critically for its fluidity. *Praia do Futuro* presents a much more complex understanding of queer identity than Pagnoni Berns suggests, rejecting utopian notions of "wholeness" and instead collapsing the dichotomies between belonging and exclusion to propose a more dynamic and contingent idea of transnational queer identity.

In Anne-Marie Fortier's work on queer affect and migration, she rejects geographically bound notions of belonging and instead suggests a relational and constitutive process of "coming home."[37] She writes: "I discuss narratives of queer migration as homecoming, where 'home' is a destination rather than an origin. [. . .] In their refusal of home, queer migrant subjects reclaim a space to be called 'home.'"[38] Indeed, as the Brazilian protagonist himself says in a voiceover to his younger brother during the closing sequence of the film: "Te escrevo pra dizer que eu não morri. Eu só voltei pra casa. Aqui nessa cidade subaquática tudo pra mim faz mais sentido" (I write to tell you that I didn't die; I just came back home. Here, in this underwater city, everything makes more sense to me). *Praia do Futuro* emphasizes home as a construct, one that is affectively transnational in scope and, in a reflection of the narrative itself, acutely non-linear in either origin or development. That is not to say, however, that conventional conceptions of home cease to be of importance for Donato: he often discusses returning to Brazil, and the appearance of his brother Ayrton only serves to accentuate the affective weight of traditional family ties. In an early scene in Berlin, Donato is asked to leave a school classroom by a caretaker, who warns him: "Sie dürfen sich hier nicht aufhalten" (You shouldn't be here). Moments later, after Donato is filmed outside with a plane suggestively flying above his head, he tells Konrad that he cannot live "em um lugar que não tenha praia" (in a place with no beach). However, for Fortier, "While narratives of migration-as-homecoming instigate a noteworthy reversal of the status of 'home' in migration, 'home' remains widely sentimentalized as a space of comfort and seamless belonging, indeed *fetishized through the movements between homes*. In other words, the movement away from home-as-origins becomes the vector for reinstating the ideal of 'home' as a site of familiarity and comfort, and for producing or entrenching 'queerness' as *away* from 'home.'"[39] In this sense, while Pagnoni Berns reads Donato's journey to Berlin as "running away from the self," I argue that it is precisely this limiting and conservative notion of origin that the film seeks to reject.[40] Water, in *Praia do Futuro*, points not to the nostalgia for a once-complete sense of self but to the intricate dynamics of queer identity that both recognize the complexity of traditional conceptions of belonging and intimate a fluidity in the formation of alternative identities outside the normative boundaries of home, family and nation.

The character of Ayrton, who arrives in Berlin as the figurative German-speaking ghost of his brother's past, vocalizes the social conservatism of Donato's hometown and the affective weight of these traditional family ties. "Por que é que tu sumiu?" he asks, after breaking the news of their mother's death. "Tu é um veado egoísta, que gosta de dar o cu, escondido na porra desse Polo Norte" (Why did you disappear? You're a selfish fag who likes to take it up the ass, hidden away in this fucking North Pole). Certain critics have understood Ayrton's character as a means of challenging the relative freedom Donato feels in Berlin, now uninhibited by the strictures of his conservative Brazilian hometown and or any familial responsibility. Simone Cavalcante da Silva notes in her article on queer masculinities that the reencounter between the brothers is steeped in aquatic imagery, "as if both characters were in a bluish liquid dream or subaquatic experience," which serves to "force the protagonist to review his past and confront his fears and identity."[41] In her reading of the ensuing confrontation between the pair, Cavalcante da Silva notes: "Donato's silence to his brother's questions may be interpreted as the shame he feels for having abandoned his family, as well as for having his sexuality exposed and being confronted about 'coming out' as a gay man. [. . .] It also recalls the 'metaphor of the closet,' suggested through Donato's migration to Berlin as a way out to hide his non-normative sexuality within the Brazilian patriarchal society."[42] An analysis such as this hinges fundamentally upon restrictive epistemologies of queerness, particularly those that see narratives of global queer mobility as the movement "from repression to freedom."[43] The invocation of the "metaphor of the closet," moreover, which itself has been challenged as a Western-centric concept by scholars such as Dennis Altman and Ben Sifuentes-Jáuregui, overlooks the film's own presentation of Donato's queerness: at no point, for instance, does he "come out" in the conventional sense of the term or voice any sense of shame or anxiety over his sexuality.[44] Furthermore, the ethical imperative of Ayrton's accusations revolve around a supposed selfishness on the part of Donato for having fled from his responsibilities, yet this specific narrative is presented in the film as itself both selfish and simplistic; though the now-adult younger brother speaks German with relative ease, his continued predilection for superhero T-shirts and his escapade on Konrad's motorcycle suggest, conversely, an enduring lack of both maturity and perspective. To reduce Donato's move to Berlin to an act of fleeing "the self," as Pagnoni Berns does, or to "a step towards liberation and freedom," as Cavalcante da Silva does, is to neglect the film's own discursive interrogation of identity, which is presented through the narrative as contingent and transnational, and which does not rely on rigid conceptions of home or restrictive notions of queerness.

In one of the film's more poignant scenes between the lovers, Donato and Konrad dance amusingly in their apartment to the French singer Christophe's 1965 song, "Aline." The lyrics of the song, which describe sandy beaches, a lost love, and painful memories, stand at odds with the joy the two protagonists display in posing with a woman's portrait and miming the words in a language that neither speaks natively. In this transnational act of translation, the two men reinscribe the song's "épave sur le sable mouillé" (flotsam and jetsam on the damp sand) with new meaning, queering the subject matter through a performance that parodies the original sentiments of loss and despair. That this extended sequence cuts immediately to a sex scene, in which the camp choreography of the song is replaced by an emphatically sexual one, is indicative both of film's domestication of queer desire and, as Schoonover and Galt contend, of the formal techniques of narrative incongruity that run throughout *Praia do Futuro*. They write: "As the lovers twist their bodies in and out of the frame, we see patterns of overlapping, lining up and separating, fitting together and moving out of sync, that metaleptically trace their trajectory of adopting the space of another or for another. [. . .] The time between these different bodily gestures has been elided: the moment of singing and the moment of fucking flash up one after another."[45] This strategy of merging incongruous scenes, truncating individual narrative strands and omitting key parts of storyline pervades the narrative of *Praia do Futuro* and serves, as Schoonover and Galt note, to "invite the asynchronous, fracture the individual, and displace linear historicity (which in its normative forms deprives queer desire of social agency and futurity)."[46] In the sequence described above, for instance, the scene cuts abruptly to an image of Donato in a park after only a few moments of foreplay; similarly, in a more perplexing fashion, around ten years pass between the second and third parts of the film with no diegetic explanation of what has happened to the protagonists in the interim or indeed of the reasons behind such a considerable gap in the story. "Where others long for progression and synchrony, our queer film spectator welcomes the intermittent but boundless embrace of atemporal affections," write Schoonover and Galt: "Where others see jump cuts, the queer film spectator sees queer historicity."[47]

These complex layers of queer historicity that are mobilized in *Praia do Futuro* function to unsettle fixed notions of identity and linear understandings of belonging. Conventional conceptions of home, represented through the character of Ayrton and evident in the aforementioned critical readings of the film, are exposed as homo-exclusionary, given that they refuse to see queer identities as anything but incomplete when displaced from normative discourses of family and nation. Indeed, in its representation of transnational queer desire, *Praia do Futuro* enacts what Fortier refers to as the "lived experience of locality" in narrations of queer migration: "Rather than seamless sites of belongings, 'homes' are locations criss-crossed by a variety of forces. [. . .] Remembrances of home at once empty it of any definitional and absolute status, while it continuously attaches it to places that acquire meaning in the process."[48] Coming "out" in *Praia do Futuro* is not figured as a single moment of contention or confrontation but is instead displaced by the provisional, future-oriented process of "coming 'home.'" According to Fortier, "The construction of queer migration as homecoming suggestively unhinges ideas of originary home(land). In queer narratives of migration, desires, memories and geographies are entangled in the creation of 'soils of significance,' that might provide, however fleetingly, a ground to rest upon."[49]

In the closing sequence of the film, Konrad, Donato, and Ayrton are filmed motorcycling across a frozen beach in northern Germany, bookending the narrative with a sequence that echoes the initial scene of Konrad and his friend speeding through the sand dunes of the Brazilian coast. This final scene of the film works to dissipate the tension between the brothers, as well as between Donato and Konrad, who are now separated for reasons the film refuses to disclose. In shots that emphasize the enormity of the beachscape, Donato reveals to his younger brother—who has lived with a fear of water since childhood—that this is a beach without water. "Eu sempre quiso trazer tu aqui," he says to Ayrton, "Eu só pensava que tu ia adorar essa praia. Sem água" (I always wanted to bring you here. I thought that you'd love this beach. It's got no water). As the soundtrack plays David Bowie's "Heroes" to images of the three men motorcycling across the open expanse of the beach at low tide, the voiceover from Donato again suggests the film's transnational, affective conceptions of home: "Te escrevo pra dizer que eu não morri. Eu só voltei pra casa. Aqui nessa cidade subaquática tudo pra mim faz mais sentido. Eu não preciso me esconder no mar pra me sentir em paz, nem preciso mergulhar pra me sentir livre" (I write to tell you that I didn't die; I just came back home. Here, in this underwater city, everything makes more sense to me. I don't need to hide myself in the ocean to feel at peace or dive to feel free). If water has been a marker of belonging—rather than of displacement, absence or secrecy—throughout the film, then here its own erasure consolidates the film's implicit queer potential. As both a queer sight (in visual terms) and a queer site (in formal terms), this beach without water suggests a sense of belonging not restricted to the coastline of Brazil, or indeed any *one* place. As the men speed across the beach with no water, the queerness of the space is thus reflected in the queerness of the new affective bonds between the three men, overcoming any purely static or originary conception of home and family with a transnational acknowledgment of queer migration as "homecoming."

Queer Excisions

The coastline and its shore, in both *Contracorriente* and *Praia do Futuro*, transcend any straightforwardly diegetic significance to function as formal and aesthetic devices in the exploration of an embodied sense of queerness. Water emphasizes the lived experience of the homosexual relationships depicted on screen in ways that problematize the characters' individual connections with the social and political environments in which they live. As Jennifer Webb remarks, "It is places like the beach, where we are so obviously embodied, that we can experience the relation of presence in the world, of belonging to and being possessed by the world, and of being attenuated as a consequence of this."[50] The films' treatment of the beach as a space that toys with notions of transience and (in)visibility brings to the fore in an embodied fashion this "relation of presence in the world," one that is often fraught with prejudice and queer- and/or homophobic discrimination. More than this, however, it is Webb's notion of "attenuation" that allows us to demarcate in a productive manner how these films engage distinctly with a politics of (queer) representation. If, at the end of *Contracorriente*'s narrative, Miguel is returned to the "safety" of heteronormative domesticity and religious community, Donato and Konrad, by contrast, reject any such attenuation of the self in *Praia do Futuro*, closing with a dynamic—though not "happy" in any conventional sense—ending that offers a more complex sense of the protagonists' place in the world.

Schoonover and Galt's notion of "queer excision" is therefore a productive lens through which to understand not only the formal and aesthetic innovations of these films (and the others in the corpus of this book) but also contemporary world cinema more generally. While they consider the notion of queer excision in *Queer Cinema in the World* to be "a mode of queer temporality," in which "queerness takes root in the splices, the glitches, and the traces of lost moments," the present study has understood such strategic omission on a broader critical plane.[51] In *Contracorriente*, it is the queer subject, Santiago, who is first excised from the narrative by drowning. His queered presence for the majority of the film, as simultaneously absent and present, dead and alive, visible and invisible, gestures toward a queer utopia in which he and Miguel can live happily ever after. It is, however, a mode of queer visibility that is predicated specifically on Santiago's invisibility and absence as a ghost. Queer excision acts here to excise the queer himself, counteracting the queer potential of the space of the beach by rendering it as the site for the religious rites of burial that restore the heteronormative values of family, community, and by extension, nation. In *Praia do Futuro*, by contrast, queer excision seeps into the very form of the film itself, realizing a queer potential that undermines linearity in terms of narrative, time and migration. Queer excision is, in this case, used to undermine any traditional concept of home, culminating in a vision of a beach-without-water that complicates any straightforward nostalgia for a lost home or identity. In its place, *Praia do Futuro* instead celebrates the dynamics of the relationships between characters as an affective, future-oriented process of "home-coming."

Chapter Four

Slow Waters

Marco Berger's *Taekwondo* and the Queer Erotics of Boredom

It was hot as hell and the windows were all steamy.

—J. D. Salinger, *Catcher in the Rye*

In the opening moments of the short British film *Baby* (WIZ, 2000), the close-up image of a hand brushing slowly against a bare chest triggers the film's interrogation of the erotic potential in screening touch. Accentuated by a shallow focus on the individual body hairs and bumps of the protagonist's skin, this suggestively haptic introduction at once emphasizes the centrality of vision in the filming of the sensual yet denies its epistemological mastery through the textural quality of its image. The film's slow narrative structure, composed entirely of a series of erotically charged flashbacks during an act of masturbation, is matched by a lack of dialogue and long, static takes of the naked and seminaked bodies in and around a public swimming pool. During these flashbacks, the protagonist—played by a twenty-year-old Ben Whishaw—negotiates the homosocial hurdles of gender-specific changing rooms and communal showers. As he does so, his constant proximity to water, which envelops bodies and distorts the senses, provides a now familiar backdrop for the exploration of a developing sexuality and its concomitant potency for queerness. Moreover, as the suggestive smirk from a confident, muscular diver implies when his gaze meets that of Whishaw, the cinematic spaces of *Baby* are conceived as sites not only where the queer subject is able to find pleasure in looking, but where the eroticism of *being looked at* can often prove to be similarly as pleasurable. When both narrative and protagonist climax in the film's closing moments—after a flashback of Whishaw removing his swimming shorts in a crowded public shower—vision, sexuality, and sensation collide through a scene that both formally embraces the spectatorial gaze and queers its relationship with the on-screen image.

To invoke the sensual, if rudimentary, formal and thematic aspects of *Baby* in a chapter on the films of the Argentine director Marco Berger is to contextualize these works within a broader cinematic lineage of slow queer film, over and above their shared emphasis on the latent eroticism of the quotidian. If *Baby* serves to represent the origins of what we might consider to be a contemporary "moment" in global queer cinema, anchored in an art-house slowness with a subdued aesthetic focus on the mundane, then it also exemplifies the recurringly haptic nature of many recent filmic explorations of queerness.[1] Strikingly, moreover, both *Baby* and Berger represent distinct junctures in a long history of combining queerness with narrative and thematic emphases on the aquatic: spaces, that is, such as swimming pools, beaches, lakes, and saunas that have come to serve as the loci of both emergent and veteran queer desires.[2] For instance, films such as Alain Guiraudie's *L'Inconnu du lac* (*Stranger by the Lake*, 2013), Barry Jenkins's *Moonlight* (2016), and Eliza Hittman's *Beach Rats* (2017) have evocatively linked water to the unpredictability, deviance, and, at times, violence connected with queer subjectivities. Other productions have instead sought to cast distinct bodies of water as sites of adolescent discovery (Céline Sciamma's *Naissance des pieuvres* [*Water Lilies*, 2007], Daniel Ribeiro's *Hoje Eu Quero Voltar Sozinho* [*The Way He Looks*, 2014], Jakob M. Erwa's *Der Mitte der Welt* [*Centre of My World*, 2016]), or as spaces for a more profound interrogation of the queer cinematic body (Lucía Puenzo's *XXY*, Julia Solomonoff's *El último verano de La Boyita* [*The Last Summer of La Boyita*, 2009]). The connections between *Baby* and these more recent films effectively shed light on an evolving formal and thematic vocabulary of global queer film, underscoring the ubiquitous preoccupation in these works with the politics inherent in screening queer corporeality. Moreover, the recurrent emphasis on a tactile, textural mode of spectatorship, provoked in large part through a shared repertoire of watery spaces, is a reminder, as Karl Schoonover and Rosalind Galt note, of queer cinema's capacity to "revise the flows and politics of world cinema and forge dissident scales of affiliation, affection, affect, and form."[3]

If slowness, then, in its varying emanations, is a frequent attribute of many, if not all, of the films mentioned above, it seems striking that such a recurring formal and narrative strategy has seldom been explored through these works in direct relation to queerness. Indeed, given that such slowness encourages—and at times even sensuously celebrates—a haptic screening of the queer body, it appears equally as surprising that recent phenomenological work on the "material turn" in film studies has been similarly myopic in its consideration of the queer. As Schoonover and Galt point out in their work on the slow, sexual politics of touch, "much film scholarship on phenomenology and the haptic brackets sexuality along with other political issues. Even when the examples are queer, cinema as a medium emerges unscathed by queerness."[4] It is this critical gap within contemporary queer film studies that I address in this chapter, through a framework that combines a phenomenological reading of Berger's work with an examination of the "sexual politics of the slow and the boring."[5] In doing so, I explore how Berger mobilizes slowness and the haptic through both the structure of the image and its sensually suggestive content, queering the relationship with the viewer not only by encouraging an erotic gaze on the naked male physique but also through a cautious deviation from the conventional formal and aesthetic registers of screening the body. Though critics of Berger's oeuvre have largely evaded these and related issues in their studies, choosing instead to focus on the director's avoidance of queer stereotype,[6] or on the narrative representation of nonheteronormative desire,[7] Berger's is undoubtedly a cinematography that demands a critical sensitivity toward the nexuses of touch and sexuality, and of slowness and queerness: these are elements inherent to the very structures of his filmic gaze.[8] From the voyeuristic inspection of the adolescent physique in the showers of *Ausente* (*Absent*, 2011) to the drawn-out contemplation of poolside bodies in *Hawaii* (2013), Berger's haptic, protracted caressing of the naked male form at once invites the spectator's gaze and queers its relationship with the sensual images of skin and sweat on screen.

On closer critical inspection, however, the stubborn visual insistence on male corporeality that pervades the majority of Berger's work belies a tension present in contemporary queer film more broadly, namely, surrounding the representational politics and queer potential of certain formal and aesthetic techniques. In Luca Guadagnino's *Call Me by Your Name* (2017), for example, the camera's elliptic movement during a pivotal scene between the two lead actors has attracted criticism for its censoring of gay sex, particularly, as critics point out, given the relative openness in screening heterosexual intercourse at an earlier point in the film. As Guy Lodge writes, "Once the two lovers begin having sex for the first time, the camera coyly drifts over to an open window, their early coital moans gentle in the background—the kind of tasteful dodge that practically nods to Code-era Hollywood."[9] While one of Berger's most recent films, *Taekwondo* (2016), codirected with Martín Farina, can certainly not be accused of shying away from homoerotic images of its protagonists, including scenes of full-frontal nudity and a sensual dwelling on bare skin and toned muscles, its formal composition nevertheless exhibits an implicit reluctance to confront queer sexuality directly or to dispense entirely with certain dramatic techniques of mainstream narrative cinema. The film's slow, relentless focus on the naked male body thus gestures toward a queer form of spectatorship while at the same time hesitating in its exploitation of the "radical potential of slowness," to use a term borrowed from Schoonover and Galt.[10] The first section of this chapter will consider *Taekwondo*'s formal structures of slowness and strategies of narrative boredom, paying close attention to how its sensual, haptic screening of the body is mobilized *in* and *through* time. The second and third sections will then explore how this collision between the haptic and the slow simultaneously incites and impedes the film's queer potential, ultimately revealing a caution on the part of the directors to fully embrace a queer undermining of normative modes of seeing—and feeling—the cinematic image.

The Politics of Slowness

In the minute-long opening sequence of *Taekwondo*, Berger and Farina introduce the film's slow, sensual tone. Through a fixed shot, the two main characters, Fernando and Germán, walk toward the camera, with their conversation progressively more audible yet never proving to be of any narrative significance. When they reach the foreground of the shot, immediately before the film's title screen appears, Fernando's toned, unclothed torso momentarily commands the screen, prefiguring the film's preference for the corporeal over the narrative, as well as its more specific aesthetic rumination on the naked male physique. This is a scene in which duration consumes narration, given that the static nature of the shot allows the spectator to focus not on the characters themselves, or on their conversation, but on their existence as bodies in time. When Fernando and Germán enter the country house in the subsequent scene, the formal aspects of the film do very little to introduce a sense of motion to the narrative: the men idly discuss the unremarkable details of the previous night, while the camera slowly maps out the seminaked bodies sleeping on the sofa and sunbathing by the poolside, all screened to the diegetic sound of trickling water. Indeed if, on the whole, any strong sense of narrative thread can be considered largely absent from the film, it can at times be deemed to be stubbornly so: shots of slumbering bodies recur frequently, as do images of glistening, athletic torsos reclining by the swimming pool (figure 4.1). The diegetic ennui of the protagonists—all childhood friends who have come to spend a relaxed vacation together in a *quinta* on the outskirts of Buenos Aires—manifests itself in a boredom on the level of content, while the composition of the shots often invites us, as spectators, to do nothing more than contemplate the beauty of the male form, dripping with water or sweat and lounging in close proximity, one body beside, or entangled with, another (figure 4.2).

Though the origins of the current trend of global slow cinema can be traced back to the turn of the twenty-first century, a more recent critical

Figure 4.1. Film still. Slumbering bodies in *Taekwondo*. *Source*: Dir. Marco Berger. Cinemilagroso, Oh My Gomez! Films (2016).

Figure 4.2. Film still. Entangled, slumbering bodies in *Taekwondo*. *Source*: Dir. Marco Berger. Cinemilagroso, Oh My Gomez! Films (2016).

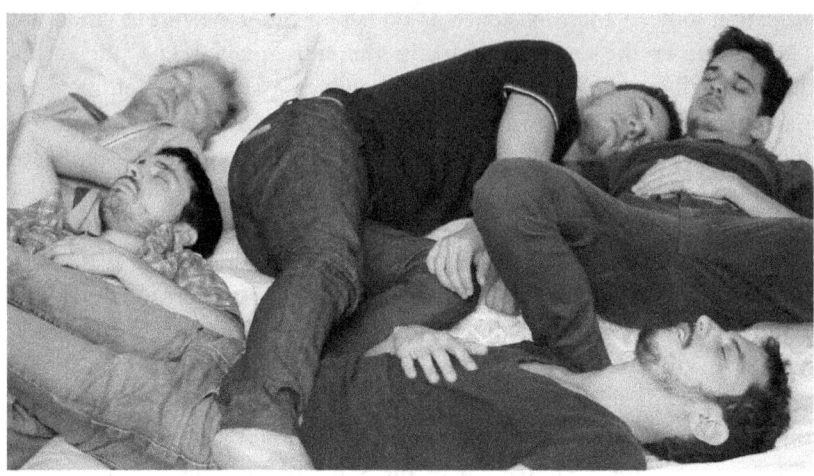

debate has unearthed specific tensions surrounding just such an aesthetic of boredom.[11] A now famous argument, labeled by one critic as "deeply parochial in its film buffery," brought to the surface the formal and political anxieties at stake in the production and reception of contemporary slow film.[12] Nick James suggested that such films are "passive-aggressive in that they demand great swathes of our precious time to achieve quite fleeting and slender aesthetic and political effects."[13] For his part, Steven Shaviro condemned the "routinized" formal aesthetic of contemporary slow cinema, which he argued had become "a sort of default international style that signifies 'serious cinema' without having to display any sort of originality or insight."[14] In an earlier, distinctly more positive critical assessment of the slow aesthetic, Matthew Flanagan drew attention to the "unique formal and structural design" of the genre, but nevertheless warned that its "sustained emptying out of deeply entrenched dramatic elements [. . .] often risks boredom on the part of the spectator, dissolving traditional components of storytelling to either the most rudimentary basis of central conflict or a series of de-centred digressive events."[15] It is this lack of dramatic narrative, with its extension of *temps morts* and nonevents, that constitutes the boredom that is inherent to *Taekwondo* and firmly woven into its very formal structures. The prolonged shots of reclining bodies are matched by formal, often overt, gestures toward narrative ellipsis. When the group of men leave one evening to go to a nightclub, for instance, they are screened walking away from the *quinta* in an extended shot before immediately being filmed returning the next morning; they each appear visibly tired, yet we are given no glimpse of the events that have taken place in-between. Here the abruptness of the change in outside light levels draws attention to an abridged form of narration, denying the spectator access to the event while explicitly emphasizing the fragmented passing of time. In its active deployment of boredom, *Taekwondo* challenges the normative criteria against which slow cinema has been judged, refusing, in any explicit sense, to "entertain" through conventional narrative structures and instead engaging the viewer in a more contemplative form of spectatorship.

As Tiago de Luca has noted in his study of the phenomenological aspects of spectatorship in the context of slow cinema, digressive shots such as those that populate *Taekwondo* allow "empty cinematic time [to come] to the fore, exposing in return the calculated temporal mechanisms by which cinema conventionally abides in its production of meaning."[16] The established filmic hierarchy that restricts duration to the service of the narrative is, as de Luca writes, reversed: "Not only does it supply the viewer with *time* to scan within and across the screen, [. . . but] it provides *too much time*, triggering a self-conscious mode of spectatorship whereby the viewer becomes aware of the viewing process and the time spent in such a process."[17] *Taekwondo* regularly makes recourse to, and capitalizes on, this cinematic realignment of shot duration over narrative resolution, imbuing the film's boredom with both formal and thematic significance. As noted above, the film habitually dwells on bodies drawn out in time, devoid of any explicit narrative consequence. Actions such as sleeping, reading,[18] and waiting take precedence via sequences that willfully withhold any sense of narrative gratification: in one instance, a cleaner's household chores are filmed in monotonous repetition, overtly drawing attention toward the tedium of our own viewing experience. Subsequently, when she has sex with one of the heterosexual men in the house, the way in which the intercourse is filmed is mechanistic, distancing, and objectifying, relying on a mere moment of eye contact as the only tangible means of narrative framing. If, as Schoonover and Galt note, "slow cinema wastes our time, asking us to spend time in visibly unproductive ways, outside efficient narrative economies of production and reproduction," then here Berger mobilizes this representational inefficiency on the levels of form as well as content, creating a sense of boredom in the very act of what might have been—in both figurative and literal terms—a point of narrative climax.[19]

While it is certainly true that *Taekwondo* mobilizes many of the slow strategies identified by the critics mentioned above, particularly in terms of such a persistent lack of narrative progression, it must be noted that Berger and Farina's direction does depart from the more radical formal uses of slowness that have conventionally been associated with the genre. The long opening take of the film, for example, replicates what Flanagan has termed "a cinema of walking," a filmic lineage that through "the mere act of walking signifies a rupture in the organisation of drama," echoing the distinctly modernist bent of films such as Roberto Rossellini's *Viaggio in Italia* (*Journey to Italy*, 1953), Michelangelo Antonioni's *L'Avventura* (1960), and Alain Resnais's *Hiroshima, mon amour* (1959). Yet despite several repetitions of the protagonists walking to and from the *quinta* over the course of the film, in very few instances are the shots left to linger statically for longer than half a minute, significantly less time than the five- or six-minute sequences associated with the directors and their films above. While, as Emre Çağlayan claims, "it would be no exaggeration to claim that walking constitutes a typical, even emblematic feature of slow cinema,"[20] these iterations of the walking scene in *Taekwondo* fall subtly into the service of the narrative. At times, they create a loose sense of anticipation, such as when Leo obliquely warns Germán that his desires for Fernando will be unrequited as the pair wander along a country path; and in the opening sequence of the film, mentioned earlier, Germán's introduction to the character of El gordo serves as a foundational illustration of the film's hesitation to release temporality from its narrative function. When the two men meet, a torso-level shot records the unremarkable routine of an introductory *saludo*; moments later, when El gordo jumps up to sit on the counter, the viewer realizes that he is naked from the waist down. The subsequent close-up of his penis, while he peels and eats an orange, lingers voyeuristically as the introductory conversation between the three men continues (figure 4.3). Thematically, the dripping juices from the orange evoke a raw sexuality and sense of virility, and the length and directness of the shot confront the spectator with an unambiguous display of male genitalia.[21] If, as Richard Misek writes in his discussion of dead cinematic time, "by imposing its own temporality onto objects, [cinema] can make possible boredom in response to objects that are not ordinarily associated with it," *Taekwondo* here intimates such boredom through its extended focus on El gordo's penis, yet ultimately

Figure 4.3. Film still. The voyeuristic gaze of *Taekwondo*. *Source*: Dir. Marco Berger. Cinemilagroso, Oh My Gomez! Films (2016).

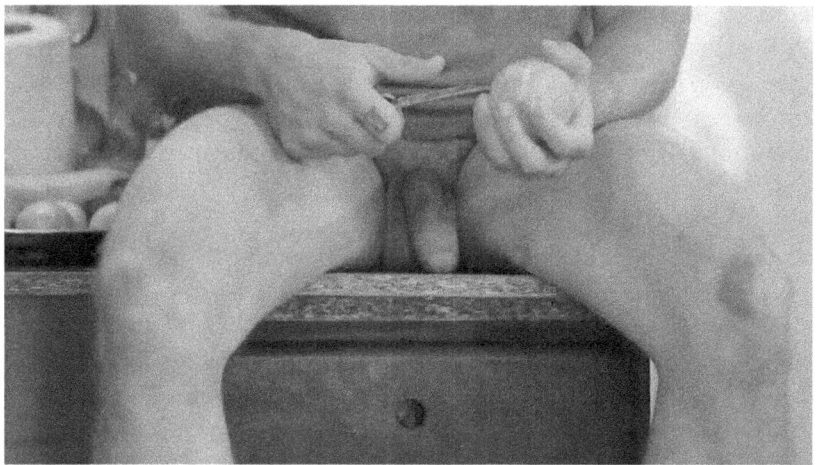

fails to "exhaust the image's representational dimension" by cutting away to the next scene after only ten seconds.[22] Furthermore, Germán's discernible surprise when first meeting El gordo thus becomes decipherable for the spectator in retrospect, allowing us to share in understanding the reason for the protagonist's initial shock. In this way the camera's intimate voyeurism serves to reflect and exacerbate Germán's sense of discomfort, imbuing the scene with an erotic hue that contrasts with the mundanity of the script. The unambiguous image of the naked male body, which at other points of the film works to defamiliarize the spectator's gaze, finds itself restricted to its function as narrative device, exposing in this instance a reliance on composition and editing that displace the slow potential of a longer, unharnessed take.

The Visual Erotics of Boredom

The quietly evolving relationship between Fernando and Germán, which one critic refers to as the film's "unrelenting hormonal ballet,"[23] provides the only impulse of what may be considered to be a sustained narrative thread in *Taekwondo*. When the country vacation draws to a close, and the pair are left alone in the *quinta*, an extended scene in the swimming pool consolidates this space as the center of gravity for the film's screening of their (as yet unexpressed) mutual desires. While the pool serves throughout the film as a site for the brazen display of the men's toned physiques, in the latter stages, it becomes the space for a more exploratory, daring interaction between the two, now released from the policing gaze of their heterosexual friends. In this particular scene, introduced via the sight and sound of Germán splashing into the water, the two men competitively hold their breath underwater and hover in close proximity, with their mouths just below the water's surface (figure 4.4). The tension is quite literally embodied in this sequence, as the two men visibly struggle to remain submerged in order to win the contest. On a broader level, the scene also expresses the ambiguity that has existed between the pair over the course of the film, and it is in many ways unsurprising that Fernando is the one who emerges victorious, reflecting his unflinching capacity to remain calm and controlled, while the younger Germán struggles to cope with the homoerotic tensions of the *quinta*. Indeed water, and specifically the water of the swimming pool, becomes a metaphor over the course of the film for the unpredictability of the pair's developing rapport, visually emphasized in this final scene by the potent image of their proximate faces and penetrating stares. If, as Fernando G. Pagnoni Berns notes in his discussion of queer Brazilian film, "water is a space that, contradictorily,

Figure 4.4. Film still. Embodied tensions in the swimming pool in *Taekwondo*. *Source*: Dir. Marco Berger. Cinemilagroso, Oh My Gomez! Films (2016).

provides intimacy but also the possibility of fleeing from it," then both the length and the composition of this sequence constitute just such an ultimatum, allowing Fernando and Germán to be intimately close to one another while wearing very little, yet still remaining within the bounds of an "acceptable" homosocial interaction.[24] In the subsequent scene, which lasts for almost two minutes and contains very little dialogue, we see Germán tacitly cycle through a range of emotions, intensifying the swimming pool's capacity to serve as "more than merely a setting, instead providing a dynamic space in which a film's central themes are played out."[25]

In their work on the cinematic swimming pool, Christopher Brown and Pam Hirsch note that the site functions as a "transitional, liminal space," in which "sexual identity becomes fluid, like the water in which the protagonists swim; it is a space of bodily and sexual metamorphosis."[26] More than a metaphor for the fluidity or unpredictability of sexuality, however, the aquatic spaces of *Taekwondo* are also sites where slowness and hapticity collide, endowed with the potential for a powerful examination of (queer) filmic embodiment. Deborah Martin has suggested in her work on the Argentine director Lucrecia Martel that the significance of the relationship between the queer and the aquatic in contemporary film lies not only in water's capacity "to be contained and controlled, or to transgress the boundaries which attempt to contain it," but also, she writes, in "its sensual qualities on the skin."[27] Indeed, during the episodes that are shot in the house's sauna and showers, the haptic nature of filming the group's naked bodies is unambiguous: a protracted shot of the men crowded into a sauna, for instance, in which the camera focuses on the sweat on the men's torsos (figure 4.5), becomes a potent means of, in Laura Marks's terms, "bringing vision close to the body and into contact with the other sense perceptions; making vision multisensory."[28] In *The Skin of the Film*, Marks explores the potential of cinema to provoke an embodied response from the viewer, arguing that visual disruptions within the frame disturb a spectator's cognitive control over the image and thus demand a more active viewing experience. Both in this scene and in *Taekwondo* more generally, the partial screening of bodies through the filmic dissection of limbs, chests, and groins means that the viewer must indeed not only "engage in [the] imaginative construction [of the image]" but also, consequently, "be aware of her or his self-involvement in the process."[29] In much the same way as the film's structures of slowness demand an increasingly contemplative response from the viewer, so too do the fragmented and textural images of the men's bodies, screened to

Figure 4.5. Film still. Haptic cinematography of sweat and skin in the sauna in *Taekwondo*. *Source*: Dir. Marco Berger. Cinemilagroso, Oh My Gomez! Films (2016).

demonstrate how "vision itself can be tactile, as though one were touching a film with one's eyes."[30]

The sweat on the men's skin thus demands a multisensory relationship from the viewer, as the spaces of the swimming pool, shower, and sauna come to function as sites of renewed queerness; queer not because of the occurrence of any nonnormative sexual act but through the prolonged and fragmented textural caressing of sweat, skin, and limbs. In this way, *Taekwondo* harnesses both the erotic potency of the haptic and the queer potential of slow spectatorship. As the protagonists are filmed in fragmented sequences, toying with their body hair or picking their toenails in scenes devoid of any explicit narrative content, the viewer becomes "bodied forth" by the image.[31] For Marks, this embodied relationship between viewer and on-screen image disrupts normative hierarchies of spectatorship, meaning that "it is not proper to speak of the *object* of a haptic look as to speak of a dynamic subjectivity between looker and image."[32] Such an embodied response in *Taekwondo* is triggered by a visual erotics of slowness that exposes normative cinematic structures of narrative, time, and perception, and reconfigures——or queers—the viewer's relationship to the image through an intersubjective dynamic that confounds conventional hierarchies of spectatorship. As I argue here, however, the film's own intersubjective drives are undercut in both temporal and affective terms. In the aforementioned sequence in the swimming pool, for instance, the haptic slowness that pervades the two-minute scene foments a sense of romantic tension, strategically positioned to directly precede the film's ultimate narrative resolution when the pair finally embrace, moments before the closing credits roll. In this sense, then, the anticipation that *Taekwondo* creates through scenes such as this one delimits the potential of its intersubjective slowness, suppressing it through an ultimate reversion to normative structures of narrative expectation.

Recent critical studies of queer cinema in Latin America have similarly observed the theoretical potential of drawing on phenomenological approaches such as that taken by Marks.[33] Vinodh Venkatesh writes in *New Maricón Cinema*, for example, that such intersubjectivity between looker and image triggers an ethically active form of spectatorship, through which the viewer is actively encouraged to confront a spectrum of nonnormative sexual potential: "We no longer simply *see* difference, we are invited to actively touch, caress, and participate in the sensuality of libidinal urges, body identifications, and often-multidirectional orientations that engender new structures of feeling vis-à-vis bodies and desires."[34] Santiago Peidro, writing specifically about the work of Berger, also notes the political potential of this more active form of spectatorship: "There is a clear interpellative impulse [. . .] that seeks to unseat the spectator from the inertia of passively accepting the cultural norms of sexual and gender intelligibility that command human relations."[35] These critics do, however, neglect to account for the intrinsic limitations of the haptic viewing processes described above, equating a capacity to queer normative structures of spectatorship with an implicitly utopian account of a more ethically active mode of viewing. In their emphasis on the ethical potential of embodied spectatorship, and its visibilization of alternative libidinal positions and recognition of pluralized sexual identities, they too eagerly overlook how these haptic strategies are mobilized—and often constrained—through time. As noted above, the formal and narrative slowness of Berger's work does indeed facilitate a haptic engagement with the cinematic body; importantly, however, it also renders such an embodied response more complex through its parallel, contingent demand via the slowness of the image that "spectatorship alter its accustomed pathways, orient itself otherwise."[36] Slowness here encourages a visual caressing of the male form at the same time as it underscores the impossibility

122 | Bodies of Water

of any such tactile engagement; it gestures toward the presence of non-normative desires just as it curtails their very modes of representation. When Fernando repeatedly touches the insect bites on Germán's chest during an extended episode in the bathroom, the haptic potential of the scene is abridged by the abrupt departure of the latter, an exit only visible through the internally framed mirror behind Fernando's head (figure 4.6). The tension that runs throughout *Taekwondo*, and through contemporary slow queer cinema more generally, between a haptic approximation of spectator to image and a reflexive recognition of the film's own "asymptotic, caressing relationship to the real," is thus problematized through the identificatory possibilities *and* limitations of cinematic slowness.[37]

Faux-Slow and the Queering of Boredom

In *Queer Cinema in the World*, Schoonover and Galt categorize Andrew Haigh's *Weekend* (2011) and Julián Hernández's *Mil nubes de paz cercan el cielo* (*A Thousand Clouds of Peace*, 2003) as recent examples of "faux-slow" cinema, a genre of films they identify with artistic pretentions that are critically at odds with their formal and aesthetic realization.[38] "Whereas these films stylistically seem to involve a loosening of narrative's grip on filmic temporality," they write, "in the long run they do not allow critical bore-

Figure 4.6. Film still. Reflections on spectatorship in *Taekwondo*. Source: Dir. Marco Berger. Cinemilagroso, Oh My Gomez! Films (2016).

dom to take hold."[39] In their analysis of how these films manipulate the spectator's gaze via specific formal techniques (such as subjective framing and narrow depth of field), Schoonover and Galt argue that such works thereby display an ultimate reluctance to confront the spectator with the "radical registers of slowness":[40] "Whenever either film comes close to depicting time emptied of narrative content, it anxiously undermines its more ambitious aesthetic impulses by overly managing the viewer's gaze, as if scrambling to counteract any wandering attention. [. . .] These faux-slow gay films trope slow-moving narration without cultivating the critical potentials of slowness, and they display nervous tics around *unleashing the gaze in time.*"[41] Schoonover and Galt posit that these tensions are fueled by concerns over the reception and distribution of contemporary queer film, reflecting a desire to appeal to consumer demands beyond the festival circuit as well as a recent impulse toward the "gentrification of gay world cinema."[42] Although, at times, their theorization of the faux-slow genre emerges as problematic, not least given the arbitrary policing of specific aesthetic and formal strategies of slowness, the anxieties they identify in contemporary queer cinema surrounding the "unleashing of the gaze in time" do nevertheless provide a productive basis for critique. While critics of Berger's films argue, in the ways explored above, that his work triggers a recognition of nonnormative desire through an embodied form of spectatorship, a more sensitive analysis of how *Taekwondo*'s haptic cinematography interacts with its slow aesthetic can thus expose a series of paradoxes that restrict the film's political potential. These paradoxes revolve around, on the one hand, modes of eroticizing the male body and, on the other, a hesitancy to dispense with certain conventionally scopic filmic techniques. That is, although the attempt to draw the spectator cognitively closer to the cinematic image through the textural, fragmented screening of the body is unmistakable, the tendency to do so through a set of eroticized images nevertheless serves to "entertain" the viewer through conventional, well-worn cinematic means. Scenes in the sauna and shower room, for example, are filmed in a suggestively warm palette, evoking the image's sensual content through tone and hue. Similarly, the subtle and intermittent recourses to traditional formal strategies, such as point-of-view framing, tactical focus, and strategic reverse-shots, all display an ultimate reluctance to deny the spectator a sense of diegetic resolution.

In relation to the distinctly erotic hue with which Berger paints his protagonists, various critics have noted a consistency in the slow, sensual emphasis on the male form throughout his oeuvre, from *Plan B*

(2009), through *Ausente* and *Hawaii*, to *Taekwondo*. Attention has been drawn in particular to Berger's progressively more pervasive reliance on close-up, static shots of the crotch area, seldom fully uncovered though often filmed in a provocative manner. Pagnoni Berns notes, for instance, that the recurrence of swimming pools, showers, and saunas in Berger's cinema legitimize in narrative terms the filming of men wearing items of clothing "that reveal more than they hide."[43] For Peidro, frames centered on the crotch area constitute the quintessential "Berger shot," which in its formal persistence "expects a distinctly participative response from the spectator, whose attention cannot be relinquished."[44] These shots appear frequently in *Taekwondo* and, for the most part, bear little relation to the film's diegetic (in)action: they surface, for example, when Germán talks on the phone to his friend or when the men wait for their turn in the shower, with their loosely draped towels barely covering their genitals and pubic hair (figure 4.7). The suggestiveness of these shots introduces an unambiguously sexual tone to the image, not simply in the visually erotic manner suggested by Marks but also in the sense of the frankly pornographic. In this regard, they reveal a fundamental tension that runs throughout much of *Taekwondo*, between the desire to defamiliarize the naked male body through stubborn, fragmented, haptic shots that withhold narrative and thematic coherence, and a parallel formal impulse to aestheticize such images of the men. On the use of these intimate shots

Figure 4.7. Film still. The "Berger shot" in *Taekwondo*. *Source*: Dir. Marco Berger. Cinemilagroso, Oh My Gomez! Films (2016).

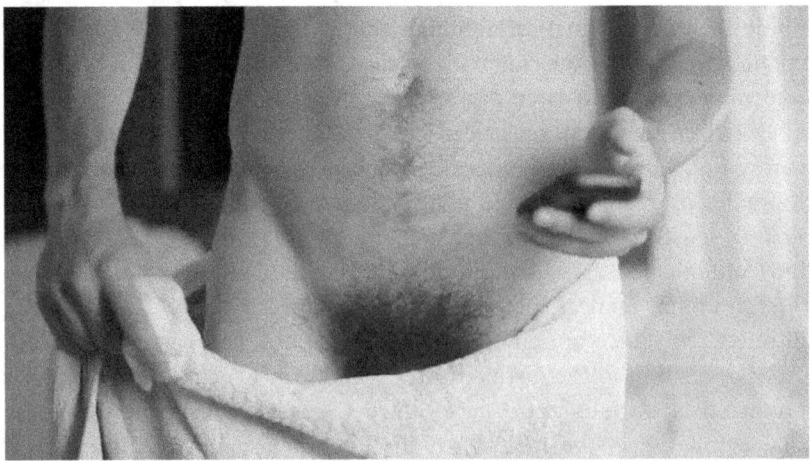

in Berger's *Ausente*, Peidro writes: "In effect, when some sort of excess, rupture, digression or emphasis emerges with respect to the logic of the narrative, the spectator's inferential process is triggered, not only interrogating the cause of such a discursive sign, as is the case with the close-up of male genitals outlined through underwear, but also becoming interpellated by it."[45] For the reasons discussed above, however, *Taekwondo*'s interpellation of the spectator through shots such as these is more intricate than Peidro here suggests. At times, the "Berger shot" is used subjectively to align the viewer with the perspective of Germán, such as when Leo actively provokes him by undressing in front of him, fueling the younger man's fears over being "outed" to the rest of the group; at other times these shots are employed only momentarily, curtailing the slow, haptic potential of the image and instead relying solely on its potential for sexual arousal. Rather than "unleashing the gaze in time," therefore, these instances of resorting to conventionally scopic means of narrative and formal framing compromise the ethical appeal that *Taekwondo* generates for its audience, undermining the film's potential to "deny [the spectator] the comfort of inhabiting the certainties of gender, sex, sexual attraction and culturally hegemonic forms of desires."[46]

As suggested above, the haptic potency of Berger and Farina's filmmaking in *Taekwondo* is diminished in terms of narrative and script. In the sauna sequence discussed above, the textural caressing of the sweat on the men's bodies, though powerful, is eventually dampened by the entrance of El gordo, who interrupts the sluggish pan across the men's chests with his conversation. Although the dialogue initially proves to be of no consequence to the narrative, the ensuing focus on the question of whether or not Germán has a girlfriend makes it clear that the viewer is intended to feel a sense of tension on the part of the younger man, exacerbated by the claustrophobic space of the sauna. This is, after all, where the men are at their most open to the homosexual (and spectatorial) gaze, an aspect that is accentuated by the deliberate, voyeuristic images of the men's torsos for much of the two-minute-long sequence. As the fragmented inspection of the men's bodies is here relegated to the narrative, the restriction of the film's slow structures cuts short the opportunity for a more ethically contemplative response. On a similar level, while the camera angles for the most part deny any explicitly subjective stance, there is a sporadic tendency toward point-of-view shots at key moments in the film. Without exception these align the viewer with the perspective of Germán, who on many levels functions as the film's outsider, reflecting our own position as voyeurs among the intimate scenes of the *quinta*. Notably, it is Germán's face that is most often presented in close-up, his eyes furtively catching glimpses of the men when they undress or shower, and his facial expressions ever-so-subtly reacting to the displays of muscular flesh that surround him. Although, admittedly, these specific narrative and formal aspects do not dominate the film, and cannot be said to undermine the more pervasive emphasis on slowness, they do represent periodic impulses, to borrow from Schoonover and Galt, to "undercut the viewer's experience of *durée* [. . .] by overly managing the viewer's gaze."[47] The film flaunts its explicit desire to prohibit narrative coherence, while, at the same time, its subtle visual cues intermittently condition the spectator's response to the emotions of the primary character(s). In this sense, although *Taekwondo* does not fall squarely into the category proposed by Schoonover and Galt, it is a film that exhibits discernible tendencies toward the faux-slow.

Slow Waters

In the final few moments of *Taekwondo*, the intimate scene of the two protagonists embracing in the shadows condenses the tensions discussed in this chapter surrounding the film's formal slowness and the potential of its queer representation. As the two men kiss, the tension that has been progressively more present in the narrative is resolved, displacing the radical uncertainty of slowness in favor of allowing spectators to confirm their suspicions that Germán's desires are indeed reciprocated. Throughout *Taekwondo*, however, Berger and Farina's cinematography represents a significant attempt to decenter queerness from conventional cinematic modes of narrative representation, reinvesting its nonnormative potential instead within filmic surface, texture, and extension. The film's haptic appeal to the viewer through the visual erotics of the fragmented images of bodies is matched by a drive to queer the relationship between spectator and text through the film's intersubjective structures of slowness. This combination of slow aesthetic and haptic cinematography not only delays, and at times proscribes, a sense of narrative gratification, but in doing so, it also creates a self-aware form of spectatorship that exposes conventional cinematic structures of time and perception. "A belaboured spectator," as Schoonover remarks, "mirrors in reverse the non-belaboured body of the character on-screen."[48] Indeed, through its "alluring account of bodies and gazes," *Taekwondo*'s unremitting screening of naked and semi-naked men in various states of repose demands that the spectator dispense with conventional modes of spectatorship.[49] However, as I have argued, rather than mounting an unwavering appeal to the spectator to acknowledge a spectrum of nonnormative desire through its embodied form of spectatorship, the politics of the slow and the boring in *Taekwondo* are both realized *and* restricted. The formal and aesthetic strategies used by Berger and Farina deny a sense of narrative rigor while also occasionally undermining the film's most challenging interpellative impulses; they queer the spectator's relationship to the image while, paradoxically, also satisfying certain expected narrative and cinematographic conventions. Ultimately, though, there is in the film's meticulous, sensual caressing of the men's skin and sweat a potent examination of the potential of queer filmic embodiment. The "threatening queer counterproductivity that simmers discursively" in the film's fusion of the haptic and the slow cautiously undermines normative structures of narrative, time, and spectatorship, gesturing toward the potential for nonnormative representation through a distinctly queer erotics of boredom.[50]

Chapter Five

Postporn Flows

Las hijas del fuego and the Queer Poetics of Sexual Pleasure

> But seeing everything—especially seeing the *truth* of sex—proves a much more difficult project than one might think, especially in the case of women's bodies, whose truths are most at stake.
>
> —Linda Williams, *Hard Core*

Barbara Hammer's *Dyketactics* (1974) is, according to the director herself, both the "first erotic lesbian film made by a lesbian" and a nascent example of the "lesbian aesthetic" that pervades much of her cinematic work.[1] In a direct challenge to what Jacques Lacan referred to as women's "lack," Hammer describes her cinema as one of "wholeness," in which "women, and especially lesbians, work from a completeness, a sense of having everything we need, a sense of recognition of the other as similar to the self and hence a sensitivity to the world around us."[2] The film's four-minute-long erotic collage of women bathing, dancing, and having sex with one another against bucolic backdrops foregrounds this sensitivity through the primacy of touch, encouraging a "tactile quality, a sensuality with sex and not sex without sensuality, that is essential to any lesbian aesthetic."[3] This intimacy with which Hammer's camera caresses her subjects and the sense of sufficiency and unbridled pleasure that pervade the work resonate with the roles that sensuality and sexuality play in the Argentine director Albertina Carri's film, *Las hijas del fuego* (*The Daughters of*

Fire, 2018). The film follows a group of women as they travel through rural Argentina, on a "viaje poliamoroso, pornográfico y antipatriarcal" (polyamorous, pornographic, and antipatriarchal journey) that confronts the spectator with visual cartographies of both the striking landscapes of Argentina's southern coastline and the bodies of the women themselves.[4] But the film also travels across genres, cutting through the conventions of experimental and pornographic media and borrowing certain narrative staples from the road movie, most notably in the "key element [that] a road movie is not just a film about people driving a vehicle, but one that focuses on a journey—irrespective of the means of transportation used—and, in particular, on the impact that journey has on the travellers."[5] It is, in the words of Griselda Soriano and Luciana Calcagno, a "*road movie* porno lesbo-feminista" (lesbian-feminist road-movie porno).[6]

The film's diegetic pretense of shooting a porn film as the women travel through Argentina is swiftly eclipsed by Carri's broader reflections on the bodily poetics of sexual pleasure, not least through the poetics of a voiceover that regularly ruminates on sex, power, history and the cinematic image. The feminist echoes of Hammer's lesbian aesthetic resonate sensuously through each and every image of the women's bodies set against rural backdrops of mountains, lakes, and the ocean.[7] *Las hijas del fuego* is, in this way, emblematic of what Hammer reads as the fundamental characteristics of radical lesbian cinema, through its intimate scenes that prioritize a "reaffirmation of the body, sexualised imagery and language, [. . .] the non-alienation from nature (landscape identification with the body), the muse as female and lesbian, and the inspiration and expansiveness that come within the context of small groupings."[8] The explicitness of the women's sexual exploits, and their notable diversity in terms of body shape and sexual preference, invite the spectator to interrogate the politics of representation that are at play in the cinematic mediatization of sexuality.[9] Carri exposes in *Las hijas del fuego* the normative taxonomies of pleasure that govern mainstream pornography, necessitating not only a reconditioning of the gaze cast toward the female body but also a recalibration of the modes employed to screen women's sexual desire.

Throughout *Las hijas del fuego*, a poetic commentary from the internal director infuses the film with a reflexivity that works to identify the body itself as a site of representational and, consequently, political radicality. During the voiceover's initial reflections, delivered by Violeta, the film's underlying preoccupation toward sexuality and the body is made clear: "El problema nunca es la representación de los cuerpos; el problema es cómo esos cuerpos vuelven territorio y paisaje frente a la cámara" (The problem is never the representation of bodies; the problem is how these bodies become territory and landscape in front of the camera). That this opening maxim is immediately followed by explicit scenes of Violeta having sex with her lover, Augustina, complete with intimate close-up shots of double-ended dildos and flows of ejaculate, is indicative of the film's broader politics of representation: Carri both appeals to the spectacular nature of the sexual act and, through the form and aesthetic of the scene, frustrates the potential of the image to communicate the women's private, hermetic sense of erotic pleasure. In this way, *Las hijas del fuego* discloses its fixation from the outset on what Linda Williams refers to in *Screening Sex* as "what is both historically and viscerally strange and intractable about sex—the many ways in which it does not submit itself to visual and aural explicitness, its incoherence, its troubling enigmas."[10] This reflexive approach to the women's sexualities challenges the parameters of the pornographic, exploring the relationship between spectatorship and the sexual act through a cinematography that is at once explicit and poetic, as much an examination of female sexuality as it is a celebration of private, unknowable pleasure. The camera's tactile, visual indulgence toward the women's bodies is matched by the similarly indulgent "masturbación mental" (mental masturbation) of the voiceover, whose lengthy poetic digressions carve, as Williams writes of feminist porn more broadly, "a path that leads to the representation of sexual pleasures becoming grounded in an economy of abundance rather than scarcity, of many rather than one."[11] By revitalizing Hammer's sense of completeness and her filmic reaffirmation of the body, *Las hijas del fuego* thus gestures toward a queer sense of pleasure that challenges normative modes of screening lesbian desire and, at the same time, exposes the intractability of "truthfully" capturing any such bodily pleasure on screen.

In *Lesbian Cinema after Queer Theory*, Clara Bradbury-Rance observes a paradox between the increased visibility of lesbian sexuality in recent mainstream media and its problematic political undercurrent: "[Visibility] fixes as it names; it dismisses some as it champions others; it distracts; it normalises; it fossilises. Palatability can sacrifice politics."[12] For Bradbury-Rance, the impulse to "make visible is to refine the spectrum of who and what is shown," leading to the sociocultural sphere's historical and "persistent framing of lesbianism in the singular."[13] This chapter acknowledges the centrality of Bradbury-Rance's assertions for any discussion surrounding the aesthetics of lesbian visibility in a film such as *Las hijas del fuego*, which overwhelmingly stakes a claim for plurality of representation and identification through an explicit abundance of sexual identities, practices, bodies, and preferences.[14] More than this, however, the chapter also seeks to address what Bradbury-Rance refers to as the "mood of sexual potential" that counteracts any such paradox of visibility, and which becomes distributed throughout a film not necessarily by "a directional relationship between subject and object" but by an "embodied dynamic" of latent sexual desire.[15] Indeed, in Carri's own words, "En *Las hijas del fuego* hay una búsqueda de lo erótico que no sólo pase por el cuerpo y lo genital, sino que lo erótico está en la palabra, en la reflexión, en la poesía, en el paisaje, en el viaje, en el afecto, en los vínculos" (There is a search for the erotic in *Las hijas del fuego* that not only passes through the body and its genitals but also finds the erotic in the verbal, in contemplation, in poetry, in landscape, in the journey, in affect, in connections).[16] In this way, the film's lesbian eroticism foregrounds a poetics of sexual pleasure that incorporates the sensuality of the women's interactions not only with each other but also, in a broader *queer* sense, with their environment. The film enacts a radical critique of normative modes of screening bodies and bodily desires, all the while queering our understanding of their embeddedness within the structures of both spectatorship and society.

This discussion therefore moves beyond the "crude parameters of shock and sensation" to which studies of cinematic sex have so often been subject. Instead, it focuses on the "embodied dynamic" of queer sexual pleasure that pervades *Las hijas del fuego* and exposes how Carri mobilizes the representation of explicit sex as a mode of critical interrogation.[17] The chapter draws on Astrid Lorange and Tim Gregory's concept of *post*pornography to argue that *Las hijas del fuego* offers a critique not only of pornographic media itself but also of the broader sociopolitical and cultural structures of repression through which women's bodies have been historically policed. The first and second sections explore the representational politics of the postpornographic through the film's layers of reflexivity, from the plot device of the internal porn film to the recurring poetic reflections from the voiceover. I then move on to consider in the final section how this reflexivity allows for an extended idea of the erotic, through which the sensuality of landscape and, in words of Teresa de Lauretis, the "technology" of gender and sexuality undermine hegemonic, normative modes of spectatorship.[18] If, as Hammer writes, "to be a lesbian today is a form of expatriation," then *Las hijas del fuego* shares in this iconoclasm by exploding the normative sociopolitical regimes of the visual that govern the ways of seeing and screening the erotic body.[19] Carri offers a radical subversion of these dominant hierarchies of spectatorship through a queer poetics of sexual pleasure that indulges in the spectacle of explicit lesbian sex and, at the same time, exposes the camera's insufficiency in capturing its potential for both pleasure and politics.

The Sexual Politics of Postpornography

The opening sequence of *Las hijas del fuego*, in which the camera sweeps across the coastal waters of Tierra del Fuego to the sounds of birds and ocean waves, foregrounds the film's central themes of movement, fluidity, and the natural environment. In the moments that follow, Carri imbues these initial images of the landscape with a latent sense of eroticism via the exposed bodies of the two protagonists, who are seen, separately, struggling to put on a wetsuit and masturbating in a glacial cavern. These visual emphases on the women's bodies are rendered all the more acute through the sounds of stretched fabric and heavy breathing, as well as through haptic shots of bare skin, uncovered breasts, and sex toys. When the women are subsequently reunited in Ushuaia, after Violeta returns by ship from an expedition to Antarctica, the film's voiceover delivers the following indictment of contemporary Argentine society: "Hay sistemas que nunca cambian, aunque el tiempo parezca modificarlo todo: la milicia y el clero son lógicas que no tienen solución. Dejan marcas indelebles por siempre. Los cuerpos son los mismos, los mismos trajes, los mismos hombres, cargando una historia de fronteras y de represión" (There are systems that never change, even if time appears to transform them completely: the military and the clergy are structures for which there is no solution. They leave indelible marks forever. The bodies remain the same, the outfits remain the same, the men remain the same, all forging a history of borders and of repression). The bodies of the women are cast by Carri throughout *Las hijas del fuego* as political counters to these hegemonic societal structures, not least of State and Church, mobilizing sexual pleasure as a radical strategy of political subversion. For instance, when the newly formed ménage-à-trois evolves into a foursome, with the addition of a childhood-friend-cum-nun, the devotional setting of a small coastal church becomes the erotic mise-en-scène for the women's sexual exploration of one another's bodies. The tableau of the women, prostrate on the altar or kneeling around it to perform oral sex, corrupts the use of the female body in the history of religious art, and the stained-glass palette and medium shot work to frame their bodily ecstasy as a religious vision against the apse of the church (figure 5.1). As the accompanying tones of organ and harpsichord swell toward a crescendo and the body of the nun writhes as she reaches climax, religious piety is subsumed by pornographic pleasure, and visions of Michelangelo's *La Pietà* are parodically exchanged for an embrace of viscerally carnal lesbian desire. At the same time, the outlandish sight of Augustina masturbating in a wetsuit not only invokes previous images of her undressing by the shoreline but also imbues the scene with a textural quality as she pleasures herself through the neoprene fabric. Her diegetic framing in this scene between two stained-glass crosses is explicit—in both senses of the word—in its subversion of "la mirada de la iglesia sobre nuestros cuerpos" (the Church's gaze over our bodies) (figure 5.2).[20] If religion remains one of the "structures for which there is no solution," as the voiceover insists, then in this sequence Carri not only suggests a momentary liberation of the women's bodies from the policing gaze of normative societal structures but also harnesses the radical power of the erotic to undo those very power structures from within.

In their article "Teaching Post-Pornography," Lorange and Gregory chart the history of pornographic representation over the past three

Figure 5.1. Film still. A sexual tableau in *Las hijas del fuego*. Source: Dir. Albertina Carri. Gentil (2018).

Figure 5.2. Film still. Neoprene pleasure in a religious setting in *Las hijas del fuego*. *Source*: Dir. Albertina Carri. Gentil (2018).

decades, proposing the term "postpornography" to denote those pornographic texts that are "characterised by three aspects: the denaturalizing of sex, the de-centring of the spectator and the recognition of media and technology as inseparable from sex."[21] Lorange and Gregory suggest that by reading cinematic sex "laterally rather than literally," contemporary critical approaches to pornographic material possess the potential not simply to expose how bodies are imaged, commodified and consumed, but also to reveal how sexual desire intersects more complexly with a range of cultural, social and political matrices.[22] They write: "Thinking of a post-pornographic sex, we're thinking of sex as *a critical encounter*, an opportunity to consider what it is that makes sex possible or not, desirable or not, pleasurable or not—and, an opportunity to think about the politics that are inextricable from sex: the politics of race, class, gender; the politics that come with technology and the politics of biologism; the politics of the state and the family; the politics of care and community, and so on."[23] Lorange and Gregory's reflections on the *criticality* of the sexual encounter resonate strongly with the role that sexual intimacy plays in *Las hijas del fuego*. The film's voiceover renders manifest the intentions of the directors (both internal and external) to explode the normativity of the spectator's gaze, and the bodies of the women, through their diversity, categorically refuse to endorse any hegemonic understanding of sexual attraction or arousal: their shapes, sizes, sexual predilections, and skin color instead establish a kaleidoscopic sense of erotic pleasure that is both unharnessed from the specificities of individual bodies and yet deeply corporeal. The film's insistence on the multiplicity of sexual preference and practice, from the recurring use of sex toys and bondage gear to the provocative repurposing of a church altar, rejects any abstract notion of sex as detached from everyday life, instead recognizing how the logics of desire and sexuality have been historically and politically coded.

The critical encounters that are imbued throughout *Las hijas del fuego* amount, over the course of the film, to a radical subversion in the historical representation of female sexuality. Through the modes of parody, provocation, and fantasy, the film embraces sexuality's "disagreements and heterogeneity, rather than consensus," reflecting the "wide range of contents and styles" that Ingrid Ryberg notes have become characteristic of contemporary queer and feminist pornography.[24] In one of the film's more playful sequences, which takes place after the group expands to include several other members, a dream scene ruptures the film's realist narrative and takes explicit aim at women's roles in mainstream pornographic production. In a wry reimagining of John Everett Millais's painting *Ophelia*, one of the women floats across the water before being awoken by a kiss from Violeta, now dressed in men's clothing (à la Drag King) and sporting a false moustache (figure 5.3). The image of the would-be Ophelia's prosthetic penis moments later parallels the scene's unsettling score,

Figure 5.3. Film still. A queer(ed) Ophelia in *Las hijas del fuego*. Source: Dir. Albertina Carri. Gentil (2018).

accentuating through its uncanniness the inauthenticity of the sexual acts being observed. That this sequence is immediately preceded by black-and-white archival footage of women reclining by a lake, diving into water, and eating fruit is significant: not only does Carri gesture overtly toward the potential for erotic pleasure in the absence of men, but here the film also demands a more implicit reconditioning of the gaze directed toward women, historically and in the present. As Lorange and Gregory note, "If feminist pornography was intent on doing porn differently, post-pornography in its more recent explorations is about doing sex differently, or, to put it even more clearly, about showing *how sex is always, has always and can always be done differently.*"[25] The queer fairy tale that Carri spins in this sequence, during which floral crowns and Hawaiian shirts are juxtaposed with the sight of oral sex being performed on a dildo, denaturalizes the sexual act, setting into stark relief the visceral authenticity of the film's other instances of unsimulated sex between the women. Moreover, as Juli A. Kroll observes in her reading of this sequence, the group's "period drag" and their "posing on an abandoned boat reference the ship-wrecked or foundering notions of the past's static genders and sexualities."[26] As Augustina and Francisca watch on from a distance, dragged up and crying performatively while they masturbate, Carri mounts a carnivalesque subversion of mainstream pornography, gesturing metacinematically toward the imbrication of sex and media with a derisory sarcasm that corrodes the conventions of the eroticized male gaze.

The distinct layers of self-awareness that are to be found in *Las hijas del fuego*, from the internal porn film to the voiceover's overt reflections on the objectification of the female body, coalesce in their purpose of exposing the insufficiency of conventional pornographic techniques in the mediation of women's sexual pleasure. For Lorange and Gregory, the framework of postpornography not only enables a more accurate description of the "complex ecology" in which erotic media now circulates, but it also allows for "a new vocabulary of sex and sexuality" that recognizes this counternormative potential of feminist and queer depictions of sex.[27] They write: "Another way to understand post-pornography is as an aesthetic mode and textural sensibility in which pornography is an ever-present subject of critique."[28] In its mobilization of erotic pleasure *as* queer political strategy, *Las hijas del fuego* aligns itself with a postpornographic intention "to deconstruct, reconfigure or deviate from pornographic tropes in order to produce different representations of sex and desire."[29] The film suggests a more capacious approach to sexuality that at times denaturalizes sex, exposing the normative frameworks through which it has been conventionally mediatized. More than this, however, as the following sections of this chapter will argue, Carri's screening of the sexual act consequently disavows the structures of voyeurism otherwise associated with pornographic material; though there *is* pleasure in looking, as the film makes abundantly clear. Instead, the film decenters the spectator through its refusal to present the women's bodies as passive commodities for the camera's gaze. As Heather Dempsey notes in her review of the film, Carri's refusal to adhere to "creative and political restraints" results in a presentation of the female body that "bypasses the male gaze and frees itself from the patriarchal tropes of possession and linearity. Emancipated, like the cyclical female pleasure depicted, it roams roundaboutly in a plane of its own."[30] In its celebratory and sensuous exploration of women's sexuality, *Las hijas del fuego* explicitly negotiates a postpornographic poetics of queer pleasure, subverting dominant modes of representing bodily desire through its reflexive focus on the radical, immanent potential of screening the sexual act.

Bodily Poetics / Queer Flows

The diegetic shooting of a porn film and the often-lyrical voiceover that accompanies the protagonists' journey north provide moments of metacinematic reflection that foreground the formal and spectatorial implications of capturing sexual desire on screen. In one scene, as Violeta and Augustina discuss a particular establishing sequence, the film wryly comments on its own narrative slowness and latent tendency to dwell on the natural landscape: "Muchos planos de leña para una porno, ¿no te parece?" asks Augustina, before adding, "Las espectadoras se nos duermen" (Lots of log shots for a porno, don't you think? Our viewers are dozing off on us). That Violeta then asks for the camera to be moved so that it no longer appears in the shot, gestures obliquely toward the desire in mainstream pornography to invisibilize the layers of mediation inherent in the screening of sexual acts. Likewise, when Violeta's voiceover initiates an extended reflection on the representational limitations of pornography with a single question—"¿Qué cuento cuando cuento porno?"—the choice of the verb *contar* exposes her own subjectivity as director and evokes the broader levels of intervention that are ordinarily concealed behind pornography's imagistic flirtation with the real.³¹ If the "perpetual purpose" of hard-core pornography is, as Williams writes, "to reveal all," then Carri goes one step further through these metacinematic facets to expose both the power dynamics inherent in such visibility and the insufficiency of these structures to capture and communicate the protagonists' sexual pleasure.³² In the internal commentary that follows, Violeta remarks:

> Hay algo del goce que es irrepresentable; no hay modo de crear un verosímil. Somos transcurrir, perdiéndonos durante horas en el antebrazo de un amado, dejando que las marcas de esa piel nos llevan al vahído. Quiero perder la cabeza, quiero perderlo todo. Que mi concha se vuelva un agujero generoso y pedigüeño. ¿Cómo mostrar esto en una porno? Si no hay truco y hay placer, sensualidad, disponibilidad, tiempo, ¿es porno? ¿O la pornografía es sólo la objetivación de los cuerpos? Si la subjetividad de esos cuerpos no está destruida, ¿dejan de pertenecer a este género?
>
> (There's something about pleasure that is unrepresentable; there's no way to craft it realistically. We're lost in time, spending hours in the arms of a lover, dizzy from the touch of her skin. I want to lose myself in her, to immerse myself completely; to let my pussy turn into a generous, imposing cavern. How do I show all of this in a porn film? If pretense is replaced by pleasure, sensuality, openness, time, is it still porn? Or is pornography only the objectification of bodies? If the subjectivity of these bodies remains intact, do they cease to belong to that genre?)

Here, Carri prioritizes the subjectivities of the protagonists over the spectacularity of explicit cinematic sex, pointing to the distinct aesthetic modes of pleasure and sensuality that lie beyond the camera's reach and outside of the scopophilic structures of the conventionally pornographic. As a critical encounter between bodies and gazes, and between private pleasure and the spectacle of pornography, the postpornographic eroticism of *Las hijas del fuego* acts critically and reflexively to identify a bodily poetics of desire that demands alternative formal and aesthetic sensibilities.

That Violeta's rumination on the limitations of pornography takes place as the women board a boat and sail across a bay, with the camera fixed on an extended shot of the boat's wake, is demonstrative of the film's broader thematic focus on bodies of water. Not only does the ocean function overtly in *Las hijas del fuego* as a metaphor for the fluidity of the women's sexualities, but the aesthetic capacities of water are also mobilized by Carri as a strategy of queer representation, one whose structures are endowed with the subversive potential to undermine the conventions of the heteronormative filmic gaze.[33] In one of the film's more experimental moments, images of fish, sea anemones, and jellyfish are superimposed onto erotic sequences of the women performing oral sex and penetrating one another with sex toys (figure 5.4). Simultaneously, the voices of Violeta and Carmen are layered on top of one another, uncannily and out of sync, as they recite the following poem:

> Yo, que sentí tu cuerpo temblar sobre el mío / Yo, que abracé tu piel mojada y tibia hasta dejar de sentir la mía / Yo, que chupé mis labios durante días buscando las rémoras de tu gusto / Yo, [. . .] que encontré todo mi ser en la inundación de tu concha erecta / que perdí todo mi ser entre tus piernas / [. . .] / y lavé con mi sangre todo lo patriarcal de tu conciencia / Yo, que me hice agua, charco, río, mar, océano sobre tu cuerpo

Figure 5.4. Film still. Sex, sea creatures, and conceptual displacement in *Las hijas del fuego*. *Source*: Dir. Albertina Carri. Gentil (2018).

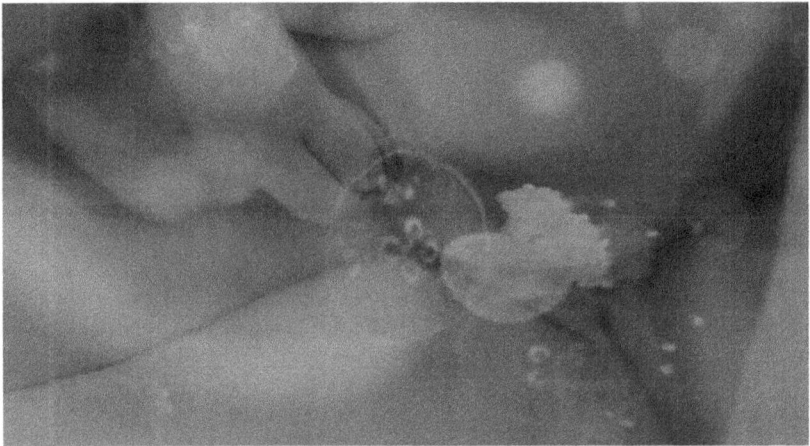

hasta dejar de ser yo / [. . .] / Porque mi sangre corre en tu agua y en tu agua corren mis venas.

(Me, who felt your body tremble on top of mine / Me, who embraced your wet, lukewarm skin until I couldn't feel my own / Me, who sucked on my lips for days, searching for the remnants of your taste / Me, who found my entire being in the flood of your erect pussy / who relinquished my entire being between your legs / and washed the patriarchy entirely from your conscience with my blood / Me, who became water, puddle, river, sea, ocean over your body until I was no longer me / Because my blood runs in your water, and in your water run my veins.)

As the poem becomes progressively more explicit in its sexual imagery, so too does the sexual contact between the women, with images of bondage gear and oral sex followed by a final, relatively longer, close-up shot of digital stimulation. The prominence throughout of the women's faces, open-mouthed and moaning in pleasure, parallels the poem's emphasis on the textural and corporeal intensities of the sexual experience. Moreover, the superimposition of explicit sex and sea creature not only extends the poem's metaphors to the visual, figuring the wetness of the lover's skin and the "flood of [her] erect pussy," but it also confounds the spectator by displacing the representation of desire to a distinct plane of reference. As Melody Jue writes in *Wild Blue Media*, "The milieu of the ocean offers an epistemological check on human knowledge formation, presenting entirely different conditions for perceptions, sensation, and life than terrestrial environments."[34] Here, the queer inscrutability of the anemone and jellyfish is mobilized as a form of "conceptual displacement," which, for Jue, "amphibiously [and] self-reflexive[ly] [. . .] humbles us into considering how our own sensory attunements are a very narrow band through which parts of the world might be perceived."[35] Carri endows water with the potential to "cleanse" the women's bodies of the patriarchal structures that would attempt to police them and to explode the rigid identity categories through which they are normatively understood. As Carmen becomes "water, puddle, river, sea [and] ocean" against the body of her lover, these watery poetics of sexual pleasure exploit the "vital materiality of water as a medium of becoming" and accentuate the film's own subversive politics of representation.[36]

This latent sense of queerness that emanates from the poetic and aesthetic interactions between bodies and water in *Las hijas del fuego* is, in this way, used to expose and challenge normative notions of sexuality, historical representation, and the cinematic gaze. In a scene introduced visually through a reflection of the women's naked bodies on the surface of a lake, Carri again draws the spectator's attention to the bodily textures of sexual desire through haptic imagery and a narrative emphasis on the senses of touch, sight, and smell. As the women kiss one another's bodies tenderly by the lakeside, Violeta's accompanying thoughts propose a radical cartography of queer politics:

> Hay que aprenderlo todo, incluso inventar nuevos aparatos para la mensura, encontrar nuevos verbos para nombrar los descubrimientos. [. . .] Culminar como un origen y derribar cualquier leyenda sobre el cuerpo sin goce. Porque aquí no hay sujeto ni sacrificio, porque no hay ofrenda ni a quien ofrendar. Porque placer y felicidad no han sido expulsado del orden cósmico, no pertenecen a una ley superior. Porque no hay desamparo en no haber culto ni imagen ni forma de representarlo. ¿Es el inicio de una nueva era? ¿El nacimiento de una nación? ¿O la idea de una nación sería demasiado patriarcal? Se va formando un pueblo que busca *una historia de contagio* y no de herencia.[37]

> (Everything must be learned anew, even new systems of measurement must be invented, new verbs to articulate our discoveries. [. . .] We culminate as an origin and demolish each and every myth of the pleasureless body. Because here there is neither subject nor sacrifice; neither offering nor anyone to be offered. Because pleasure and happiness have not been expelled from the cosmic order; they do not belong to any higher law. Because there is no neglect in the absence of devotion, of the image, of representation. Is this the dawn of a new era? The birth of a nation? Or would the idea of a nation be too patriarchal? A people is forming that seeks *a history of contagion* and not of inheritance.)

The queer potentiality that Carri invokes in this sequence resonates strongly with what José Esteban Muñoz describes in *Cruising Utopia* as the necessary futurity of subaltern politics, the "anticipatory illumination of a queer world, a sign of an actually existing queer reality, a kernel of political possibility within a stultifying heterosexual present."[38] This "future in the present," as Muñoz terms it, works throughout *Las hijas del fuego* to signal alternative modes of being that harness "the glimpses and moments of contact" that "let us feel that this world is not enough, that indeed something is missing."[39] Violeta's rejection of the normative strictures of nation and inheritance for a nonlinear, nonhierarchal *history of contagion* is calibrated through a bodily pleasure that refuses to submit "to any higher law" and exists outwith the normative constraints "of the image, of representation." Indeed, as the women mobilize "su arte y su cuerpo, su territorio y su paisaje como herejes antorchas a iluminar un nuevo cielo" (their art and their body, their territory and their landscape, as heretic torches to illuminate a new horizon), *Las hijas del fuego* enacts an "embodied and performed queer politics" that foregrounds the radical horizontality of contagion as a queer political strategy, one driven by, in Muñoz's terms, an "insistence on potentiality or concrete possibility for another world."[40]

In the closing stages of the film, once the women reach their destination of Puerto Madryn, a drug-induced reverie in the home of Augustina's mother consolidates the queer, antinormative thrust of the sequences explored above. As two separate couples begin to have sex, one in Augustina's childhood bedroom and the other by the poolside, the metanarrative and the metacinematic again coalesce when Violeta's voiceover delivers the following analysis of the film's own nonlinear composition:

> Un personaje nuevo entra en escena y modifica toda la trama, o un incidente mínimo hace que la trama vuelque. Así sucedería en un texto que todavía abraza ideales de trama y no de urdimbre. En cambio, si la trama altera la estructura, y se vuelven tramado, costura, vórtice, fluido, sólo puedo entregarme a su paisaje, a los pequeños hilos de su territorio gozoso, al cuerpo que chilla desde la pantalla, al cuerpo que es goce y no otra cosa. Y así, volverme porno.
>
> (A new character enters the scene and modifies the entire plot, or a minimal incident affects the plot in some way. At least that's what would happen in a text that still embraces ideas of plot over schema. However, if the plot alters the structure,

and they become a framework, a seam, a vortex, a flow, all I can do is surrender to its landscape, to the small threads of its joyful territory, to the body that screams from the screen; to the body that is pure pleasure and nothing else. And in this way, I become porn.)

The identification in this passage of "flows" and "vortices" as structures for the representation of "pure pleasure and nothing else" rejects a linearity of narrative and endorses the antinormative and nonhierarchical thrust of the film's queer aesthetic. That these representational tactics permit the protagonist to "become porn" is crucial: here, Carri displaces any scopic approach to sexual pleasure with a politics of contagion and becoming that point to the insufficiencies of mediatized representations of sex, offering a momentary vision of Muñoz's "future in the present." The hallucinogenic sequence that follows this scene, during which images of the women on swings and dancing around a swimming pool are repeated, slowed down, sped up, and paused, both formally reflects their drug-induced state and emphasizes the film's queer impulses: in Muñoz's terms, "Take ecstasy with me thus becomes a request to stand out of time together, to resist the stultifying temporality and time that is not ours, that is saturated with violence both visceral and emotional, a time that is not queerness."[41] Carri's formal jump cuts, narrative instability, and reflexive refusal to participate in a linear presentation of time in this sequence are closing reminders of the film's broader refusal to adhere to normative expectations of sexuality. If, as Violeta remarks, the women's bodies become "insurgencia y vértigo" (rebellion and vertigo), they do so through a postpornographic representational regime that embraces a radical queer politics of flows, vortices, contagion, and becoming.

Landscape and the Technologies of Desire

The ever-present coastal imagery and natural landscapes of *Las hijas del fuego* cease to be, in the ways explored thus far, merely passive settings for the unfolding of the film's plot. Unconstrained to any superficial role as symbolic reflections of the women's raw beauty or the naturalness of their sexual desire for one another, the images of mountains, lakes, rivers, and shorelines formally and aesthetically condition the spectator to contemplate sexuality on a broader discursive plane. One critic writes that

Carri's "cinematography helps to illuminate curious parallels between the bodies and landscapes, [and that] the camera's caress bestows upon forests and mountains a carnality which elevates sex to the transcendent."[42] Yet, while the film does indeed imbue the landscape with an undeniable sensuality, transcendence is neither the objective nor the outcome of Carri's bucolic representations of explicit sex: paradoxically, the film's impulse to engage sensuously with landscape instead "de-eroticises sex," to use Lorange and Gregory's term, "in order to engage with the erotic in an extended or expanded idea of sex, a gesture that reconfigures the capacity for an erotics that includes but is not limited to sexual acts."[43] In doing so, the film's postpornographic perception of the erotic recasts the gaze directed toward the women and their bodies, interrogating the film's own explicitly stated concern that it is not the representation of bodies itself that is inherently problematic but rather how "esos cuerpos vuelven territorio y paisaje frente a la cámara" (these bodies become territory and landscape in front of the camera).

The territorializing force of the camera is thus central to Carri's concerns throughout *Las hijas del fuego*. Midway through the film, for instance, as the women travel through the Patagonian countryside, the voiceover sketches out an initial scene of the diegetic porn film, focusing suggestively on the parallel mediatization of body and landscape. Alongside extended tracking shots of fields and mountains, filmed from the women's minivan as it drives along the highway, Violeta says: "Escena 1: Carmen camina por las inmediaciones de un lago. El lago se muestra brillante y la superficie es como un cuerpo inmaculado. La cámara se eleva y la tierra se torna un cuerpo resistente; el paisaje se desvela erótico, sexual, salvaje y tierno" (Scene 1: Carmen walks along the banks of a lake. The lake appears shiny, and its surface is like an immaculate body. The camera rises and the land turns into a resistant body; the landscape reveals itself as erotic, sexual, wild, and tender). In this reflection on the sensuality of both body and landscape, and crucially their relationship with media, the simultaneity of resistance and revelation when faced with the camera problematizes the spectacularity of the women's sexual acts: "El paisaje," continues Violeta, "se vuelve un animal herido según los ojos que lo devoran" (The landscape becomes a wounded animal to the eyes that devour it). Here, Carri reflexively presents the body and the landscape not as sites (or sights) of poetic transcendence but as the battlegrounds for a politics of representation, harnessing "the idea of nature and culture as co-constitutive and the idea of sexuality as determined by the natural-cultural mediation of bodies but rejecting the notion that a more 'authentic' sex can be experienced and represented by pornography."[44]

In *Hard Core*, Williams writes, "For women, one constant in the history of sexuality has been a failure to imagine their pleasures outside a dominant male economy," and she advocates for the "strategic value to a feminist scrutinizing of pornography that seeks the seeds to a different sexual economy in the limitations and inadequacies of the reigning one."[45] Building on Williams's work on the critical potential of pornographic sex almost three decades later, Lorange and Gregory argue that "if pornography is, by now, a way of thinking about the way sex and desire are imaged, consumed, learned, reproduced, and so on, in the context of the long history of capitalism, then post-pornography is a way of thinking about how to engage with sex and desire without imagining sex as a natural resource mined by capital in the production of desire-as-commodity."[46] In its reflexive interrogation of sexual pleasure, *Las hijas del fuego* resists the scopophilic territorialization of the women's bodies, undermining the notion of "desire-as-commodity" and rejecting sexuality's abstraction from the normalizing economies of society and the image. The film's queer aesthetic registers the "limitations and inadequacies" of historically hegemonic representations of sex, not only revealing the insufficiency of the camera lens in capturing the intimacy and intensities of the sexual act, but also disclosing how "sexuality *itself is a technology*, that is, sexuality is that which allows for meaningful encounters between a subject and their world, or between sex as a bodily experience and sex as a socially situated encounter."[47] To give a striking example, when the character of Francisca is first introduced by the voiceover, immediately following the reflections on body and landscape discussed above, Violeta says:

> Nota de personaje: Francisca. A ella lo que más le gusta es que la miren. Todo su cuerpo se llena de espasmos cuando sienta una mirada externa a la escena. La primera mirada fue la de la madre, una madre que le espiaba, y ella jugaba no verla mientras el chorro del bidet golpeaba su lozana vulva. [. . .] Luego se sucedieron las cerraduras del sistema, las lecturas de la madre, las imposiciones del padre, la reclusión definitiva del goce, o que el goce se vuelva a la imposibilidad misma.
>
> (Character note. Francisca: what she enjoys most is being watched. Her entire body spasms when she feels a gaze external

to the scene. The first gaze was that of her mother, a mother who used to spy on her, and she would pretend not to see her while the jet of water from the bidet pounded her glowing vulva. [. . .] Then came the system's lockdowns, the mother's lectures, the father's impositions, the definitive repression of pleasure, or rather pleasure itself became an impossibility.)

The explicitly detailed description of Francisca's early sexual experience and the policing nature of the lockdowns and impositions that followed are rendered all the more acute when the possibility of any subsequent sexual pleasure is bound to this formative moment of transgression: "La vida, el sexo: una búsqueda desaforada por recomponer aquella mirada" (Life, sex: a frenzied search to repair that gaze). In another instance, during an episode entitled "Sobre el territorio de amor" (On the Territory of Love), one of the women is described as having internalized this bodily repression to the point of circumscribing her capacity to experience sexual pleasure in the presence of another: "A Rosario sólo le gusta el sexo consigo misma. [. . .] Sólo puede concentrarse en la pérdida de conciencia a solas. De ser posible, completamente sola" (Rosario only enjoys sex with herself. [. . .] She can only concentrate on the loss of consciousness when she is alone. Completely alone, if possible). In this way, sexuality functions throughout *Las hijas del fuego* not only as a "technology" that mediates between the women and the world around them, but also one whose capacity to negotiate private pleasure and the external gaze exposes both the structural violence that governs women's bodies and, more implicitly, the hierarchies of spectatorship to which these bodies are exposed.

The political valency of Carri's queer opposition to the repression of the gaze—be it structural, societal or cinematic—culminates in the film's intimate closing sequence. Here, "the definitive repression of pleasure" is challenged in a carnivalesque fashion by a thematic and formal celebration of the women's sexual agency. The scene's initial images, in which the women pose in an overly fabricated fashion to signal the beginning of the internal porn film, resonate with the film's broader reflexive key, before the distinction between *Las hijas del fuego* itself and the diegetic film is blurred and, ultimately, collapsed.[48] As the camera follows a dildo-laden roller-skater as she moves uncannily between the rooms and garden of the country house, it documents a range of sexual positions, groupings, and BDSM practices, from inflatable mouth gags and head masks to plastic-wrap mummification. In line with Williams's assertion that "fetishes are short-term, short-sighted solutions to more fundamental problems of power and pleasure in social relations," here Carri cultivates—though refuses to sensationalize—the subversive potential of these alternative sexual practices, not least through Francisca, the former nun, who is pictured in bondage and receiving oral sex, with her arms outstretched and bound in the shape of a cross (figure 5.5).[49]

Crucially, a single fixed shot of Rosario commands the closing six minutes of the film, as she sits on a red chair and begins to masturbate, repeatedly—it appears—reaching climax.[50] In Carri's own words, the force of this final scene results not from "la masturbación misma, sino porque lo que esa actriz le entrega a la cámara tiene un poder político, una potencia vital y una materialidad tal que justifica todo el desparramo de goces y voces anterior. [. . .] Las mujeres también tenemos derecho al voyerismo, si así lo deseamos" (the masturbation itself, but because of the political power of what this actress surrenders to the camera, a vital potency and a materiality that justifies the deluge of pleasures and voices that have come before. Us women have the right to voyeurism, if we so desire).[51] As Williams has argued, the image of the masturbatory woman is far from radical in itself and indeed "haunts a great deal of pornography," a woman who is "simultaneously insatiable *and* satisfied, capable of both continuing her pleasure indefinitely and of satisfying herself through her own efforts at clitoral stimulation."[52] Conversely, the "political power" and

Figure 5.5. Film still. Bondage in a religious pose in *Las hijas del. Source*: Dir. Albertina Carri. Gentil (2018).

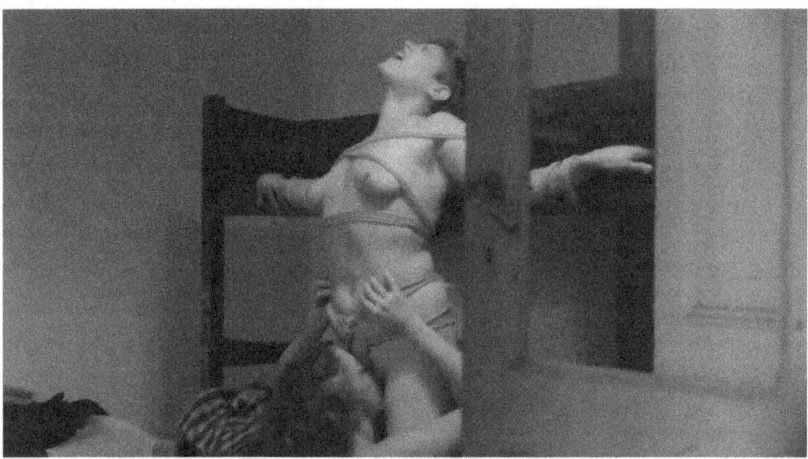

"vital potency" of this concluding scene are formal rather than thematic: Rosario's central framing and the direct, open-legged view of her body as she masturbates suggests the presence of a spectator, yet her closed eyes and the formal cut in sound when she puts on a pair of headphones prohibits any performance of connection beyond the screen (figure 5.6). Moreover, the voiceover's previous declaration that Rosario can only reach climax when alone—*completely* alone—renders the gaze intentionally passive; here, the spectator is not excluded from the eroticism of voyeurism, which is often overtly celebrated throughout the film, but the agency of Rosario herself is prioritized over any potential spectatorial pleasure. In this sense, though Kroll argues in her reading of the film that the extended length of the scene and its static focus on Rosario "erases the spectator effect, thus collapsing the breach between signified and signifier, viewer and on-screen spectacle," I argue instead that it is instead precisely this distance between spectator and spectacle that finds itself maintained and interrogated in this sequence.[53] This is not a pleasure "without artifice," as Kroll contends, but a mediatized eroticism that is fundamentally and reflexively inextricable from its formal exposition on the screen.

If, as Williams writes of heterosexual pornography, the male "money shot" is not only "undeniably spectacular" but also "hopelessly spectacular," given its inability to "access knowledge of women's pleasure," then here Carri seeks a distinct type of intimate visibility through this six-min-

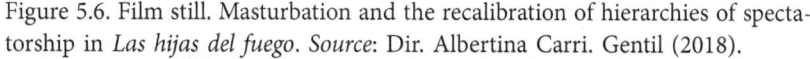

Figure 5.6. Film still. Masturbation and the recalibration of hierarchies of spectatorship in *Las hijas del fuego*. *Source*: Dir. Albertina Carri. Gentil (2018).

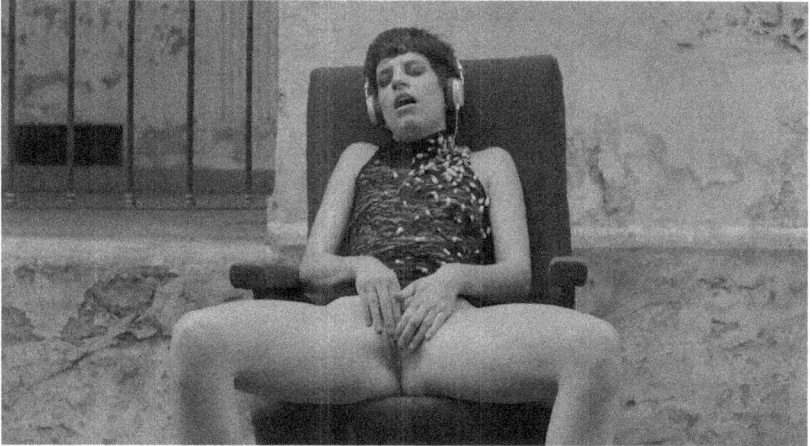

ute, direct focus on Rosario's self-sufficient onanism.[54] The explicitness of the shot's composition belies a more fundamentally private and unknowable pleasure experienced by the actor and *only* by the actor. Carri spectacularizes a lack of spectacle through Rosario's masturbation and, more implicitly, consolidates the film's broader critique of the visceral insufficiency of mediatized sexuality. As the silence of scene is replaced with the sounds of flowing water, which continue when the scene cuts and the credits begin to roll, the film's queer strategies of conceptual displacement are yoked to a bodily poetics of explicit sex. This is strategy that allows Carri to embrace the heterogeneity of sexuality and its iterations, and one that enacts a postpornographic critique of the territorialization of women's bodies and their sexual pleasure.

A Postporn Manifesto

In her writing on the sexual "counter-currencies" of Barbara Hammer's early cinema, Jacquelyn Zita reflects on the "symbolic burial of the lesbian body" within the cultural imaginary of patriarchal societies.[55] "Initially, the lesbian body has no meaning," she writes. "The presumption of difference is a cultural artefact, composed of signs and images that have been bartered for the meaning of a lesbian's experience and the use of her body. The currency for the most part has belonged to men, as has the exchange."[56] For Zita, the context of progressive queer politics in which Hammer's films were made witnessed a "new iconography of the lesbian body, an iconography to carry the spectator into forbidden and revelatory terrain," and which allowed the lesbian experience to "enter the public sphere under a new currency of signs which abrasively refused misreading and invisibility."[57] As this chapter has argued, *Las hijas del fuego* is driven by similar aesthetic and political impulses, offering a contemporary cartography of this "forbidden and revelatory terrain" and refusing to consent to the impositions of dominant hierarchies of representation and spectatorship.

Through both its poetic reflections on the structural and institutional repression enacted toward women's bodies and the queer formal strategies of screening explicit sex that it mobilizes, *Las hijas del fuego* positions its protagonists—as the internal director remarks at the beginning of the film—as "las nietas, bisnietas, hijas y hermanas de aquellas que pusieron su arte y su cuerpo, su territorio y su paisaje como herejes antorchas a iluminar un nuevo cielo" (the granddaughters, great-granddaughters, daughters, and sisters of those who raised their art and their body, their territory and their landscape, as heretic torches to illuminate a new horizon). In doing so, Carri corroborates Williams's assertion that "what is sometimes most challenging about art films is not their explicit sex but the drive to push aesthetics into unfamiliar emotional territory."[58] The queer representational strategies that this chapter has explored, from the conceptual displacement of the film's postporn flows to its politically utopian ideation of a liberatory "future in the present," enables *Las hijas del fuego* to consolidate a nonhierarchical, nonlinear notion of sexual desire that embraces heterogeneity and rejects the scopophilic thrust of the pornographic lens. If, for Carri, the film's closing sequence represents "un bucle, una incertidumbre, la carencia total de certezas y, por tanto, la entrega a otros modos de percepción del mundo" (a loop, a doubt, the total lack of certainties and, as such, the surrender to other modes of perceiving the world), then these alternative modes are driven not simply by the latent potential of women's sexual pleasure with and in the presence of other women. They are, more significantly, fueled by the critical, mediatory "technology" of sexuality and its capacity to expose the territorializing and structural repression of the societal—and cinematic—gaze.[59]

Coda

After *XXY*

> To access queer visuality we may need to squint, to strain our vision and force it to see otherwise, beyond the limited vista of the here and now.[1]
>
> —José Esteban Muñoz, *Cruising Utopia*

In the opening credit sequence of Lucía Puenzo's *XXY* (2007), repeated images of adolescent body parts are juxtaposed with the sights and sounds of underwater life. These intercalated images of creatures, both human and nonhuman, and of terrains, both wet and dry, foreshadow the ambiguity that attends the life of film's intersexed teenage protagonist. As the narrative unfolds, Alex finds herself caught as much between the stages of childhood and adulthood as between supposedly discrete biological categories.[2] This initial sequence has been a source of stimulating critical discussion among film scholars, some of whom note in its watery and aural appeal to the senses a distinctly haptic potential, one that conditions the spectator to *feel* the film and its narrative through a synesthetic and embodied richness. Deborah Martin writes that, through its treatment of fluidity, "the film figures the intersex body as a site of becoming and rejects the idea of a fixed subjectivity or corporeality."[3] Vinodh Venkatesh, for his part, suggests that the decoupling of sound and image in this introductory sequence "evokes the violent decentring force that is at the core of the film's phenomenology."[4] The inability on the part of the spectator to discern the narrative significance of either adolescent body or marine creature, or, moreover, to decipher any connection between them, is consolidated by the sequence's final ax chop, which appears to sever the last letter of the film's title from an X to a Y. In this way, *XXY* emphasizes from the outset the act of cutting—in narrative, filmic, and theoretical terms—as one of destabilization and violence, and it becomes over the course of the film a threat that is as much material as it is ideological. This is, in short, a sequence whose *form* is queer, even if its narrative content at such an early stage is not.

It may seem somewhat paradoxical to conclude *Bodies of Water* with a discussion of the haptically aquatic beginnings of its filmic corpus. Yet *XXY* is, in the ways I discuss below, an important foundation for the films that have occupied the focus of these chapters, as well as for much contemporary queer cinema from Latin America more broadly. The film's innovative impulse toward queering the filmic form, alongside what Martin terms "a quite unprecedented intervention on the part of Argentine cinema into international debates on intersexuality," positions *XXY* firmly at the forefront of what I have argued has become a recognizable queer cultural movement within Latin America.[5] If, as José Esteban Muñoz compels us to do in *Cruising Utopia*, we "squint [and] strain our vision" toward the queer aesthetics of *XXY*, then it becomes comparatively clear how "a posterior glance at different moments, objects, and spaces might offer us an anticipatory illumination of queerness."[6] It is precisely this "illumination of queerness" that I discern and explore in the films analyzed in this book, all of which realize the "anticipatory" nature of queerness through innovations in narrative content, temporal structure, representational mode, and/or aesthetic technique. Moreover, through their collective emphasis on the body (in water), these films strategically mobilize the aquatic and its haptic potential to augment embodiment, in order to pay closer and more complex attention to the dynamics and realities of queerness, as well as to their cinematic figurations.

In both narrative and structural terms, *XXY* exhibits, and indeed capitalizes on, many of the defining features of what I term in the first chapter of this book New Queer Realism. From its long, meditative shots of Alex floating in seawater to the realistically mundane treatment of sex and sexuality, the film displays in a nascent fashion the embodied realities of adolescent life and a formal engagement with the "politics of the slow and boring."[7] Similarly, though the film is undoubtedly critical of the societal prejudice that is directed toward nonnormative bodies and identities, at moments presenting such discrimination in intensely affecting and affective ways, the primary focus remains not on society as a whole but on the microcosm in which Alex both exists and resists. In fact, the film's move away from the urban center to the coastline—a notable attribute of much contemporary queer world cinema, in contrast to the city-focused narratives of New Queer Cinema—is reinforced by a parallel movement on a broader critical plane. For Venkatesh, "the sea and the maritime function [in *XXY*] as heuristic vectors that gesture towards the queer and plural possibilities of leaving heteronormativity behind."[8] More than this, however, not only are the interstitial settings of the beach and its secluded coastline integral to *XXY* for a theoretical notion of fluidity beyond the strictures of cisnormativity, but they also allow for a critically *embodied* understanding of adolescence more broadly. The coast provides a thematic, theoretical, and formal setting for the concerns of a film that center on the normalizing violence of boundaries and borders, and, in turn, on the political potential of inhabiting the peripheries of convention.

For Moira Fradinger, the relationship between "cuerpo, sexo y género" (bodies, sex, and gender) that *XXY* examines is one that is calibrated fundamentally by "el ambiente costero uruguayo, poblado de anfibios y reptiles en peligro de extinción" (the coastal environment of Uruguay, which is filled with amphibians and reptiles at risk of extinction).[9] Fradinger identifies in her study a substantive, coconstitutive relationship between Alex and her surroundings, and between the film's overarching critical concerns and the formal and aesthetic possibilities of the coast. She writes: "Analizo el medio ambiente no como telón de fondo de la película, sino como el fondo desde donde surge su núcleo respecto a la diversidad humana" (I analyze the environment not as the background of the film but rather as the very ground from which its central concerns regarding human diversity emerge).[10] This is precisely the mode of environmental embedding that takes place in many of the films discussed in this book, not least those in the second and third chapters, which exploit the coast's materiality and peripherality in order to foreground, respectively, the textures and tensions of adolescent sexualities and the affective experience of (trans)national belonging and "home" for queer characters. In these two chapters specifically, the beach—or rather the instability of its demarcations as tides ebb, flow, and crash—harnesses a sense of epistemological potential. Land-based categories of sex, gender, and belonging, like tidal currents, cease to be discrete or resolute, and identities, through their exposure to the elements, are *felt* and embodied in radical ways.

It is, however, not only the space of the coast and the materiality of its wetness that are mobilized by queer directors but also, as *XXY* demonstrates, often the life forms that dwell within the ocean or subsist on the water's edge. As Lourdes Estrada-López notes in relation to the introductory sequence of *XXY*, the presence of sea anemones—that is, those queer, amorphous, at-times hermaphroditic creatures—"expresa la complejidad de la sexualidad en el mundo natural."[11] For Estrada-López, the superimposition of the film's title in this sequence—whose typography she notes is "de color metálico" (of a metallic color) rather than of a natural script or hue—over the watery depths of the ocean "refuerza la idea de la imposición de esta nomenclatura artificial ilustrando como la inteligibilidad de los sujetos [humanos] se construye a partir del discurso de la biología/genética" (reinforces the idea of the imposition of an artificial nomenclature that exposes how the intelligibility of human beings is constructed from biological/genetic discourse).[12] The film broadens its invocation to the diverse sexualities, epistemologies, and modes of being within the animal kingdom through the repeated parallels it sets up in the unfolding of its narrative between Alex and various reptiles and amphibians. Indeed, turtles, in particular, recur frequently, both figuratively through the tag that Alex wears around her neck (and then gifts to Álvaro) and literally via the image of broken turtle shells, with the latter evoking a sense of vulnerability and exposure that closely matches her own feelings of defenselessness once her "secret" is exposed to the coastal community. This recourse to the amphibious consolidates the notion at the core of the film's treatment of Alex's intersexuality, crystalized in her own response to her father's reassurance that he will support whichever gender (of two, it is implied) she "chooses": "¿Y si no hay nada que elegir?" (And what if there isn't a choice to make?). As Debra A. Castillo notes, "Implicitly, in the context of the film's symbolic structure, the positing of an obligatory choice—to be either man or woman—along with the self-mutilation attendant upon this decision, is like asking an amphibian to choose between sea and land, or—even more extreme—aquarium and desert."[13]

There is, to be sure, in the appeal to nonhuman forms of sexuality and gender a fundamental danger, just as there is more broadly in the film's petition to an unbridled sense of political and identarian fluidity. As the second chapter of this book has argued, we must be careful to avoid what I term the "fallacy of fluidity," whose utopian gesture toward an essential rejection of fixed identities would also wash away the very material realities of queerness and its intersections. Similarly, here, the metaphoric turn toward nonhuman forms of sexuality flirts uncomfortably with histories of understanding nonnormativity as monstrous and, paradoxically, *un*natural. Though this risk has, for the most part, gone unaddressed in critical readings of the film, *XXY* itself is implicitly aware of such dangers: it largely avoids these pitfalls, if not entirely, through both its sustained and complex treatment of watery imagery and an avoidance of clichés and stereotypes otherwise associated with intersexuality. The recurring image of Alex floating in the water, for instance, often formally dissects her body, refusing to offer an idealized meditative image of the adolescent that is somehow liberated from the specter of the cut (figure C.1). Likewise, though the parallels between Alex and the lizard are, at times, somewhat heavy handed, the film's broader treatment of dead turtles and squashed insects maintains a firm sense of the violence, both literal and symbolic, that haunts Alex's existence. Far from making fluidity "a fetish," as Brad Epps has suggested more broadly of queer theory, or, indeed, from rendering "the body so discursive as to matter little, if at all," Puenzo places the materiality of adolescent body and the violence it is subjected to both narratively and formally at the forefront of the film's structures and concerns.[14]

We can therefore see in *XXY*, on the levels of cinematography, aesthetics, form, and narrative, the epistemological potential of watery spaces and their environs, which this book has argued is present, in various guises and to varying extents, in much contemporary queer film from Latin America. What Fradinger refers to as *ectoentidad* in her article,

Figure C.1. Film still. Formal cuts to the body in *XXY*. *Source*: Dir. Lucía Puenzo. Historias Cinematográficas, Wanda Visión S.A., Pyramide Productions (2007).

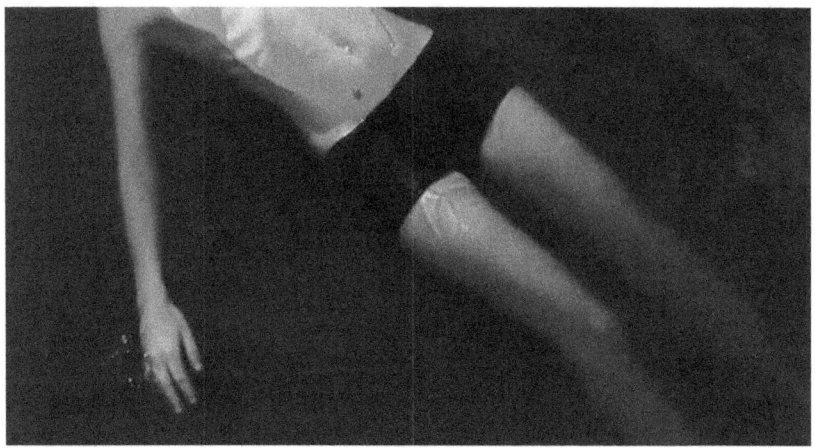

and indeed what Venkatesh and Martin respectively term in their studies of *XXY* as "often-multidirectional orientations" and a "postmodernistic corporeal undecidability," are, I would argue, localized iterations of what can be understood more broadly as water's potential for "conceptual displacement," a framework explored in chapter 5 of this book to analyze the politics and poetics of postpornography.[15] In *Wild Blue Media*, Melody Jue argues that the "methodology of *conceptual displacement* [. . .] involves imaginatively submerging media terms into the ocean to see how they hold up in a liquid milieu of pressure, salinity, and coldness (among other qualities)."[16] In a broad sense, *Bodies of Water* has attempted to reorient what is a highly incisive and productive framework for media studies toward the realm of queer cinematic representation, asking what happens culturally and politically to concepts of sexuality and gender, as well as those of embodiment, identity, and temporality, when they find themselves submerged within bodies of water. Filmic strategies of slowness, boredom, hapticity, excision, embodiment, and displacement intersect in innovative ways in these films to offer new possibilities for the cinematic figuration of queerness, opening up affective and political pathways for identification with and through the queer subject.

In the ways described above, *XXY* can be understood, however cautiously, as a point of departure for the aesthetic trends explored in *Bodies of Water*. Yet we must also be conscious to contextualize it within its broader queer cinematic lineage, which, as the introduction to this book makes clear, is one that has long turned to water to symbolize the dynamism and fluidity of human sexuality. The intersecting characteristics that I have identified through this primary corpus—a cinematic fascination with the body, a thematic and formal embrace of watery spaces, the focus on nonnormative sexualities and genders, a slowness of narrative pace and structure, and a mundane focus on the everyday realities of queer lives—collectively cohere into an identifiable wave of contemporary queer Latin American film, one marked as much by a shared sense of the urgency of queer representation as by the coconstitutive impulse toward aesthetic and formal innovation. These, I suggest, are the trends and registers of New Queer Realism in Latin American cinema and beyond. It is my hope that *Bodies of Water* will open up new lines of flight for analyzing how contemporary queer representation has positioned itself at the confluence of theoretical debates surrounding fluidity, embodiment, sexuality, and gender. By ending the book in this way, with a backward glance at the watery origins of the present moment of queer Latin American cinema, my aim is to express how these films persistently invite us to "squint" and "strain our vision," to "force it to see otherwise, beyond the limited vista of the here and now."[17] Through their cinematic imaginings of more diverse worlds and ways of being, these queer films elucidate how bodies—be they of flesh, of film, or of water—act as innovative, dynamic, and politically insistent sites for representing the contemporary queer experience.

Notes

Introduction

1. Melody Jue, *Wild Blue Media: Thinking through Seawater* (Durham: Duke University Press, 2020), 10.

2. Jue, *Wild Blue Media*, 18.

3. According to Steve Mentz, the blue humanities "comprises a current of scholarly and artistic discourses that foreground human relationships with water in all its forms. [. . .] It] self-consciously distinguishes itself from terrestrial (or 'green') models of the relationship with the nonhuman environment" (*An Introduction to the Blue Humanities*). While Mentz notes that "neologisms have been proposed, from hydro-criticism to critical ocean studies to ocean history," he nevertheless writes that "the sub-disciplinary modes of cultural and literary studies in the early 2020s mostly gather under the banner of the 'blue humanities'" (*An Introduction to the Blue Humanities*). For Elizabeth DeLoughrey, this "oceanic turn" "reflects an important shift from a long-term concern with mobility across transoceanic surfaces to theorizing oceanic submersion, thus rendering vast oceanic space into ontological place" ("Submarine Futures of the Anthropocene," 32).

4. Following Lúcia Nagib, I understand the term "world film" not in the "restrictive and negative" sense of "the non-Hollywood cinema," but instead as a "world cinema [that] is simply the cinema of the world" ("Towards a Positive Definition of World Cinema," 26, 31). For Nagib, as for my own analysis in *Bodies of Water*, "World cinema is not a discipline, but a method, a way of cutting across film history according to waves of relevant films and movements, thus creating flexible geographies" ("Towards a Positive Definition of World Cinema," 31).

5. Karl Schoonover and Rosalind Galt, *Queer Cinema in the World* (Durham: Duke University Press, 2016), 5.

6. Lisa Blackmore and Liliana Gómez, "Beyond the Blue: Notes on the Liquid Turn," in *Liquid Ecologies in Latin American and Caribbean Art*, ed. Lisa Blackmore and Liliana Gómez (New York: Routledge, 2020), 2.

7. Giulio Boccaletti, *Water: A Biography* (London: Pantheon Books, 2021), 41, italics added.

8. Boccaletti, *Water*, 13–14.

9. Lúcia Nagib, *Brazil on Screen: Cinema Novo, New Cinema, Utopia* (London, New York: I.B. Tauris, 2007), 6.

10. Stefan Helmreich, "Nature/Culture/Seawater," *American Anthropologist* 113, no. 1 (2011): 133.

11. Gaston Bachelard, *Water and Dreams: An Essay on the Imagination of Matter*, trans. Edith R. Farrell (Dallas: Pegasus Foundation, 1983), 6.

12. Bachelard, *Water and Dreams*, 14, 6, 5.

13. Bachelard, *Water and Dreams*, 15.

14. Timothy Morton, *Hyperobjects: Philosophy and Ecology after the End of the World* (Minneapolis: University of Minnesota Press, 2013).

15. Morton, *Hyperobjects*, 1.

16. Adam O'Brien, "In and around *The Bay*: Water, Fish, Infrastructure," *Film Studies* 19, no. 1 (2018): 22–23.

17. Maite Conde, *Foundational Films: Early Cinema and Modernity in Brazil* (Oakland: University of California Press, 2018), 54.

18. "A Meditative Cinepoem from 1929 Captures the Reflective, Ethereal Wonders of Water," *Aeon*, accessed August 17, 2022, https://aeon.co/videos/a-meditative-cinepoem-from-1929-captures-the-reflective-ethereal-wonders-of-water.

19. "A Striking Classic from an Early Documentary Explores Amsterdam in the Rain," *Aeon*, accessed August 17, 2022, https://aeon.co/videos/a-striking-classic-from-an-early-documentary-master-explores-amsterdam-in-the-rain.

20. Béla Balázs, *Theory of the Film*, trans. Edith Bone (London: Dennis Dobson, 1951), 176.

21. Balázs, *Theory of the Film*, 176.

22. Eva S. Hayward, "Enfolded Vision: Refracting *the Love Life of the Octopus*," *Octopus: A Visual Studies Journal* 1 (2005), 50.

23. Nicole Starosielski, "Beyond Fluidity: A Cultural History of Cinema under Water," in *Ecocinema Theory and Practice*, ed. Stephen Rust, Salma Monani, and Sean Cubitt (New York: Routledge, 2013), 150.

24. Starosielski, "Beyond Fluidity," 149–50.

25. Elizabeth DeLoughrey, "Submarine Futures of the Anthropocene," *Comparative Literatures* 69, no. 1 (2017): 35.

26. It is worth noting the recent work of historians such as Sujit Sivasundaram to recalibrate the importance of bodies of water within discussions of global historical events. In *Waves Across the South*, Sivasundaram writes: "There is a quarter of this planet which is often forgotten in the histories that are told in the West. This quarter is an oceanic one, pulsating with winds and waves, tides and coastlines, and islands and beaches. [. . .] These watery spaces [. . .] occupy centre stage in what follows. They are cast as the makers of world history and

the modern condition" (Sivasundaram, *Waves Across the South: A New History of Revolution and Empire* [Chicago: University of Chicago Press, 2020], 1).

27. Starosielski, "Beyond Fluidity," 164.

28. Barbara Hammer, *HAMMER! Making Movies out of Sex and Life* (New York: Feminist Press, City University of New York, 2010), 119.

29. Kathleen Hulser, "Frames of Passage: Nine Recent Films of Barbara Hammer," accessed October 23, 2023, https://barbarahammer.com/wp-content/uploads/2020/05/1988_Frames-Of-Passages_CentrePompidou_KathrynHulser.pdf.

30. Hulser, "Frames of Passage."

31. Gustave Flaubert, quoted in Rupert Wright, *Take Me to the Source: In Search of Water* (London: Vintage, 2009), 119; Paul Valéry, quoted in Jennifer Webb, "Beaches and Bodies," *Body, Space & Technology* 2, no. 1 (2001).

32. Veronica Strang, "Common Senses: Water, Sensory Experience and the Generation of Meaning," *Journal of Material Culture* 10, no. 1 (2005): 98.

33. Strang, "Common Senses," 97.

34. Strang, "Common Senses," 99.

35. Céline Sciamma, "Press Release," accessed August 26, 2022, https://s3.eu-west-3.amazonaws.com/storage.playtime.group/asset/5e87acb2a878b9000426ce1e/upload_a22a3a5b8ba32f7d59dc5699b5934875.pdf; Christopher Brown and Pam Hirsch, "Introduction: The Cinema of the Swimming Pool," in *The Cinema of the Swimming Pool*, ed. Christopher Brown and Pam Hirsch (Oxford: Peter Lang, 2014), 20; Peter Bradshaw, "A Bigger Splash: My 10 Favourite Films about Swimming," *The Guardian*, March 13, 2008, accessed August 22, 2022, https://www.theguardian.com/film/filmblog/2008/mar/13/swimmingmoviesletspoolour.

36. Geoffrey Maguire, "Visual Displeasure: Adolescence and the Erotics of the Queer Male Gaze in Marco Berger's *Ausente*," in *New Visions of Adolescence in Contemporary Latin America Cinema*, ed. Geoffrey Maguire and Rachell Randall (New York: Palgrave Macmillan, 2018), 42.

37. Jack Halberstam, *The Queer Art of Failure* (Durham: Duke University Press, 2011), 111.

38. As many critics have noted, the public swimming pool also has a long history as a site of racial segregation and class and gender discrimination. See, for instance, Jeff Wiltse, *Contested Waters: A Social History of Swimming Pools in America*.

39. Henning Eichberg, quoted in Miranda Ward, "Swimming in a Contained Space: Understanding the Experience of Indoor Lap Swimmers," *Health & Place* 46 (2017): 318.

40. Fernando G. Pagnoni Berns, "Cartographies of Desire: Swimming Pools and the Queer Gaze," in *Cinema of the Swimming Pool*, ed. Christopher Brown and Pam Hirsch (Oxford: Peter Lang, 2014), 230.

41. Ward, "Swimming in a Contained Space," 319.

42. Brown and Hirsch, "Introduction," 4.

43. Pagnoni Berns, "Cartographies of Desire," 230.
44. Pagnoni Berns, "Cartographies of Desire," 235.
45. Christopher Connery, "The Oceanic Feeling and the Regional Imaginary," in *Global/Local: Cultural Production and the Transnational Imaginary*, ed. Rob Wilson (Durham: Duke University Press, 1996), 289; Sean Redmond, "Death and Life at the Cinematic Beach," *Journal of Media & Cinema Studies* 29, no. 5 (2013): 719.
46. Roland Barthes, *Mythologies*, trans. Annette Lavers (London: Paladin, 1972), 2.
47. Hester Blum, "The Prospect of Oceanic Studies," *PMLA* 125, no. 3 (May 2010): 670.
48. Blum, "The Prospect of Oceanic Studies," 670.
49. Alison Ribeiro de Menezes, "Memory beyond the Anthropocene: The Tactile Rhetorics of Patricio Guzmán's *Nostalgia de la luz* and *El botón de nácar*," in *Beyond the Rhetoric of Pain*, ed. Berenike Jung and Stella Bruzzi (New York: Routledge, 2019), 115.
50. Irene Depetris Chauvin, "Memories in the Present: Affect and Spectrality in Contemporary Aquatic Imaginaries," trans. Kate Wilson, in *Liquid Ecologies in Latin American and Caribbean Art*, ed. Lisa Blackmore and Liliana Gómez (London: Routledge, 2020), 146.
51. Erika Balsom, *An Oceanic Feeling: Cinema and the Sea* (New Plymouth, New Zealand: Govett-Brewster Art Gallery, 2018), 11.
52. Balsom, *An Oceanic Feeling*, 14–15, italics added.
53. Steve Mentz, *Ocean* (New York and London: Bloomsbury Academic, 2020), 33.
54. Mentz, *Ocean*, 33–34.
55. Édouard Glissant, *Poetics of Relation*, trans. Betsy Wing (Ann Arbor: University of Michigan Press, 1997), 6.
56. Glissant, *Poetics of Relation*, 6.
57. Mentz, *Ocean*, 7.
58. Balsom, *An Oceanic Feeling*, 28.
59. Astrida Neimanis, *Bodies of Water: Posthuman Feminist Phenomenology* (London: Bloomsbury Academic, 2016), 129–30.
60. Barthes, *Mythologies*, 2.
61. Brady Hammond, "The Shoreline and the Sea: Liminal Spaces in the Films of James Cameron," *Continuum: Journal of Media & Cultural Studies* 27, no. 5 (2013): 90.
62. Hammond, "The Shoreline and the Sea," 690.
63. Henri Lefebvre, *The Production of Space*, trans. Donald Nicholson-Smith (Oxford: Blackwell, 1991), 383.
64. Lefebvre, *The Production of Space*, 383–85.

65. Lefebvre, *The Production of Space*, 384.
66. Jean-Didier Urbain, *At the Beach*, trans. Catherine Porter (Minneapolis: University of Minnesota Press, 2003), 6.
67. Fiona Handyside, *Cinema at the Shore: The Beach in French Film* (Bern, Switzerland: Peter Lang, 2014), 188; Jennifer Webb, "Beaches, Bodies, and Being in the World," in *Some Like It Hot: The Beach as Cultural Dimension*, ed. James Skinner, Keith Gilbert, and Allan Edwards (Aachen Germany: Meyer & Meyer Sport, 2003), 80.
68. Papu Curotto, quoted in "Niños jugando: Entrevista a Papu Curotto y Andi Nachón," *Página/12,* accessed August 26, 2022, https://www.pagina12.com.ar/20629-ninos-jugando.
69. Ben Bollig, "The Poet as Screenwriter: Landscape and Protagonism in Papu Curotto's *Esteros*," *New Cinemas: Journal of Contemporary Film* 15, no. 2 (September 2017): 131, italics added.
70. Philip, E. Steinberg, "Of Other Seas: Metaphors and Materialities in Maritime Regions," *Atlantic Studies* 10, no. 2 (2013): 163.
71. Jue, *Wild Blue Media*, 2.
72. Balsom, *An Oceanic Feeling*, 10.
73. Jue, *Wild Blue Media*, 2.
74. Adam O'Brien, "In and around *The Bay*: Water, Fish, Infrastructure," *Film Studies* 19, no. 1 (Autumn 2018): 24.
75. O'Brien, "In and around *The Bay*," 24.
76. O'Brien, "In and around *The Bay*," 25, italics added.
77. Ian Gordon and Simon Inglis, *Great Lengths: The Historic Indoor Swimming Pools of Britain* (Swindon: English Heritage, 2009), 16.
78. Strang, "Common Senses," 100; Webb, "Beaches, Bodies, and Being in the World," 84, italics in the original.
79. Webb, "Beaches, Bodies, and Being in the World," 84.
80. Laura U. Marks, *The Skin of the Film* (Durham: Duke University Press, 2000), 152; Vivian Sobchack, *Carnal Thoughts: Embodiment and Moving Image Culture* (Berkeley: University of California Press, 2004), 63.
81. Sobchack, *Carnal Thoughts*, 60, italics added.
82. Sobchack, *Carnal Thoughts*, 76.
83. Jennifer Barker, *The Tactile Eye: Touch and the Cinematic Experience* (Berkeley: University of California Press, 2009), 4.
84. Paul Stoller, *Sensuous Scholarship* (Philadelphia: University of Pennsylvania Press, 1997); Barker, *The Tactile Eye*, 2, italics added.
85. Barker, *The Tactile Eye*, 3.
86. Marks, *The Skin of the Film*, 129.
87. Marks, *The Skin of the Film*, 159.
88. Marks, *The Skin of the Film*, 94.

89. Marks, *The Skin of the Film*, 188, italics added.
90. Marks, *The Skin of the Film*, 190.
91. Marks, *The Skin of the Film*, 191.
92. Katharina Lindner, *Film Bodies: Queer Feminist Encounters with Gender and Sexuality in Cinema* (London: I.B. Tauris, 2017), 55.
93. Lindner, *Film Bodies*, 55, italics in the original.
94. Marks, *The Skin of the Film*, 164.
95. Marks, *The Skin of the Film*, 164.
96. Lee Edelman, *No Future: Queer Theory and the Death Drive* (Durham: Duke University Press, 2004), 29, 2.
97. Edelman, *No Future*, 29.
98. José Esteban Muñoz, *Cruising Utopia: The Then and There of Queer Futurity* (New York: New York University Press, 2009), 1, italics added.
99. Muñoz, *Cruising Utopia*, 1, italics added.
100. Muñoz, *Cruising Utopia*, 1.
101. Muñoz, *Cruising Utopia*, 4.
102. Muñoz, *Cruising Utopia*, 1.
103. Muñoz, *Cruising Utopia*, 185, italics added.
104. Muñoz, *Cruising Utopia*, 22, italics added.
105. Robin Campillo, quoted in Nick Chen, "*120 BPM*: The Magical Must-See Movie about AIDS, Love and Clubbing in Paris," *Dazed*, accessed August 29, 2022, https://www.dazeddigital.com/film-tv/article/39530/1/120-bpm-robin-campillo-interview.
106. It is worth noting in passing how Campillo's treatment of the hospital bed in *120 BPM* works to reclaim it as a site of queer experience, eschewing the overwhelmingly negative, "unambiguously morbid" images that saturated the media of bedridden men who were "debilitated, sick, and almost dead" (Lawrence, "AIDS, the Impossibility of Representation and Plurality," *Social Text* 52/53 [Autumn 1997]: 243). For Tim Lawrence, "Such representations play into deep and reactionary cultural narratives. [. . .] Doom, powerlessness, and hopelessness are central themes: there is little chance of the diseased person having a productive life; the overdetermined body images of the person with AIDS are evidence of inner depravity" (Lawrence, "AIDS," 243). Rather than picturing its protagonists in this way, as "desexualized, [. . .] stripped of power and silenced," and exclusively surrounded by grieving family members, *120 BPM* instead imag(in)es them embraced by their queer communities, actively discussing queer politics and activism and even, as the particular scene I mention here demonstrates, continuing to engage in sexual acts. They are active, politically aware and desiring agents rather than (solely) victims (Lawrence, "AIDS," 243).
107. Michele Aaron, "New Queer Cinema: An Introduction," in *New Queer Cinema: A Critical Reader*, ed. Michele Aaron (Edinburgh: University of Edinburgh Press, 2004), 5.

108. Monica B. Pearl, "AIDS and New Queer Cinema," in *New Queer Cinema: A Critical Reader,* ed. Michele Aaron (Edinburgh: University of Edinburgh Press, 2004), 23; José Arroyo, "Death, Desire and Identity: The Political Unconscious of 'New Queer Cinema,'" in *Activating Theory: Lesbian, Gay, Bisexual Politics,* ed. Joseph Bristow and Angelina R. Wilson (London: Lawrence and Wishart, 1993), 90.

109. Arroyo, "Death, Desire and Identity," 92.

110. For an overview of the development of LGBTQ+ rights in Latin America during the first two decades of the twenty-first century, see Javier Corrales, "The Expansion of LGBT Rights in Latin America and the Backlash," in *The Oxford Handbook of Global LGBT and Sexual Diversity Politics,* ed. Michael J. Bosia, Sandra M. McEvoy, and Momin Rahman (Oxford: Oxford University Press, 2020), 185–200.

111. Aaron, "New Queer Cinema," 4.

112. B. Ruby Rich, *New Queer Cinema: The Director's Cut* (Durham: Duke University Press, 2013), 142.

113. Rich, *New Queer Cinema,* 143.

114. Vinodh Venkatesh, *New Maricón Cinema: Outing Latin American Film* (Austin: University of Texas Press, 2016), 7.

115. David William Foster, *Queer Issues in Contemporary Latin American Cinema* (Houston: University of Texas Press, 2003), xvii.

116. Foster, *Queer Issues,* xvii.

117. Gus Subero, *Queer Masculinities in Latin American Cinema: Male Bodies and Narrative Representations* (London: I.B. Tauris, 2014), 18.

118. Subero, *Queer Masculinities,* 19.

119. Subero, *Queer Masculinities,* 5, 19.

120. Venkatesh, *New Maricón Cinema,* 21.

121. Venkatesh, *New Maricón Cinema,* 21.

122. Venkatesh, *New Maricón Cinema,* 60, 61.

123. Venkatesh, *New Maricón Cinema,* 6, 7, 8.

124. Venkatesh, *New Maricón Cinema,* 7.

125. Gonzalo Aguilar, *Other Worlds: New Argentine Film,* trans. Sarah Ann Wells (New York: Palgrave Macmillan, 2008), 22–23; Joanna Page, *Crisis and Capitalism in Contemporary Argentine Cinema* (Durham: Duke University Press, 2009), 182.

126. Brad Epps, "The Fetish of Fluidity," in *Homosexuality and Psychoanalysis,* ed. Tim Dean and Christopher Lane (Chicago: University of Chicago Press, 2006), 413.

127. Geoffrey Maguire and Rachel Randall, "Introduction: Visualising Adolescence in Contemporary Latin American Cinema. Gender, Class and Politics," in *New Visions of Adolescence in Contemporary Latin American Cinema,* ed. Geoffrey Maguire and Rachell Randall (New York: Palgrave Macmillan, 2018), 16.

128. Balsom, *An Oceanic Feeling,* 11.

129. Inderpal Grewel and Caren Kaplan, "Global Identities: Theorizing Transnational Studies of Sexuality," *GLQ: A Journal of Lesbian and Gay Studies* 7, no. 4, (2001): 670.

130. Anne-Marie Fortier, "'Coming Home': Queer Migrations and Multiple Evocations of Home," *European Journal of Cultural Studies* 4, no. 4 (2001).

131. Schoonover and Galt, *Queer Cinema in the World*, 277.

132. Astrid Lorange and Tim Gregory, "Teaching Post-Pornography," *Cultural Studies Review* 24, no. 1 (2018).

133. Jue, *Wild Blue Media*, 11.

Chapter 1

1. Manuel Betancourt, "Argentine Drama *Fin de siglo* and the Changing Face of Gay Male Intimacy," *ReMezcla*, accessed October 23, 2023, https://remezcla.com/features/film/review-fin-de-siglo-end-of-century/; Sara Ahmed, *The Promise of Happiness* (Durham, NC: Duke University Press, 2010), 65.

2. Fiona Handyside, *Cinema at the Shore: The Beach in French Film* (Bern, Switzerland: Peter Lang, 2014), 13.

3. The following films, among many others, all contain moments in which directors emphasize the strength and athleticism of the gay male body through formal techniques that involve entering or exiting water: Javier Fuentes-León's *Contracorriente* (*Undertow*, 2009); Marco Berger's *Ausente* (*Absent*, 2011), *Hawaii* (2013), and *Taekwondo* (2016); Alain Guiraudie's *L'Inconnu du lac* (*Stranger by the Lake*, 2013); Karim Aïnouz's *Praia do Futuro* (*Futuro Beach*, 2014); and Jakob M. Erwa's *Der Mitte der Welt* (*Center of My World*, 2016).

4. Lucio Castro, quoted in Mireira Mullor, "Lucio Castro: 'No hay nada que entender en el cine, no es una clase de matemáticas,'" *Fotogramas*, accessed October 23, 2023, https://www.fotogramas.es/noticias-cine/a29821657/fin-de-siglo-pelicula-gay-filmin-entrevista/. Unless otherwise stated, all translations from Spanish, Portuguese, and French are my own.

5. Stuart Richards, "A New Queer Cinema Renaissance," *Queer Studies in Media & Popular Culture* 1, no. 2 (2016): 221; Monica B. Pearl, "AIDS and New Queer Cinema," in *New Queer Cinema: A Critical Reader*, ed. Michele Aaron (Edinburgh: Edinburgh University Press, 2004), 23.

6. These aspects of New Queer Realism are present in many contemporary queer films from beyond the Latin American context, such as in the work of Céline Sciamma, Francis Lee, Xavier Dolan, Apichatpong Weerasethakul, Tsai Ming-liang, Yen Tan, and Alain Guiraudie, among many others.

7. Andrew Moor, "'New Gay Sincerity' and Andrew Haigh's *Weekend* (UK, 2011)," *Film Studies* 19, no. 1 (Autumn 2018): 9.

8. See, for instance: Chris Drew, "Brief Encounters in Barcelona," *Dog and Wolf*, accessed October 23, 2023, https://www.dogandwolf.com/2020/02/end-of-the-century-2019-film-review/; Jude Dry, "*End of the Century*: Swooning Gay Romance Is the Argentine Answer to *Weekend*," *Indiewire*, accessed October 23, 2023, https://www.indiewire.com/2019/07/end-of-the-century-trailer-gay-movie-weekend-1202158735/. There have also been less-convincing links made by critics with Richard Linklater's *Before* trilogy (*Before Sunrise*, 1995; *Before Sunset*, 2004; and *Before Midnight*, 2013), but these largely fail to note the significant distinctions between the films in terms of genre, queer context, and realist modes.

9. José Esteban Muñoz, *Cruising Utopia: The Then and There of Queer Futurity* (New York and London: New York University Press, 2009), 186.

10. Muñoz, *Cruising Utopia*, 10.

11. Ben Qureshi, "Romance Redux in Barcelona: *End of the Century*," *Film Quarterly* 73, no. 3 (Spring 2020): 81.

12. Qureshi, "Romance Redux," 81.

13. Ahmed, *The Promise of Happiness*, 117.

14. Leo Bersani, "Is the Rectum a Grave?," *AIDS: Cultural Analysis/Cultural Activism* 43 (Winter 1987): 197–222; Leo Bersani, *Homos* (Cambridge: Harvard University Press, 1995); Lee Edelman, *No Future: Queer Theory and the Death Drive* (Durham, NC: Duke University Press, 2004).

15. Ahmed, 89, italics added.

16. Muñoz, *Cruising Utopia*, 10; Ahmed, *The Promise of Happiness*, 89.

17. Glenn Kenny, "*End of the Century* Review: A Vacation Veers into Existential States," *The New York Times*, accessed October 23, 2023, https://www.nytimes.com/2019/08/15/movies/end-of-the-century-review.html.

18. Richard Dyer, "Male Porn: Coming to Terms," *Jump Cut*, no. 30 (March 1985); Linda Williams, *Screening Sex* (Durham, NC: Duke University Press, 1999).

19. Cüneyt Çakirlar and Gary Needham, "The Monogamous/Promiscuous Options in Contemporary Gay Film: Registering the Amorous Couple in *Weekend* (2011) and *Paris 05:59: Théo & Hugo* (2016)," *New Review of Film and Television Studies* 18, no. 4 (Winter 2020): 402.

20. Dyer, "Male Porn," 28; Williams, *Screening Sex*, 5.

21. Ben Walters, "New-Wave Queer Cinema: 'Gay Experience in All Its Complexity,'" *The Guardian*, October 4, 2012.

22. Walters, "New-Wave Queer Cinema."

23. Moor, "New Gay Sincerity," 5.

24. Moor, "New Gay Sincerity," 10.

25. Moor, "New Gay Sincerity," 10.

26. B. Ruby Rich, "New Queer Cinema," in *New Queer Cinema: A Critical Reader*, ed. Michele Aaron (Edinburgh: Edinburgh University Press, 2004), 16.

27. Michele Aaron, "New Queer Cinema: An Introduction," in *New Queer Cinema: A Critical Reader*, ed. Michele Aaron (Edinburgh: Edinburgh University Press, 2004), 3–4.

28. Pearl, "AIDS and New Queer Cinema," 34.

29. Edelman, *No Future*.

30. In his chapter, Moor defends the use of "gay" in the term "New Gay Sincerity" by arguing that "Gayness, here conceived, refers to modes of identity that are figured around same-sex desire. [. . .] Because New Gay Sincerity acknowledges but tones down the postmodern play associated with New Queer Cinema in favour of a more studied and unblinking realism, the adjective 'gay' is a better fit than 'queer'" ("New Gay Sincerity," 6, 7). This chapter instead adopts the term "queer" in its discussion of New Queer Realism for several reasons: first, it refers more broadly to a wave of contemporary queer cinema that adopts the realist modes of representation described herein to depict queer relationships not simply between members of the same gender; second, its analysis of New Queer Realism expands beyond any exclusive focus on queer thematics or content to encompass queer aspects of film on the levels of style, form, and aesthetic, none of which could straightforwardly be termed as "gay."

31. Moor, "New Gay Sincerity," 17.

32. Ed Gonzalez, "Review: *End of the Century* Tells a Sexy and Haunted Riddle of a Romance," *Slant*, March 25, 2019, https://www.slantmagazine.com/film/review-end-of-the-century-tells-a-sexy-and-haunted-riddle-of-a-romance/.

33. Gonzalez, "Review."

34. Moor, "New Gay Sincerity," 5.

35. Moor, "New Gay Sincerity," 8.

36. Karl Schoonover and Rosalind Galt, *Queer Cinema in the World* (Durham, NC: Duke University Press, 2016), 272, italics added.

37. The painting the men consider is *La batalla de Tetuán*, by the Catalan artist Marià Fortuny. In a manner that resonates with the film's own ruminations on time, the painting was left unfinished by the artist and considered to be "a very unorthodox History painting, not following at all the traditional structures of this genre, a fact that makes it both singular and extraordinary" ("La batalla de Tetuán," *Catálogo*, Museu Nacional d'Art de Catalunya, https://www.museunacional.cat/es/colleccio/la-batalla-de-tetuan/maria-fortuny/010695-000).

38. Betancourt, "Argentine Drama *Fin de siglo*."

39. The irony of analyzing this scene (and indeed of offering an analysis of the film as a whole) in light of Ocho's remarks about subjective interpretation is not lost on the author of this book.

40. Jack Halberstam, *The Queer Art of Failure* (Durham, NC: Duke University Press, 2011), 2–3.

41. Halberstam, *The Queer Art of Failure*, 3.

42. Halberstam, *The Queer Art of Failure*, 3.
43. Halberstam, *The Queer Art of Failure*, 88.
44. Ahmed, *The Promise of Happiness*, 59.
45. Elizabeth Freeman, *Time Binds: Queer Temporalities, Queer Histories* (Durham, NC: Duke University Press, 2010), 5.
46. Ahmed, *The Promise of Happiness*, 195–96.
47. Ahmed, *The Promise of Happiness*, 197–98.
48. Ahmed, *The Promise of Happiness*, 117.
49. Freeman, *Time Binds*, xv.
50. Ahmed, *The Promise of Happiness*, 198.
51. Ahmed, *The Promise of Happiness*, 198.
52. Ahmed, *The Promise of Happiness*, 197.
53. Ahmed, *The Promise of Happiness*, 218.
54. Ahmed, *The Promise of Happiness*, 220.
55. Freeman, *Time Binds*, xv.
56. Freeman, *Time Binds*, xv.
57. Gonzalez, "Review: *End of the Century*."
58. Freeman, *Time Binds*, xv.
59. Stephanie Deborah Clare, "(Homo)normativity's Romance: Happiness and Indigestion in Andrew Haigh's *Weekend*," *Continuum: Journal of Media & Cultural Studies* 27, no. 6 (Spring 2013): 786, 785.
60. Clare, "(Homo)normativity's Romance," 786.
61. Michael Snediker, "Queer Optimism," *Postmodern Culture* 16, no. 3 (Spring 2006), italics in the original.
62. David Wojnarowicz, *Close to the Knives: A Memoir of Disintegration* (London: Serpent's Tail, 1992), 61.
63. Muñoz, *Cruising Utopia*, 1.
64. Muñoz, *Cruising Utopia*, 49.

Chapter 2

1. Gaston Bachelard, *Water and Dreams: An Essay on the Imagination of Matter* (Dallas: Pegasus Foundation, 2006 [1983]), 6.
2. Laura U. Marks, *The Skin of the Film* (Durham and London: Duke University Press, 2000), 159.
3. Fernando G. Pagnoni Berns, "Water and Queer Intimacy," in *Space and Subjectivity in Contemporary Brazilian Cinema*, ed. Antônio Márcio da Silva and Mariana Cunha (Cham, Switzerland: Palgrave Macmillan, 2017), 190.
4. Pagnoni Berns, "Water and Queer Intimacy," 198.
5. See Judith Butler, *Gender Trouble: Feminism and the Subversion of Identity* (London: Routledge, 1990); Judith Butler, *Bodies That Matter: On the Discursive*

Limits of "Sex" (New York: Routledge, 1993); Judith Butler, *Undoing Gender* (New York: Routledge, 2004).

6. See Claudia Castañeda, *Figurations: Child, Bodies, Worlds* (Durham, NC: Duke University Press, 2002); Emma Wilson, *Cinema's Missing Children* (London: Wallflower, 2003); Vicky Lebeau, *Childhood and Cinema* (London: Reaktion Books, 2008); Karen Lury, *The Child in Film: Tears, Fears and Fairy Tales* (London: I.B. Tauris, 2010).

7. Kathryn Bond Stockton, *The Queer Child, or Growing Sideways in the Twentieth Century* (Durham: Duke University Press, 2009).

8. Brad Epps, "The Fetish of Fluidity," in *Homosexuality and Psychoanalysis*, ed. Tim Dean and Christopher Lane (Chicago: University of Chicago Press, 2006), 413; Epps is keen to stress that the fluidity of which he talks "does not have the same function in feminism and AIDS activism as it does in most academic queer theory, where it tends to be—to echo and expand Warner's criticism of Butler—metaphysical" ("The Fetish of Fluidity," 417).

9. Epps, "The Fetish of Fluidity," 414.

10. Geoffrey Maguire and Rachel Randall, eds., *New Visions of Adolescence in Contemporary Latin American Cinema* (New York: Palgrave Macmillan, 2018), 16.

11. On the differentiation of adolescence from childhood in the Latin American context, see Carolina Rocha and Georgia Seminet, *Screening Minors in Latin American Cinema* (Lanham, Maryland: Rowman & Littlefield, 2014); Rachel Randall, *Children on the Threshold in Contemporary Latin American Cinema: Nature, Gender, and Agency* (Lanham: Lexington Books, 2017).

12. Maguire and Randall, *New Visions of Adolescence*, 17.

13. The term "queer" is used in this chapter to refer to nonnormative sexual and gender identities, which fall under the broadly defined umbrella of LGBTQI+ identities. It is important to note, as João Nemi Neto does in his work, the number and range of localized terms used to describe nonnormative sexualities and identities in Brazil and their complex interactions. For an extended discussion of this, please see João Nemi Neto, "Brazilian Queer Cinema," in *Oxford Research Encyclopedia of Communication,* 2021, accessed January 15, 2022, https://doi.org/10.1093/acrefore/9780190228613.013.1205; and Simone Cavalcante da Silva, "A Delicate Balance: Queer Masculinities in Contemporary Brazilian Film," in *Locating Queerness in the Media: A New Look*, ed. Jane Campbell and Theresa Carilli (Lanham: Lexington Books, 2017).

14. Lúcia Nagib, *Brazil on Screen: Cinema Novo, New Cinema, Utopia* (London: I.B. Tauris, 2007), 3.

15. José Esteban Muñoz, *Cruising Utopia: The Then and There of Queer Futurity* (New York: New York University Press, 2009), 1.

16. Nagib, *Brazil on Screen*, 4.

17. Maite Conde, *Foundational Films: Early Cinema and Modernity in Brazil* (Oakland: University of California Press, 2018), 54.

18. Conde, *Foundational Films*, 54.
19. Nagib, *Brazil on Screen*, 3.
20. Nagib, *Brazil on Screen*, 4.
21. Ivana Bentes, "The *sertão* and the *favela* in Contemporary Brazilian Film," in *The New Brazilian Film*, ed. Lúcia Nagib (London: I.B. Tauris, 2003), 124.
22. This *sertão*-sea formulation is repeated throughout the film's script and in its soundtrack, via lyrics written by Rocha and set to music by Sérgio Ricardo. The dictum is based on a prophecy from a speech by the religious leader Antônio Conselheiro, as discussed in Euclides da Cunha's *Os Sertões* from 1902.
23. Nagib, *Brazil on Screen*, 3; Bentes, "The *sertão* and the *favela*," 121; Nagib, *Brazil on Screen*, 4; It is worth pointing out that Bentes understands the *sertão* and the *favela* to have "always been the 'other side' of modern and positivist Brazil," going on to argue: "They are both real and symbolic lands which to a large degree invoke Brazilian imagery; they are lands in crisis, where desperate or rebellious characters live or wander; they are signs of a revolution to come or of a failed modernity" ("The *sertão* and the *favela*," 121).
24. Nagib, *Brazil on Screen*, 3; Nagib, "Death on the Beach: The Recycled Utopia of *Midnight*," in *The New Brazilian Film*, ed. Lúcia Nagib (London: I.B. Tauris, 2003), 168.
25. Nagib, *Brazil on Screen*, 12; Lúcia Nagib, "Back to the Margins in Search of the Core: *Foreign Land*'s Geography of Exclusion," in *The Brazilian Road Movie: Journeys of (Self) Discovery*, ed. Sara Brandellero (Cardiff: University of Wales Press, 2013), 168.
26. Marilena Chaui, "Brazil: The Foundational Myth," in *Between Conformity and Resistance: Essays on Politics, Culture, and the State*, trans. and ed. Maite Conde (New York: Palgrave Macmillan, 2011), 122, 120.
27. Nagib, "Back to the Margins," 174, italics added.
28. Muñoz, *Cruising Utopia*, 1, italics in the original.
29. Jasbir K. Puar, *Terrorist Assemblages: Homonationalism in Queer Times* (Durham and London: Duke University Press, 2007 [2017]), 2.
30. Simone Cavalcante da Silva, "A Delicate Balance," 164; Interestingly, although homosexual representation *on screen* was scant, James N. Green notes that the physical space of the cinema was the site of queer acts: "The darkness of the cinema house, the focused attention of the audience on the silver screen, and the luxurious and expansive multiple waiting rooms, hallways, and bathrooms typical of the modern movie palaces provided an ideal location for same-sex erotic adventures. One could escape from work for an hour to two during the day and engage in a clandestine and anonymous liaison in this dimly lit space" (*Beyond Carnival: Male Homosexuality in Twentieth-Century Brazil* [Chicago: University of Chicago Press, 1999], 96).
31. Stephanie Dennison and Lisa Shaw, *Popular Cinema in Brazil, 1930–2001* (Manchester, Manchester University Press, 2004), 161.

32. Dennison and Shaw, *Popular Cinema*, 161.
33. Nemi Neto, "Brazilian Queer Cinema."
34. Nemi Neto goes so far as to avoid referring to these characters as "queer," given the inherent misogyny involved: "The author resist [*sic*] identifying these characters as queer, for they represent a *clownesque* version of women, with the sole intent of ridicule or to make the audience laugh. [. . .] The popular appeal of a man being ridiculed and demoralized by acting as a woman even today proves a recipe for easy laughs in Brazilian culture" ("Brazilian Queer Cinema").
35. B. Ruby Rich, *New Queer Cinema: The Director's Cut* (Durham: Duke University Press, 2013), 176.
36. Rich, *New Queer Cinema*, 175.
37. Marcus D. Welsh, "Cross-Dressing and Transgressing: The Queer Body in *Madame Satã*," *Latin American Perspectives* 48, no. 2 (March 2021): 124, 126, italics added.
38. Welsh, "Cross-Dressing," 124.
39. Rich, *New Queer Cinema*, x.
40. Cavalcante Da Silva, "A Delicate Balance," 164–65.
41. Stuart Richards, "A New Queer Cinema Renaissance," *Queer Studies in Media & Popular Culture* 1, no. 2 (2016): 221; Monica B. Pearl, "AIDS and New Queer Cinema," in *New Queer Cinema: A Critical Reader*, ed. Michele Aaron (Edinburgh: Edinburgh University Press, 2004), 23.
42. Christopher Pullen, "Queer Male Bodies and the Cinematic Liminal Beach," *Film International* 16, no. 3 (2018): 29.
43. Pullen, "Queer Male Bodies," 29.
44. Pullen, "Queer Male Bodies," 29.
45. Pullen, "Queer Male Bodies," 31.
46. Laura Podalsky, *The Politics of Affect and Emotion in Contemporary Latin American Cinema: Argentina, Brazil, Cuba and Mexico* (New York: Palgrave Macmillan, 2011), 103.
47. Podalsky, *The Politics of Affect and Emotion*, 103.
48. Maguire and Randall, *New Visions of Adolescence*, 17.
49. Podalsky, *The Politics of Affect and Emotion*, 103.
50. Deborah Martin, "*Planeta ciénaga*: Lucrecia Martel and Contemporary Argentine Women's Filmmaking," in *Latin American Women Filmmakers: Production, Politics, Poetics*, ed. Deborah Martin and Deborah Shaw (London: I.B. Tauris, 2017), 248.
51. Martin, "*Planeta ciénaga*," 253–54.
52. Martin, "*Planeta ciénaga*," 254–55.
53. Nagib, "Back to the Margins," 168.
54. Nemi Neto, "Brazilian Queer Cinema."

55. One critic astutely notes the connection between the character Sócrates and the famed captain of the 1982 Brazilian World Cup football team: "The image of Sócrates the footballer provides a stark contrast not only to the experiences of the central character but to the flawed male figures he encounters. Each of the men in Sócrates's life appears to fail him: his homophobic father disowns him, his love interest rejects him, his cousin refuses to house him, and one older gay male seeks to exploit his situation for sexual favours" (Matthew Barrington, "*Sócrates* Review," *Sight and Sound*, accessed October 23, 2023, https://www.bfi.org.uk/sight-and-sound/reviews/socrates-brazilian-teenager-loss-homophobia).

56. Nick Gómez, "*Sócrates* Review," *Culturefly*, accessed April 17, 2022, https://culturefly.co.uk/socrates-review/.

57. Barrington, "*Sócrates* Review."

58. Barrington, "*Sócrates* Review."

59. Barrington, "*Sócrates* Review."

60. Alessandra Brandão and Ramayana Lira da Souza, "*Bodylands* para além da in/visibilidade lésbica no cinema: Brincando com água," *Revista Brasileira de Estudos de Cinema e Audiovisual* 9, no. 2 (July 2020): 114.

61. Fiona Handyside, *Cinema at the Shore: The Beach in French Film* (Bern, Switzerland: Peter Lang, 2014), 55, 56.

62. Jennifer Webb, "Beaches, Bodies, and Being in the World," in *Some Like It Hot: The Beach as a Cultural Dimension*, ed. Allan Edwards, Keith Gilbert, and James Skinner (Oxford: Meyer and Meyer Sport, 2003), 84.

63. Webb, "Beaches," 83, italics added.

64. Epps, "The Fetish of Fluidity," 413–14.

65. Lisa Downing, "Perversion and the Problem of Fluidity and Fixity," in *Clinical Encounters in Sexuality: Psychoanalytic Practice and Queer Theory*, ed. Noreen Giffney and Eve Watson (Baltimore, Maryland: Punctum Books, 2017), 124.

66. Lisa Blackmore and Liliana Gómez, eds., *Liquid Ecologies in Latin American and Caribbean Art* (New York: Routledge, 2020), 2.

67. Hester Blum, "The Prospect of Oceanic Studies," *PMLA* 125, no. 3 (May 2010): 670.

68. Epps, "The Fetish of Fluidity," 414.

69. Nagib, *Brazil on Screen*, 3.

Chapter 3

1. Veronica Strang, *Water* (London: Reaktion Books, 2015), 59–60.

2. Erika Balsom, *An Oceanic Feeling: Cinema and the Sea* (Wellington, New Zealand: Govett-Brewster, 2018), 11.

3. Balsom, *An Oceanic Feeling*, 11.

4. Strang, *Water*, 175.

5. Inderpal Grewal and Caren Kaplan, "Global Identities: Theorizing Transnational Studies of Sexuality," *GLQ: A Journal of Lesbian and Gay Studies* 7, no. 4 (2001): 670.

6. Steven Dillon, *Derek Jarman and Lyric Film: The Mirror and the Sea* (Austin: University of Texas Press, 2004), 67.

7. Dillon, *Derek Jarman*, 110.

8. Jennifer Webb, "Beaches, Bodies, and Being in the World," in *Some Like It Hot: The Beach as Cultural Dimension*, ed. James Skinner, Keith Gilbert, and Allan Edwards (Aachen Germany, Meyer & Meyer Sport, 2003), 85, italics added.

9. Fiona Handyside, *Cinema at the Shore: The Beach in French Film* (Bern, Switzerland: Peter Lang, 2014), 5; Fiona Handyside, "The Possibilities of a Beach: Queerness and François Ozon's Beaches," *Screen* 53, no. 1 (Spring 2012): 56.

10. Handyside, "The Possibilities of a Beach," 71.

11. Laura U. Marks, *The Skin of the Film* (Durham: Duke University Press, 2000), 183.

12. Marks, *The Skin of the Film*, 162.

13. Fernando Gabriel Pagnoni Berns, "Water and Queer Intimacy," in *Space and Subjectivity in Contemporary Brazilian Cinema*, ed. Antônio Márcio da Silva and Mariana Cunha (Cham: Palgrave Macmillan, 2017), 188.

14. For examples outside the Latin American context, see, for instance, Alain Guiraudie's *L'Innconu du lac* (*Stranger by the Lake*, 2013), Barry Jenkins's *Moonlight* (2016), and Céline Sciamma's *Portrait d'une jeune fille en feu* (*Portrait of a Lady on Fire*, 2019).

15. Handyside, "The Possibilities of a Beach," 71.

16. Handyside, *Cinema at the Shore*, 13.

17. Handyside, "The Possibilities of a Beach," 56.

18. Laura Mulvey, "Visual Pleasure and Narrative Pleasure," *Screen* 16, no. 3 (Autumn 1975).

19. Mulvey, "Visual Pleasure," 838.

20. David Greven, *Ghost Faces: Hollywood and Post-Millennial Masculinity* (Albany: State University of New York Press, 2016), 2.

21. Greven, *Ghost Faces*, 19, 35.

22. Greven, *Ghost Faces*, 47, italics in the original.

23. Greven, *Ghost Faces*, 54.

24. Greven, *Ghost Faces*, 53.

25. Greven, *Ghost Faces*, 4.

26. Pierre Losson, "De *No se lo digas a nadie* a *Contracorriente*: Representaciones de la homosexualidad en el cine peruano contemporáneo," *El ojo que piensa* no. 5 (2012).

27. James Rawson, "Why Are Gay Characters at the Top of Hollywood's Kill List?," *The Guardian*, accessed October 23, 2023, https://www.theguardian.com/film/filmblog/2013/jun/11/gay-characters-hollywood-films.

28. Rawson, "Why Are Gay Characters?"

29. Karl Schoonover and Rosalind Galt, *Queer Cinema in the World* (Durham: Duke University Press, 2016), 45, 47.

30. Schoonover and Galt, *Queer Cinema in the World*, 46.

31. Schoonover and Galt, *Queer Cinema in the World*, 14.

32. Greven, *Ghost Faces*, 9.

33. These scenes are reminiscent of, if not direct citations of, scenes from Claire Denis's *Beau Travail* (1999), in which soldiers from the French Foreign Legion conduct military training on beaches.

34. Balsom, *An Oceanic Feeling*, 28, 51.

35. Cavalcante da Silva and Pagnoni Berns note that the Oberbaum Bridge separated East and West Germany, and they consequently suggest that this may be linked to a transition period of Donato's life.

36. Pagnoni Berns, "Water and Queer Intimacy," 196, italics added.

37. Anne-Marie Fortier, "'Coming Home': Queer Migrations and Multiple Evocations of Home," *European Journal of Cultural Studies* 4, no. 4 (2001).

38. Fortier, "Coming Home," 407, 410.

39. Fortier, "Coming Home," 412, italics in the original.

40. Pagnoni Berns, "Water and Queer Intimacy," 194.

41. Simone Cavalcante da Silva, "The Space of Queer Masculinities in Karim Aïnouz's *Praia do Futuro*," in *Space and Subjectivity in Contemporary Brazilian Cinema,* ed. Antônio Márcio da Silva and Mariana Cunha (Cham: Palgrave Macmillan, 2017), 177.

42. Cavalcante da Silva, "The Space of Queer Masculinities," 178.

43. Grewel and Kaplan, "Global Identities," 670.

44. Dennis Altman, "Global Gaze/Global Gays," *GLQ* 3, no. 4 (1997); Ben Sifuentes-Jáuregui, *The Avowal of Difference: Queer Latino American Narratives* (Albany: State University of New York Press, 2014).

45. Schoonover and Galt, *Queer Cinema in the World*, 298.

46. Schoonover and Galt, *Queer Cinema in the World*, 295.

47. Schoonover and Galt, *Queer Cinema in the World*, 296, italics added.

48. Fortier, "Coming Home," 415.

49. Fortier, "Coming Home," 420.

50. Webb, "Beaches, Bodies, and Being in the World," 86.

51. Schoonover and Galt, *Queer Cinema in the World*, 286.

Chapter 4

1. For example, Ben Walters suggested that Ira Sachs's *Keep the Lights On* (2012), Andrew Haigh's *Weekend* (2012), and Tavis Matthews's *I Want Your Love* (2012) represented a "new-wave queer cinema [. . .] rejecting stereotypical roles and predictable plots [and representing] a welcome shift in queer cinema—an

embrace of the real" (Walters, "New-Wave Queer Cinema: Gay Experience in All Its Complexity," *The Guardian*, October 4, 2012, https://www.theguardian.com/film/2012/oct/04/new-wave-gay-cinema).

2. As mentioned in the introduction, perhaps one of the most striking early examples of this combination of water and queerness can be found in Derek Jarman's *Sebastiane* (1976), in which the characters of Adrian and Anthony are filmed in an intimate four-minute sequence that focuses haptically on their arms, torsos, heads, and buttocks as they splash in the water of a rock pool by the ocean.

3. Karl Schoonover and Rosalind Galt, *Queer Cinema in the World* (Durham, NC: Duke University Press, 2016), 5.

4. Schoonover and Galt, *Queer Cinema in the World*, 236–37.

5. Schoonover and Galt, *Queer Cinema in the World*, 277.

6. See, for instance, David William Foster, "Marco Berger: Filmar las masculinidades *queer* en Argentina," *Imagofagia*, no. 9 (2014): 1–17; Diego Moreiras, "Educación sexual integral, Marco Berger y *Ausente*. Miradas en conflicto desde una didáctica de la comunicación," *Anagramas* 14, no. 28 (2016): 97–114.

7. See, for instance, Santiago Peidro, "Un deseo que interpela: subvirtiendo las normas morales de la erogenia masculina," *Ética y Cine Journal* 3, no. 3 (2013): 43–53; Fernando Gabriel Pagnoni Berns, "Cartographies of Desire: Swimming Pools and the Queer Gaze," in *The Cinema of the Swimming Pool*, ed. Christopher Brown and Pam Hirsch (Oxford: Peter Lang, 2014), 229–37.

8. See Geoffrey Maguire, "Visual Displeasure: Adolescence and the Queer Male Gaze in Marco Berger's *Ausente*," in *New Visions of Adolescence in Contemporary Latin American Cinema*, ed. Geoffrey Maguire and Rachel Randall (New York: Palgrave Macmillan, 2018), 33–59.

9. Guy Lodge, "Why Is Oscar-Buzzed Romance *Call Me by Your Name* So Coy about Gay Sex?," *The Guardian*, accessed October 23, 2023, https://www.theguardian.com/film/2017/nov/23/call-me-by-your-name-gay-sex-oscars.

10. Schoonover and Galt, *Queer Cinema in the World*, 278.

11. Jonathan Romney reflects on the ideological motivations that underpin contemporary slow film: "Apart from filling the gap left by philosophical-poetic auteurs such as Bergman and Tarkovsky, the current Slow Cinema might be seen as a response to a bruisingly pragmatic decade in which, post-9/11, the oppressive everyday awareness of life as overwhelmingly political, economic and ecological would seem to preclude (in the West, at least) any spiritual dimension in art" (Romney, "In Search of Lost Time," *Sight and Sound*, February, 2010, 43).

12. Danny Leigh, "The View: Is It OK to Be a Film Philistine?," *The Guardian*, accessed March 14, 2020, https://www.theguardian.com/film/filmblog/2010/may/21/film-philistine.

13. Nick James, "Passive Aggressive," *Sight and Sound* 20, no. 4 (2010): 5.

14. Steven Shaviro, "Slow Cinema vs Fast Films," *The Pinocchio Theory*, May 12, 2010.

15. Matthew Flanagan, "Towards an Aesthetic of Slow in Contemporary Cinema," *Danmarks Klogeste Filmtidsskrift* 6, no. 29 (2008).
16. Tiago de Luca, "Slow Time, Visible Cinema: Duration, Experience, and Spectatorship," *Cinema Journal* 56, no. 1 (2016): 31.
17. De Luca, "Slow Time," 29, italics in the original.
18. Germán can often be seen reading J. D. Salinger's *Catcher in the Rye*, providing a fertile intertext given the novel's periodic descriptions of male bodies and, as some critics have noted, a certain ambiguity in the protagonist's sexuality. See Pia Livia Hekanaho, "Queering *Catcher*: Flits, Straights, and Other Morons," in *J. D. Salinger's "The Catcher in the Rye": A Study Guide*, ed. Sarah Graham (New York: Routledge, 2007), 89–97.
19. Schoonover and Galt, *Queer Cinema in the World*, 277.
20. Emre Çağlayan, *Poetics of Slow Cinema: Nostalgia, Absurdism, Boredom* (Basingstoke: Palgrave Macmillan, 2018), 81.
21. The passing use of fruit here is reminiscent of similar symbols in contemporary queer film, perhaps most notably the (distinctly less subtle) presence of peaches in Luca Guadagnino's *Call Me by Your Name* (2017).
22. Richard Misek, "Dead Time: Cinema, Heidegger and Boredom," *Continuum* 24, no. 5 (2010): 778–79; de Luca, "Slow Time, Visible Cinema," 38.
23. Diego Lerer, "Estrenos: *Taekwondo* de Marco Berger y Martín Farina," *Micropsia*, accessed March 17, 2020, http://www.micropsiacine.com/2016/08/estrenos-taekwondo-marco-berger-martin-farina/.
24. Fernando Gabriel Pagnoni Berns, "Water and Queer Intimacy," in *Space and Subjectivity in Contemporary Brazilian Cinema*, ed. Antônio Márcio da Silva and Mariana Cunha (Cham: Palgrave Macmillan, 2017), 186.
25. Christopher Brown and Pam Hirsch, "Introduction: The Cinema of the Swimming Pool," in *The Cinema of the Swimming Pool*, ed. Christopher Brown and Pam Hirsch (Oxford: Peter Lang, 2014), 1.
26. Brown and Hirsch, "Introduction," 17–18.
27. Deborah Martin, "*Planeta ciénaga*: Lucrecia Martel and Contemporary Argentine Women's Filmmaking," in *Latin American Women Filmmakers: Production, Politics, Poetics*, ed. Deborah Martin and Deborah Shaw (London: I.B. Tauris, 2017), 255.
28. Laura Marks, *The Skin of the Film: Intercultural Cinema, Embodiment and the Senses* (Durham, NC: Duke University Press, 2000), 159.
29. Laura Marks, "Video Haptics and Erotics," *Screen* 39, no. 4 (1998): 342.
30. Marks, *The Skin of the Film*, xi.
31. Marks, *The Skin of the Film*, 193.
32. Marks, *The Skin of the Film*, 164, italics in the original.
33. See, for instance: Gustavo Subero, *Queer Masculinities in Latin American Cinema: Male Bodies and Narrative Representations* (London: I.B. Tauris, 2013);

Vinodh Venkatesh *New Maricón Cinema: Outing Latin American Film* (Austin: University of Texas Press, 2016).

34. Venkatesh, *New Maricón Cinema*, 7, italics in the original.
35. Peidro, "Un deseo que interpela," 46, 49.
36. Schoonover and Galt, *Queer Cinema in the World*, 277.
37. Schoonover and Galt, *Queer Cinema in the World*, 192, italics added.
38. Schoonover and Galt also mention and Xavier Dolan's *Tom à la ferme* (*Tom at the Farm*, 2013) and Ira Sachs's *Keep the Lights On* (2012) as examples of "slow-faux" cinema (*Queer Cinema in the World*, 276–81).
39. Schoonover and Galt, *Queer Cinema in the World*, 278.
40. Schoonover and Galt, *Queer Cinema in the World*, 278.
41. Schoonover and Galt, *Queer Cinema in the World*, 278, 280, italics added.
42. Schoonover and Galt, *Queer Cinema in the World*, 278.
43. Pagnoni Berns, "Cartographies of Desire," 230.
44. Peidro, "Un deseo que interpela," 50.
45. Peidro, "Un deseo que interpela," 50.
46. Peidro, "Un deseo que interpela," 49.
47. Schoonover and Galt, *Queer Cinema in the World*, 278.
48. Karl Schoonover, "Wastrels of Time: Slow Cinema's Laboring Body, the Political Spectator and the Queer," *Framework: The Journal of Cinema and Media* 53, no. 1 (2012): 70.
49. Natalia Trzenko, "Bafici: *Taekwondo* es un atrapante relato hecho de cuerpos y miradas," *La Nación*, accessed April 18, 2018, https://www.lanacion.com.ar/espectaculos/cine/atrapante-relato-hecho-de-cuerpos-y-miradas-nid1890261/.
50. Schoonover and Galt, *Queer Cinema in the World*, 276.

Chapter 5

1. Barbara Hammer, *HAMMER! Making Movies out of Sex and Life* (New York: Feminist Press, City University of New York, 2010), 99, 119.
2. Hammer, *HAMMER!*, 119–20.
3. Barbara Hammer, quoted in Jacquelyn Zita, "The Films of Barbara Hammer: Counter-Currencies of a Lesbian Iconography," *Jump Cut. Journal of Contemporary Media*, nos. 24–25 (2005 [1981]), accessed July 16, 2020, https://www.ejumpcut.org/archive/onlinessays/JC24-25folder/BarbaraHammerZita.html.
4. Albertina Carri, "Sinopsis: *Las hijas del fuego*," AlbertinaCarri.com, accessed July 16, 2020, http://www.albertinacarri.com/?fbclid=IwAR111rllSAr9MCQ3HqPRALd3Jbul1bf5h40g0wTb9zAj1plB7kzIOYcro_k.
5. Verónica Garibotto and Jorge Pérez, eds., *The Latin American Road Movie* (New York: Palgrave Macmillan 2016), 2.

6. Griselda Soriano and Luciana Calcagno, "Dos textos sobre *Las hijas del fuego* de Albertina Carri. TEXTO 1," *Otros Cines*, accessed July 16, 2020, https://www.otroscines.com/nota?idnota=13954.

7. It is worth noting that the sexualities of the women in Carri's film are not presented as fixed and, in many ways, transcend the necessity for any such discrete identification. In this chapter, "lesbian" refers to sex and sexual acts performed between women rather than necessarily denoting any fixed category of sexuality or sexual orientation.

8. Barbara Hammer, quoted in "The SPIT! Manifesto Reader," accessed July 16, 2020, http://www.carlosmariaromero.com/spit-manifesto, 9.

9. This chapter focuses on the radical nature of Carri's work and does not offer any extended reflection on the generic limitations of pornography or enter into existing debates regarding porn's artistic or narrative value. For an extended discussion of these issues, see Linda Williams, "Cinema's Sex Acts," and Jacob M. Held, "What Is and Is Not Porn: Sex, Narrative, and *Baise-Moi*."

10. Linda Williams, *Screening Sex* (Durham: Duke University Press, 2008), 11.

11. Albertina Carri, quoted in Juan Pablo Cinelli, "Una forma de estar en el mundo más poética," *Página 12*, accessed 16 July 16, 2020, https://www.pagina12.com.ar/152342-una-forma-de-estar-en-el-mundo-mas-poetica; Linda Williams, *Hard Core: Power, Pleasure, and the "Frenzy of the Visible"* (Berkeley: University of California Press, 1989), 117.

12. Clara Bradbury-Rance, *Lesbian Cinema after Queer Theory* (Edinburgh: Edinburgh University Press, 2019), 3.

13. Bradbury-Rance, *Lesbian Cinema*, 3, 4.

14. In *Hard Core*, Williams writes: "It is thus precisely because heterosexual pornography has begun to address me [as a heterosexual woman] that I may very well be its ideal reader. Conversely, because lesbian and gay pornography do not address me personally, their initial mappings as genres properly belongs to those who can read them better" (Williams, *Hard Core*, 7). As a cisgendered gay man, the author of this book is not the primary target of the eroticism of *Las hijas del fuego*. The film is, however, of central importance to the formal and aesthetic tendencies examined in *Bodies of Water*. As the introduction points out, it has become commonplace in critical studies of queer cultural texts, not least in the Latin American context (David William Foster, *Queer Issues in Contemporary Latin American Cinema*; Gus Subero, *Queer Masculinities in Latin American Cinema: Male Bodies and Narrative Representation*), to collapse the notion of queerness into a framework that takes the gay (white) male body as representative of the collective, reproducing in critical material the relative hypervisibility of the gay man as a marker or symbol of queerness. My approach to Carri's work necessarily attends to the more complex representational politics of screening explicit lesbian sex, as well as to the limitations of my own subject position, which I hope

are mitigated to some degree by the exclusive reliance in this chapter on work authored or coauthored by critics who identify as women (with the one exception of José Esteban Muñoz), several of whom also identify in their work as lesbians.

15. Bradbury-Rance, *Lesbian Cinema*, 13.

16. Albertina Carri, quoted in Marisol Aguila, "Entrevista a Albertina Carri: La hija del fuego," *El Agente: Crítica de cine*, accessed July 16, 2020, http://elagentecine.cl/entrevista/entrevista-a-albertina-carri-la-hija-del-fuego/.

17. Williams, *Screening Sex*, 1.

18. Teresa de Lauretis, *Technologies of Gender: Essays on Theory, Film and Fiction* (Bloomington: Indiana University Press, 1987).

19. Hammer, *HAMMER!*, 100.

20. Carri, quoted in Aguila, "Entrevista."

21. Astrid Lorange and Tim Gregory, "Teaching Post-Pornography," *Cultural Studies Review* 24, no. 1 (2018): 137.

22. Lorange and Gregory, "Teaching Post-Pornography," 141.

23. Lorange and Gregory, "Teaching Post-Pornography," 146, italics added.

24. Ingrid Ryberg, "The Ethics of Shared Embodiment in Queer, Feminist and Lesbian Pornography," *Studies in European Cinema* 12, no. 3 (2015): 263.

25. Lorange and Gregory, "Teaching Post-Pornography," 139, italics in the original.

26. Juli A. Kroll, *Body, Gender and Sexuality in Latin American Cinema: Insurgent Skin* (Cham, Switzerland: Palgrave Macmillan, 2022), 96, 97.

27. Lorange and Gregory, "Teaching Post-Pornography," 141, 142.

28. Lorange and Gregory, "Teaching Post-Pornography," 141.

29. Lorange and Gregory, "Teaching Post-Pornography," 141.

30. Heather Dempsey, "The Daughters of Fire," *Savage Journal*, accessed July 16, 2020, http://www.savageonline.co.uk/our-journal/the-daughters-of-fire/.

31. The Spanish verb "contar," meaning "to tell," "to narrate," or "to relate," is difficult to render into English in this particular instance. A possible translation of this question, which takes into account the deliberate ambiguities of the voiceover, might be: "What stories do I tell when I tell the story of porn?"

32. Linda Williams, "Cinema's Sex Acts," *Film Quarterly* 67, no. 4 (2014): 14.

33. It is interesting to note that this scene initially shows the women contemplating the sea, with a grounded boat with a damaged hull in the background, before panning to them boarding a ship and sailing across the bay. Moreover, the final image of the previous scene has the word "RENACER," meaning "to be reborn" as a verb or "rebirth" as a noun, written on a sign outside a building.

34. Melody Jue, *Wild Blue Media: Thinking through Seawater* (Durham: Duke University Press, 2020), 10.

35. Jue, *Wild Blue Media*, 7, 10.

36. Jue, *Wild Blue Media*, 19.

37. Italics added.

38. Muñoz, *Cruising Utopia*, 49; In a satisfying stroke of queer coincidence, the front cover of Muñoz's *Cruising Utopia* uses an untitled image from the artist Luke Dowd, in which koi fish of differently enhanced colors appear swimming underwater.

39. José Esteban Muñoz, *Cruising Utopia: The Then and There of Queer Futurity* (New York: New York University Press, 2009), 49, 55, 1.

40. Muñoz, *Cruising Utopia*, 49, 1.

41. Muñoz, *Cruising Utopia*, 187.

42. Dempsey, "The Daughters of Fire."

43. Lorange and Gregory, "Teaching Post-Pornography," 141.

44. Lorange and Gregory, "Teaching Post-Pornography," 139.

45. Williams, *Hard Core*, 4, 117.

46. Lorange and Gregory, "Teaching Post-Pornography," 146.

47. Lorange and Gregory, "Teaching Post-Pornography," 140, italics in the original.

48. At several points in the closing sequence, one of the women can be seen wearing a moustache and using an Apple MacBook, gesturing to the contemporary circulation of pornographic media among men, as well as to the imbrication of sex and media more generally.

49. Williams, *Hard Core*, 105.

50. Deborah Shaw, in conversation with José Arroyo, notes that this scene in itself marks a journey in the film's treatment of sex, from Violeta's covert masturbation in a glacial cavern at the beginning of the film to the explicit, openly masturbatory act of Rosario in this final scene (quoted in José Arroyo, "In Conversation with Deborah Shaw on *The Daughters of Fire*," *First Impressions: Notes on Film and Culture*, March 30, 2020). https://notesonfilm1.com/2020/03/30/in-conversation-with-deborah-shaw-on-the-daughters-of-fire-albertina-carri-argentina-2018/).

51. Carri, quoted in Cinelli, "Una forma de estar."

52. Williams, *Hard Core*, 109.

53. Kroll, *Body, Gender and Sexuality*, 104.

54. Williams, *Hard Core*, 109.

55. Zita, "The Films of Barbara Hammer."

56. Zita, "The Films of Barbara Hammer."

57. Zita, "The Films of Barbara Hammer."

58. Williams, "Cinema's Sex Acts," 16.

59. Carri, quoted in Cinelli, "Una forma de estar."

Coda

1. José Esteban Muñoz, *Cruising Utopia: The Then and There of Queer Futurity* (New York: New York University Press, 2009), 22.

2. It is important to note that Alex's diagnosis in *XXY* does not correspond biologically to Klinefelter syndrome, the medical condition often known as XXY (or KS). Klinefelter syndrome refers specifically to boys and men who are born with an extra X chromosome. The UK's NHS website notes: "Boys and men with Klinefelter syndrome are still genetically male, and often will not realise they have this extra chromosome. [. . .] The [extra] X chromosome is not a 'female' chromosome and is present in everyone" ("Klinefelter syndrome," NHS website, February 20, 2023, https://www.nhs.uk/conditions/klinefelters-syndrome/). In an interview for REALFIC(c/t)ION, Puenzo has remarked on the misnomer of the film's title: "There was an internal conflict to decide if I had to use that title or not because the title doesn't respond to the diagnosis of Alex, and it was part of my own conflicts: having an extreme medical realism or making a fiction out of the subject. [. . .] I decided to make a respectful fiction and because it was respectful, I was able to use a title that wasn't exactly the diagnosis" (Puenzo, quoted in Pablo Goldbarg, "*XXY*: Interview with Lucía Puenzo," REALFIC(c/t)ION, April 29, 2008, http://pablogoldbarg.blogspot.com/2008/04/interview-with-luca-puenzo-xxy.html). Alex is therefore more accurately to be considered intersex, which is the term I use in this chapter. Any discussion of the character's "queerness" refers to her condition as intersex rather than the erroneous reference to Klinefelter syndrome.

3. Deborah Martin, "Growing Sideways in Argentine Cinema: Lucía Puenzo's *XXY* and Julia Solomonoff's *El último verano de la Boyita*," *Journal of Romance Studies* 13, no. 1 (Spring 2013): 38.

4. Vinodh Venkatesh, *New Maricón Cinema: Outing Latin American Film* (Austin: University of Texas Press, 2016), 115.

5. Martin, "Growing Sideways," 38.

6. Muñoz, *Cruising Utopia*, 22.

7. Karl Schoonover and Rosalind Galt, *Queer Cinema in the World* (Durham, NC: Duke University Press, 2016), 277.

8. Venkatesh, *New Maricón Cinema*, 119.

9. Moira Fradinger, "Cuerpos anfibios: Metamorfosis y *ectoentidad* sexual en *XXY* (2007) de Lucía Puenzo," *Cuadernos de literatura* 20, no. 40 (2016): 359.

10. Fradinger, "Cuerpos anfibios," 359.

11. Lourdes Estrada-López, "Deconstrucción sexual e intersexualidad en *XXY* de Lucía Puenzo," *Bulletin of Spanish Studies* 91, no. 3 (2014): 430.

12. Estrada-López, "Deconstrucción sexual," 430.

13. Debra A. Castillo, "Haunted: *XXY*," in *Despite All Adversities: Spanish-American Queer Cinema*, ed. Andrés Lema-Hincapié and Debra A. Castillo (Albany: State University of New York Press, 2015), 163.

14. Brad Epps, "The Fetish of Fluidity," in *Homosexuality and Psychoanalysis*, ed. Tim Dean and Christopher Lane (Chicago: University of Chicago Press, 2006), 413.

15. Fradinger, "Cuerpos anfibios," 359; Venkatesh, *New Maricón Cinema*, 7; Martin, "Growing Sideways," 36.

16. Melody Jue, *Wild Blue Media: Thinking through Seawater* (Durham: Duke University Press, 2020), 4–5, italics in the original.

17. Muñoz, *Cruising Utopia*, 22.

Bibliography

Aaron, Michele. "New Queer Cinema: An Introduction." In *New Queer Cinema: A Critical Reader*, edited by Michele Aaron, 3–14. Edinburgh: University of Edinburgh Press, 2004.
Aeon. "A Meditative Cinepoem from 1929 Captures the Reflective, Ethereal Wonders of Water." *Aeon*, November 9, 2018. https://aeon.co/videos/a-meditative-cinepoem-from-1929-captures-the-reflective-ethereal-wonders-of-water.
Aeon. "A Striking Classic from an Early Documentary Explores Amsterdam in the Rain." *Aeon*, November 9, 2018. https://aeon.co/videos/a-striking-classic-from-an-early-documentary-master-explores-amsterdam-in-the-rain.
Aguila, Marisol. "Entrevista a Albertina Carri: La hija del fuego." *El Agente: Crítica de cine,* May 31, 2019. http://elagentecine.cl/entrevista/entrevista-a-albertina-carri-la-hija-del-fuego/.
Aguilar, Gonzalo. *Other Worlds: New Argentine Film.* Translated by Sarah Ann Wells. New York: Palgrave Macmillan, 2008.
Ahmed, Sara. *The Promise of Happiness*. Durham, NC: Duke University Press, 2010.
Altman, Dennis. "Global Gaze/Global Gays." *GLQ* 3, no. 4 (1997): 417–36.
Arroyo, José. "Death, Desire and Identity: The Political Unconscious of 'New Queer Cinema.'" In *Activating Theory: Lesbian, Gay, Bisexual Politics*, edited by Joseph Bristow and Angelina R. Wilson, 70–96. London: Lawrence and Wishart, 1993.
Arroyo, José. "In Conversation with Deborah Shaw on *The Daughters of Fire* (Albertina Carri, Argentina, 2018)." *First Impressions: Notes on Film and Culture*, March 30, 2020. https://notesonfilm1.com/2020/03/30/in-conversation-with-deborah-shaw-on-the-daughters-of-fire-albertina-carri-argentina-2018/.
Bachelard, Gaston. *Water and Dreams: An Essay on the Imagination of Matter.* Translated by Edith R. Farrell. Dallas: Pegasus Foundation, 1983.
Balázs, Béla. *Theory of the Film.* Translated by Edith Bone. London: Dennis Dobson, 1951.
Balsom, Erika. *An Oceanic Feeling: Cinema and the Sea.* New Plymouth, New Zealand: Govett-Brewster Art Gallery, 2018.

Barker, Jennifer. *The Tactile Eye: Touch and the Cinematic Experience*. Berkeley: University of California Press, 2009.

Barrington, Matthew. "*Sócrates* Review." *Sight and Sound*, September 2, 2020. https://www.bfi.org.uk/sight-and-sound/reviews/socrates-brazilian-teenager-loss-homophobia.

Barthes, Roland. *Mythologies*. Translated by Annette Lavers. London: Paladin, 1972.

Bentes, Ivana. "The *Sertão* and the *Favela* in Contemporary Brazilian Film." In *The New Brazilian Film*, edited by Lúcia Nagib, 121–37. London: I.B. Tauris, 2003.

Bersani, Leo. *Homos*. Cambridge: Harvard University Press, 1995.

Bersani, Leo. "Is the Rectum a Grave?" *AIDS: Cultural Analysis/Cultural Activism* 43 (Winter 1987): 197–222.

Betancourt, Manuel. "Argentine Drama *Fin de Siglo* and the Changing Face of Gay Male Intimacy." *ReMezcla*, November 7, 2019. https://remezcla.com/features/film/review-fin-de-siglo-end-of-century/.

Blackmore, Lisa, and Liliana Gómez, eds. *Liquid Ecologies in Latin American and Caribbean Art*. New York: Routledge, 2020.

Blum, Hester. "The Prospect of Oceanic Studies." *PMLA* 125, no. 3 (May 2010): 670–77.

Boccaletti, Giulio. *Water: A Biography*. London: Pantheon Books, 2021.

Bollig, Ben. "The Poet as Screenwriter: Landscape and Protagonism in Papu Curotto's *Esteros*." *New Cinemas: Journal of Contemporary Film* 15, no. 2 (September 2017): 123–39.

Bond Stockton, Kathryn. *The Queer Child, or Growing Sideways in the Twentieth Century*. Durham: Duke University Press, 2009.

Bradbury-Rance, Clara. *Lesbian Cinema after Queer Theory*. Edinburgh: Edinburgh University Press, 2018.

Bradshaw, Peter. "A Bigger Splash: My 10 Favourite Films about Swimming." *The Guardian*, March 13, 2008. https://www.theguardian.com/film/filmblog/2008/mar/13/swimmingmoviesletspoolour.

Brandão, Alessandra, and Ramayana Lira da Souza. "*Bodylands* para além da in/visibilidade lésbica no cinema: Brincando com água." *Revista Brasileira de Estudos de Cinema e Audiovisual* 9, no. 2 (July 2020): 98–118.

Brown, Christopher, and Pam Hirsch. "Introduction: The Cinema of the Swimming Pool." In *The Cinema of the Swimming Pool*, edited by Christopher Brown and Pam Hirsch, 23–42. Oxford: Peter Lang, 2014.

Butler, Judith. *Bodies That Matter: On the Discursive Limits of "Sex."* New York: Routledge, 1993.

Butler, Judith. *Gender Trouble: Feminism and the Subversion of Identity*. London: Routledge, 1990.

Butler, Judith. *Undoing Gender*. New York: Routledge, 2004.

Çağlayan, Emre. *Poetics of Slow Cinema: Nostalgia, Absurdism, Boredom*. Basingstoke: Palgrave Macmillan, 2018.

Çakırlar, Cüneyt, and Gary Needham. "The Monogamous/Promiscuous Options in Contemporary Gay Film: Registering the Amorous Couple in *Weekend* (2011) and *Paris 05:59: Théo & Hugo* (2016)." *New Review of Film and Television Studies* 18, no. 4 (Winter 2020): 402–30.

Carri, Albertina. "Sinopsis: *Las hijas del fuego*." AlbertinaCarri.com, accessed July 16, 2020. http://www.albertinacarri.com/?fbclid=IwAR111rllSAr9MCQ3HqPRALd3Jbul1bf5h40g0wTb9zAj1plB7kzIOYcro_k.

Castañeda, Claudia. *Figurations: Child, Bodies, Worlds*. Durham, NC: Duke University Press, 2002.

Castillo, Debra A. "Haunted: *XXY*." In *Despite All Adversities: Spanish-American Queer Cinema*, edited by Andrés Lema-Hincapié and Debra A. Castillo, 155–72. Albany: State University of New York Press, 2015.

Cavalcante da Silva, Simone. "A Delicate Balance: Queer Masculinities in Contemporary Brazilian Film." In *Locating Queerness in the Media: A New Look*, edited by Jane Campbell and Theresa Carilli, 161–77. Lanham: Lexington Books, 2017.

Cavalcante da Silva, Simone. "The Space of Queer Masculinities in Karim Aïnouz's *Praia do Futuro*." In *Space and Subjectivity in Contemporary Brazilian Cinema*, edited by Antônio Márcio da Silva and Mariana Cunha, 169–83. Cham, Switzerland: Palgrave Macmillan, 2017.

Chaui, Marilena. "Brazil: The Foundational Myth." In *Between Conformity and Resistance: Essays on Politics, Culture, and the State*. Translated and edited by Maite Conde, 113–40. New York: Palgrave Macmillan, 2011.

Chen, Nick. "*120 BPM*: The Magical Must-See Movie about AIDS, Love and Clubbing in Paris." *Dazed*, April 2, 2018. https://www.dazeddigital.com/film-tv/article/39530/1/120-bpm-robin-campillo-interview.

Cinelli, Juan Pablo. "Una forma de estar en el mundo más poética." *Página 12*, June 16, 2018. https://www.pagina12.com.ar/152342-una-forma-de-estar-en-el-mundo-mas-poetica.

Clare, Stephanie Deborah. "(Homo)normativity's Romance: Happiness and Indigestion in Andrew Haigh's *Weekend*." *Continuum: Journal of Media & Cultural Studies* 27, no. 6 (Spring 2013): 785–98.

Conde, Maite. *Foundational Films: Early Cinema and Modernity in Brazil*. Oakland: University of California Press, 2018.

Connery, Christopher. "The Oceanic Feeling and the Regional Imaginary." In *Global/Local: Cultural Production and the Transnational Imaginary*, edited by Rob Wilson, 284–311. Durham: Duke University Press, 1996.

Corrales, Javier. "The Expansion of LGBT Rights in Latin America and the Backlash." In *The Oxford Handbook of Global LGBT and Sexual Diversity Politics*, edited by Michael J. Bosia, Sandra M. McEvoy, and Momin Rahman, 185–200. Oxford: Oxford University Press, 2020.

Cunha, Euclides da. *Os Sertões*. London, UK: Mogul Classics, 2014 [1902].

Curotto, Papu. "Niños jugando: Entrevista a Papu Curotto y Andi Nachón." *Página 12*, February 22, 2017. https://www.pagina12.com.ar/20629-ninos-jugando.
de Lauretis, Teresa. *Technologies of Gender: Essays on Theory, Film and Fiction*. Bloomington: Indiana University Press, 1987.
DeLoughrey, Elizabeth. "Submarine Futures of the Anthropocene." *Comparative Literatures* 69, no. 1 (2017): 32–44.
de Luca, Tiago. "Slow Time, Visible Cinema: Duration, Experience, and Spectatorship." *Cinema Journal* 56, no. 1 (2016): 23–42.
Dempsey, Heather. "The Daughters of Fire." *Savage Journal*, December 12, 2018. http://www.savageonline.co.uk/our-journal/the-daughters-of-fire/.
Dennison, Stephanie, and Lisa Shaw, eds. *Popular Cinema in Brazil, 1930–2001*. Manchester, Manchester University Press, 2004.
Depetris Chauvin, Irene. "Memories in the Present: Affect and Spectrality in Contemporary Aquatic Imaginaries." Translated by Kate Wilson. In *Liquid Ecologies in Latin American and Caribbean Art*, edited by Lisa Blackmore and Liliana Gómez, 144–59. London: Routledge, 2020.
Dillon, Steven. *Derek Jarman and Lyric Film: The Mirror and the Sea*. Austin: University of Texas Press, 2004.
Downing, Lisa. "Perversion and the Problem of Fluidity and Fixity." In *Clinical Encounters in Sexuality: Psychoanalytic Practice and Queer Theory*, edited by Noreen Giffney and Eve Watson, 124–44. Baltimore, Maryland: Punctum Books, 2017.
Drew, Chris. "Brief Encounters in Barcelona." *Dog And Wolf*, February 21, 2020. https://www.dogandwolf.com/2020/02/end-of-the-century-2019-film-review/.
Dry, Jude. "*End of the Century*: Swooning Gay Romance Is the Argentine Answer to *Weekend*." *Indiewire*, July 17, 2019. https://www.indiewire.com/2019/07/end-of-the-century-trailer-gay-movie-weekend-1202158735/.
Dyer, Richard. "Male Porn: Coming to Terms." *Jump Cut* 30 (March 1985): 27–29.
Edelman, Lee. *No Future: Queer Theory and the Death Drive*. Durham: Duke University Press, 2004.
Epps, Brad. "The Fetish of Fluidity." In *Homosexuality and Psychoanalysis*, edited by Tim Dean and Christopher Lane, 412–31. Chicago: University of Chicago Press, 2006.
Estrada-López, Lourdes. "Deconstrucción sexual e intersexualidad en *XXY* de Lucía Puenzo." *Bulletin of Spanish Studies* 91, no. 3 (2014): 419–43.
Flanagan, Matthew. "Towards An Aesthetic of Slow in Contemporary Cinema." *Danmarks Klogeste Filmtidsskrift* 6, no. 29 (2008).
Fortier, Anne-Marie. "'Coming Home': Queer Migrations and Multiple Evocations of Home." *European Journal of Cultural Studies* 4, no. 4 (2001): 405–24.
Foster, David William. "Marco Berger: Filmar las masculinidades *queer* en Argentina." *Imagofagia*, no. 9 (2014): 1–17.
Foster, David William. *Queer Issues in Contemporary Latin American Cinema*. Austin: University of Texas Press, 2003.

Fradinger, Moira. "Cuerpos anfibios: Metamorfosis y *ectoentidad* sexual en *XXY* (2007) de Lucía Puenzo." *Cuadernos de literatura* 20, no. 40 (2016): 357–81.
Freeman, Elizabeth. *Time Binds: Queer Temporalities, Queer Histories.* Durham, NC: Duke University Press, 2010.
Garibotto, Verónica, and Jorge Pérez. *The Latin American Road Movie.* New York: Palgrave Macmillan, 2016.
Glissant, Édouard. *Poetics of Relation.* Translated by Betsy Wing. Ann Arbor: University of Michigan Press, 1997.
Goldbarg, Pablo. "*XXY*: Interview with Lucía Puenzo." REALFIC(c/t)ION, April 29, 2008. http://pablogoldbarg.blogspot.com/2008/04/interview-with-luca-puenzo-xxy.html.
Gómez, Nick. "*Sócrates* Review." *Culturefly*, September 4, 2020. https://culturefly.co.uk/socrates-review/.
Gonzalez, Ed. "Review: *End of the Century* Tells a Sexy and Haunted Riddle of a Romance." *Slant*, March 25, 2019. https://www.slantmagazine.com/film/review-end-of-the-century-tells-a-sexy-and-haunted-riddle-of-a-romance/.
Gordon, Ian, and Simon Inglis. *Great Lengths: The Historic Indoor Swimming Pools of Britain.* Swindon: English Heritage, 2009.
Green, James N. *Beyond Carnival: Male Homosexuality in Twentieth-Century Brazil.* Chicago: University of Chicago Press, 1999.
Greven, David. *Ghost Faces: Hollywood and Post-Millennial Masculinity.* Albany: State University of New York Press, 2016.
Grewel, Inderpal, and Caren Kaplan "Global Identities: Theorizing Transnational Studies of Sexuality." *GLQ: A Journal of Lesbian and Gay Studies* 7, no. 4, (2001): 663–79.
Halberstam, Jack. *The Queer Art of Failure.* Durham: Duke University Press, 2011.
Hammer, Barbara. *HAMMER! Making Movies out of Sex and Life.* New York: Feminist Press, City University of New York, 2010.
Hammond, Brady. "The Shoreline and the Sea: Liminal Spaces in the Films of James Cameron." *Continuum: Journal of Media & Cultural Studies* 27, no. 5 (2013): 690–703.
Handyside, Fiona. *Cinema at the Shore: The Beach in French Film.* Bern, Switzerland: Peter Lang, 2014.
Handyside, Fiona. "The Possibilities of a Beach: Queerness and François Ozon's Beaches." *Screen* 53, no. 1 (Spring 2012): 54–71.
Hayward, Eva S. "Enfolded Vision: Refracting the *Love Life of the Octopus*." *Octopus: A Visual Studies Journal* 1 (2005): 48–57.
Hekanaho, Pia Livia. "Queering *Catcher*: Flits, Straights, and Other Morons." In *J. D. Salinger's "The Catcher in the Rye": A Study Guide*, edited by Sarah Graham, 89–97. New York: Routledge, 2007.
Held, Jacob M. "What Is and Is Not Porn: Sex, Narrative, and *Baise-Moi*." In *Sex and Storytelling in Modern Cinema: Explicit Sex, Performance and Cinematic Technique*, edited by Lindsay Coleman, 25–48. London: I.B. Tauris, 2016.

Helmreich, Stefan. "Nature/Culture/Seawater." *American Anthropologist* 113, no. 1 (2011): 132–44.
Hulser, Kathleen. "Frames of Passage: Nine Recent Films of Barbara Hammer." *BarbaraHammer.com*, accessed October 23, 2023. https://barbarahammer.com/wp-content/uploads/2020/05/1988_Frames-Of-Passages_Centre Pompidou_KathrynHulser.pdf.
James, Nick. "Passive Aggressive." *Sight and Sound* 20, no. 4 (2010).
Jue, Melody. *Wild Blue Media: Thinking through Seawater*. Durham: Duke University Press, 2020.
Kenny, Glenn. "'End of the Century' Review: A Vacation Veers into Existential States." *The New York Times*, August 15, 2019. https://www.nytimes.com/2019/08/15/movies/end-of-the-century-review.html.
"La batalla de Tetuán." *Catálogo*, Museu Nacional d'Art de Catalunya, accessed February 9, 2023. https://www.museunacional.cat/es/colleccio/la-batalla-de-tetuan/maria-fortuny/010695-000.
Lawrence, Tim. "AIDS, the Impossibility of Representation and Plurality in Derek Jarman's *Blue*." *Social Text* 52/53 (Winter 1997): 241–64.
Lebeau, Vicky. *Childhood and Cinema*. London: Reaktion Books, 2008.
Lefebvre, Henri. *The Production of Space*. Translated by Donald Nicholson-Smith. Oxford: Blackwell, 1991.
Leigh, Danny. "The View: Is It OK to Be a Film Philistine?" *The Guardian*, May 21, 2010. https://www.theguardian.com/film/filmblog/2010/may/21/film-philistine.
Lerer, Diego. "Estrenos: *Taekwondo* de Marco Berger y Martín Farina." *Micropsia*, August 17, 2016. http://www.micropsiacine.com/2016/08/estrenos-taekwondo-marco-berger-martin-farina/.
Lindner, Katharina. *Film Bodies: Queer Feminist Encounters with Gender and Sexuality in Cinema*. London: I.B. Tauris, 2017.
Lodge, Guy. "Why Is Oscar-Buzzed Romance *Call Me by Your Name* So Coy about Gay Sex?" *The Guardian*, November 23, 2017. https://www.theguardian.com/film/2017/nov/23/call-me-by-your-name-gay-sex-oscars.
Lodge, Oliver. *Ether and Reality: A Series of Discourses on the Many Functions of the Ether of Space*. Cambridge: University of Cambridge Press, 2012 [1925].
Lorange, Astrid, and Tim Gregory. "Teaching Post-Pornography." *Cultural Studies Review* 24, no. 1 (2018): 137–49.
Losson, Pierre. "De *No se lo digas a nadie* a *Contracorriente*: Representaciones de la homosexualidad en el cine peruano contemporáneo." *El ojo que piensa* 5 (2012).
Lury, Karen. *The Child in Film: Tears, Fears and Fairy Tales*. London: I.B. Tauris, 2010.
Maguire, Geoffrey. "Visual Displeasure: Adolescence and the Erotics of the Queer Male Gaze in Marco Berger's *Ausente*." In *New Visions of Adolescence in*

Contemporary Latin America Cinema, edited by Geoffrey Maguire and Rachell Randall, 37–57. New York: Palgrave Macmillan, 2018.
Maguire, Geoffrey, and Rachel Randall. "Introduction: Visualising Adolescence in Contemporary Latin American Cinema. Gender, Class and Politics." In *New Visions of Adolescence in Contemporary Latin America Cinema*, edited by Geoffrey Maguire and Rachell Randall, 1–33. New York: Palgrave Macmillan, 2018.
Marks, Laura U. *The Skin of the Film*. Durham: Duke University Press, 2000.
Marks, Laura U. "Video haptics and erotics." *Screen* 39, no. 4 (1998): 331–48.
Martin, Deborah. "Growing Sideways in Argentine Cinema: Lucía Puenzo's *XXY* and Julia Solomonoff's *El último verano de La Boyita*." *Journal of Romance Studies* 13, no. 1 (Spring 2013): 34–48.
Martin, Deborah. "*Planeta ciénaga*: Lucrecia Martel and Contemporary Argentine Women's Filmmaking." In *Latin American Women Filmmakers: Production, Politics, Poetics*, edited by Deborah Martin and Deborah Shaw, 241–62. London: I.B. Tauris, 2017.
Mentz, Steve. *An Introduction to the Blue Humanities*. London: Routledge, 2023.
Mentz, Steve. *Ocean*. New York and London: Bloomsbury Academic, 2020.
Misek, Richard "Dead Time: Cinema, Heidegger and Boredom." *Continuum* 24, no. 5 (2010): 777–85.
Moor, Andrew. "'New Gay Sincerity' and Andrew Haigh's *Weekend* (UK, 2011)." *Film Studies* 19, no. 1 (Autumn 2018): 4–19.
Moreiras, Diego. "Educación sexual integral, Marco Berger y *Ausente*. Miradas en conflicto desde una didáctica de la comunicación." *Anagramas* 14, no. 28 (2016): 97–114.
Morton, Timothy. *Hyperobjects: Philosophy and Ecology after the End of the World*. Minneapolis: University of Minnesota Press, 2013.
Mullor, Mireira. "Lucio Castro: 'No hay nada que entender en el cine, no es una clase de matemáticas.'" *Fotogramas*, November 18, 2019. https://www.fotogramas.es/noticias-cine/a29821657/fin-de-siglo-pelicula-gay-filmin-entrevista/.
Mulvey, Laura. "Visual Pleasure and Narrative Pleasure." *Screen* 16, no. 3 (Autumn 1975): 6–18.
Muñoz, José Esteban. *Cruising Utopia: The Then and There of Queer Futurity*. New York: New York University Press, 2009.
Nagib, Lúcia. "Back to the Margins in Search of the Core: *Foreign Land*'s Geography of Exclusion." In *The Brazilian Road Movie: Journeys of (Self) Discovery*, edited by Sara Brandellero, 162–83. Cardiff: University of Wales Press, 2013.
Nagib, Lúcia. *Brazil on Screen: Cinema Novo, New Cinema, Utopia*. London, New York: I.B. Tauris, 2007.
Nagib, Lúcia. "Death on the Beach: The Recycled Utopia of *Midnight*." In *The New Brazilian Film*, edited by Lúcia Nagib, 157–72. London: I.B. Tauris, 2003.

Nagib, Lúcia. "Towards a Positive Definition of World Cinema." In *Remapping World Cinema: Identity, Culture and Politics in Film*, edited by Stephanie Dennison and Song Hwee Lim, 26–33. London, New York: Wallflower, 2006.

Neimanis, Astrida. *Bodies of Water: Posthuman Feminist Phenomenology*. London: Bloomsbury Academic, 2016.

Nemi Neto, João. "Brazilian Queer Cinema." In *Oxford Research Encyclopedia of Communication*, 2021, accessed January 15, 2022. https://doi.org/10.1093/acrefore/9780190228613.013.1205.

NHS. "Klinefelter Syndrome." NHS website, February 20, 2023. https://www.nhs.uk/conditions/klinefelters-syndrome/.

O'Brien, Adam. "In and around *The Bay*: Water, Fish, Infrastructure." *Film Studies* 19, no. 1 (2018): 20–33.

Page, Joanna. *Crisis and Capitalism in Contemporary Argentine Cinema*. Durham: Duke University Press, 2009.

Pagnoni Berns, Fernando G. "Cartographies of Desire: Swimming Pools and the Queer Gaze." In *Cinema of the Swimming Pool*, edited by Christopher Brown and Pam Hirsch, 229–37. Oxford: Peter Lang, 2014.

Pagnoni Berns, Fernando G. "Water and Queer Intimacy." In *Space and Subjectivity in Contemporary Brazilian Cinema*, edited by Antônio Márcio da Silva and Mariana Cunha, 185–200. Cham, Switzerland: Palgrave Macmillan, 2017.

Pearl, Monica B. "AIDS and New Queer Cinema." In *New Queer Cinema: A Critical Reader*, edited by Michele Aaron, 23–36. Edinburgh: University of Edinburgh Press, 2004.

Peidro, Santiago. "Un deseo que interpela: subvirtiendo las normas morales de la erogenia masculina." *Ética y Cine Journal* 3, no. 3 (2013): 43–53.

Podalsky, Laura. *The Politics of Affect and Emotion in Contemporary Latin American Cinema: Argentina, Brazil, Cuba and Mexico*. New York: Palgrave Macmillan, 2011.

Probyn, Elspeth, cit. "Eating the Ocean, by Elspeth Probyn." In *Times Higher Education*, edited by Philip Hoare, December 1, 2016. https://www.timeshighereducation.com/books/review-eating-the-ocean-elspeth-probyn-duke-university-press#.

Puar, Jasbir K. *Terrorist Assemblages: Homonationalism in Queer Times*. Durham and London: Duke University Press, 2007.

Pullen, Christopher. "Queer Male Bodies and the Cinematic Liminal Beach." *Film International* 16, no. 3 (2018): 27–36.

Qureshi, Bilal. "Romance Redux in Barcelona: End of the Century." *Film Quarterly* 73, no. 3 (Spring 2020).

Randall, Rachel. *Children on the Threshold in Contemporary Latin American Cinema: Nature, Gender, and Agency*. Lanham: Lexington Books, 2017.

Rawson, James. "Why Are Gay Characters at the Top of Hollywood's Kill List?" *The Guardian*, June 11, 2013. https://www.theguardian.com/film/filmblog/2013/jun/11/gay-characters-hollywood-films.

Redmond, Sean. "Death and Life at the Cinematic Beach." *Journal of Media & Cinema Studies* 27, no. 5 (2013): 715–28.
Ribeiro de Menezes, Alison. "Memory beyond the Anthropocene: The Tactile Rhetorics of Patricio Guzmán's *Nostalgia de la luz* and *El botón de nácar*." In *Beyond the Rhetoric of Pain*, edited by Berenike Jung and Stella Bruzzi, 105–19. New York: Routledge, 2019.
Rich, Ruby. "New Queer Cinema." In *New Queer Cinema: A Critical Reader*, edited by Michele Aaron, 3–14. Edinburgh: Edinburgh University Press, 2004.
Rich, Ruby. *New Queer Cinema: The Director's Cut*. Durham: Duke University Press, 2013.
Richards, Stuart. "A New Queer Cinema Renaissance." *Queer Studies in Media & Popular Culture* 1, no. 2 (2016): 215–29.
Rocha, Carolina, and Georgia Seminet, eds. *Screening Minors in Latin American Cinema*. Lanham, Maryland: Rowman & Littlefield, 2014.
Romney, Jonathan. "In Search of Lost Time." *Sight and Sound* 20, no. 2 (2010).
Ryberg, Ingrid. "The Ethics of Shared Embodiment in Queer, Feminist and Lesbian Pornography." *Studies in European Cinema* 12, no. 3 (2015): 261–74.
Schoonover, Karl. "Wastrels of Time: Slow Cinema's Laboring Body, the Political Spectator and the Queer." *Framework: The Journal of Cinema and Media* 53, no. 1 (2012): 65–78.
Schoonover, Karl, and Rosalind Galt. *Queer Cinema in the World*. Durham: Duke University Press, 2016.
Sciamma, Céline. Press Release for *Naissance des pieuvres*, accessed August 26, 2022. https://s3.eu-west-3.amazonaws.com/storage.playtime.group/asset/5e87ac-b2a878b9000426ce1e/upload_a22a3a5b8ba32f7d59dc5699b5934875.pdf.
Shaviro, Steven. "Slow Cinema vs Fast Films." *The Pinocchio Theory*, May 12, 2010. http://www.shaviro.com/Blog/?p=891.
Sifuentes-Jáuregui, Ben. *The Avowal of Difference: Queer Latino American Narratives*. Albany: State University of New York Press, 2014.
Sivasundaram, Sujit. *Waves across the South: A New History of Revolution and Empire* Chicago: University of Chicago Press, 2020.
Snediker, Michael. "Queer Optimism." *Postmodern Culture* 16, no. 3 (Spring 2006).
Sobchack, Vivian. *Carnal Thoughts: Embodiment and Moving Image Culture*. Berkeley: University of California Press, 2004.
Soriano, Griselda, and Luciana Calcagno. "Dos textos sobre *Las hijas del fuego* de Albertina Carri. TEXTO 1." *Otros Cines*, October 30, 2018. https://www.otroscines.com/nota?idnota=13954.
SPIT! "The SPIT! Manifesto Reader," accessed July 16, 2020, 1–66. http://www.carlosmariaromero.com/spit-manifesto.
Starosielski, Nicole. "Beyond Fluidity: A Cultural History of Cinema under Water." In *Ecocinema Theory and Practice*, edited by Stephen Rust, Salma Monani, and Sean Cubitt, 149–68. New York: Routledge, 2013.

Steinberg, Philip E. "Of Other Seas: Metaphors and Materialities in Maritime Regions." *Atlantic Studies* 10, no. 2 (2013): 156–69.
Stoller, Paul. *Sensuous Scholarship*. Philadelphia: University of Pennsylvania Press, 1997.
Strang, Veronica. *Water*. London: Reaktion Books, 2015.
Strang, Veronica. "Common Senses: Water, Sensory Experience and the Generation of Meaning." *Journal of Material Culture* 10, no. 1 (2005): 92–120.
Subero, Gustavo. *Queer Masculinities in Latin American Cinema: Male Bodies and Narrative Representations*. London: I.B. Tauris, 2013.
Urbain, Jean-Didier. *At the Beach*. Translated by Catherine Porter. Minneapolis: University of Minnesota Press, 2003.
Venkatesh, Vinodh. *New Maricón Cinema: Outing Latin American Film*. Austin: University of Texas Press, 2016.
Walters, Ben. "New-Wave Queer Cinema: Gay Experience in All Its Complexity." *The Guardian*, October 4, 2012. https://www.theguardian.com/film/2012/oct/04/new-wave-gay-cinema.
Ward, Miranda. "Swimming in a Contained Space: Understanding the Experience of Indoor Lap Swimmers." *Health & Place* 46 (2017): 315–31.
Webb, Jennifer. "Beaches and Bodies." *Body, Space & Technology* 2, no. 1 (2001).
Webb, Jennifer. "Beaches, Bodies, and Being in the World." In *Some Like It Hot: The Beach as Cultural Dimension*, edited by James Skinner, Keith Gilbert, and Allan Edwards, 77–90. Aachen Germany, Meyer & Meyer Sport, 2003.
Welsh, Marcus D. "Cross-Dressing and Transgressing: The Queer Body in *Madame Satã*." *Latin American Perspectives* 48, no. 2 (March 2021): 123–36.
Williams, Linda. "Cinema's Sex Acts." *Film Quarterly* 67, no. 4 (2014): 9–25.
Williams, Linda. *Hard Core: Power, Pleasure, and the "Frenzy of the Visible."* Berkeley: University of California Press, 1989.
Williams, Linda. *Screening Sex*. Durham: Duke University Press, 2008.
Wilson, Emma. *Cinema's Missing Children*. London: Wallflower, 2003.
Wiltse, Jeff. *Contested Waters: A Social History of Swimming Pools in America*. Chapel Hill: University of North Carolina Press, 2007.
Wright, Rupert. *Take Me to the Source: In Search of Water*. London: Vintage, 2009.
Zita, Jacquelyn. "The Films of Barbara Hammer: Counter-Currencies of a Lesbian Iconography." *Jump Cut: A Review of Contemporary Media* 24–25 (2005 [1981]). https://www.ejumpcut.org/archive/onlinessays/JC24-25folder/BarbaraHammerZita.html.

Index

120 BPM, 24–26, 166n106

activism, 24–26, 26, 37–38, 166n106
ACT UP, 24–25
adolescence: sexuality, 11, 16, 31–32, 59–60, 71–74, 83, 111, 155; queer, 16, 31–23, 62–63, 64, 153–155; theories of, 62–63, 70–71, 77, 81–82, 157
aesthetics: adolescent, 72–73; Cinema Novo, 65; lesbian, 6–7, 78–79, 129–130, 131–133, 139; queer, 23–24, 24–30, 34, 38–39, 56–58, 64, 106–107, 110, 144, 154; realist, 42–45; slow, 111–112, 113–117; watery, 2–3, 19–20, 24–26, 34, 60–61, 77, 78–79, 140–141, 142–143, 154, 158–159
affect, 3, 11, 23, 27–28, 29, 39–40, 45, 48–49, 50, 55–56, 56–58, 69–74, 81, 101–102, 104, 106–107, 154–155, 158
Ahmed, Sara, 22, 36, 40–41, 50–52, 54–55
AIDS, 8, 24–26, 26, 37–38, 94–95, 166n106, 172n8. *See also* HIV
Aïnouz, Karim, 3, 38, 61, 67–68, 83–84
Airbnb, 41, 52, 56

animals, 5–6, 13, 14, 140–141, 155–156. *See also* sea creatures
antisocial thesis, the, 22–23, 40–41, 55–57
art house, 110–111
Ausente, 32–33, 111, 123–124, 125, 168n3

Baby, 109–110
Bachelard, Gaston, 1, 4–5, 59, 63–64
Balsom, Erika, 13–14, 17–18, 84, 97
Barcelona, 35–36, 44, 53–54
Barker, Jennifer, 20–21
Barthes, Roland, 12, 15
Beach: cinematic, 1–2, 8–9, 15–17, 19, 36, 69–72, 74–76, 79, 83–84, 86–88, 89–91, 97–98, 99–100, 105–106, 106–107, 154–155; sex on the, 89–90
Beira-mar, 64, 69–74, 81–82, 83
Berger, Marco, 3, 9, 12, 27, 38, 109–111, 126–127, 168n3
Bersani, Leo, 22–23, 40
blue humanities, 2–3, 161n2. *See also* blue turn
blue turn, 2–3, 161n2
Blum, Hester, 12, 81
bondage, 136, 147–148
boredom, 9, 112–116, 117, 122, 127

Buenos Aires, 113
Butler, Judith, 171n5

Call Me by Your Name, 112, 179n21
camming, online, 59–60
Campillo, Robin, 24–26
Carri, Albertina, 3, 38, 129–130, 132, 148, 151
Castro, Lucio, 3, 35–36, 37
Catcher in the Rye, 109, 179n18
children, 44, 49, 56, 63–64. *See also* reproductive futurity
church, 90–91, 92, 133–134, 136
Cinema Novo, 64–65
coming out, 56, 72, 84–85, 101–103, 105
conceptual displacement, 141, 150–151, 158
Contracorriente, 69, 84, 86–96
cruising, 11–12, 16, 36–37, 41
currents, 1, 3, 6, 88, 155

death, 24–26, 57, 74, 84, 87–89, 94, 95–96, 157, 166n106. *See also* drowning
DeLoughrey, Elizabeth, 6, 161n3
delta, 16–17
de Luca, Tiago, 115–116
documentary, 5, 13, 48, 57, 77–78
domesticity, 9, 39, 40–4, 45, 53, 54–56, 56–58, 89–91, 106
Downing, Lisa, 80–81
drowning, 21, 60, 84, 88, 97, 96, 106–107
Dyer, Richard, 42–43

Edelmann, Lee, 22–23, 40, 44
embodiment: water and, 2–3, 17–20, 24, 30, 78–79, 81–82, 117–121, 158–159; theories of, 20–22, 24, 29, 34, 119–122, 131–133, 143, 154–155

Epps, Brad, 31–32, 63, 79–81, 157, 172n8
estuary, 16–17
excision, queer, 106–107

faciality, 92–93
fallacy, of fluidity, 61–62, 63–64, 156–157
fish, 14–15, 17–18, 33, 91, 140–141
Freeman, Elizabeth, 22, 51, 52, 55, 57
Foster, David William, 28–30
Fortier, Anne-Marie, 101–102, 104–105
Fuentes-León, Javier, 3, 27, 69, 83–84, 168n3
futurity, queer, 23–24, 30, 36, 39, 53–54, 56–58, 66, 96, 142–143

Galt, Rosalind, 3, 46–47, 95–96, 104, 106–107, 110–112, 115, 122–123, 126
ghost, 84, 88–89, 91–93, 94, 97, 98, 102–103, 107
ghost face, 92–94
Grindr, 31, 37, 38, 41, 46, 57. *See also* hook-up apps
Guiraudie, Alain, 16, 69, 110, 168n3, 176n14

Halberstam, Jack, 9–10, 22, 49–50
Haigh, Andrew, 35, 38–39, 55–56, 122
Hammer, Barbara, 6–7, 129–132, 150
happiness, queer, 36, 40–41, 45, 50–52, 54–58, 142
hapticity, 2–3, 7, 9, 21–23, 27–28, 59–61, 71–73, 75–76, 78–79, 86–87, 96–97, 119–121, 124–126, 126–127, 133, 153–154, 158
Hayward, Eva, 6, 14
Helmreich, Stefan, 4
heteronormativity, 22, 28–29, 36, 40–41, 54–55, 67–68, 80–81, 89–90, 94–95, 106–107, 140, 155

historicity, queer, 104–106
Hittman, Eliza, 16, 110
HIV, 8, 24–26, 26, 37–38, 94–95, 166n106, 172n8. *See also* AIDS
home-coming, 102, 105–106
homonormativity, 39, 45, 55–56
homophobia, 36, 56, 74, 79, 83, 96, 106, 175n55
hook-up apps, 31, 38, 50, 57. *See also* Grindr
hyperobject, 4–5

immersion, 17–19, 20–22, 139
internet, 37, 59–60
intersexuality, 152–157
intersubjectivity, 120–121, 126–127

Jarman, Derek, 7, 85, 178n2
Jenkins, Barry, 110, 176n14
Jue, Melody, 2, 17–18, 141, 158. *See also* conceptual displacement

Klinefelter syndrome, 184n2

lake, 1, 8, 110, 130, 137, 142, 145–146
landscape, 17, 44, 47, 69–70, 87–88, 130–133, 138, 143–146, 151
lesbianism, 6–7, 28–29, 77, 129–133, 150–151. *See also* aesthetic, lesbian
Lindner, Katherina, 21–22
locker room, 11–12, 109–110
Lumière, Louis, 5
Lyra, Cris, 3, 64, 74–81

machismo, 27, 66
Madame Satã, 67–68
male gaze, 7, 12, 18, 91–92, 111, 117, 122–123
maricón, 27–28, 29, 121
Marks, Laura U., 19–20, 21–22, 87, 119–120, 121, 124

marriage, same-sex, 26, 31, 38, 40, 44, 51, 55, 57
Martel, Lucrecia, 9, 27, 30, 38, 71, 119
Martin, Deborah, 73–74, 119, 153–154, 158
Masculinity, 28–29, 59–60, 66–67, 90–96, 103
masturbation, 10, 25, 46, 106–107, 131, 134, 137, 148–150, 183n50
Matzembacher, Filipe, 27, 59–60, 83
melodrama, 50, 56, 72, 93
memory, 16, 17–18, 21–22, 84, 96
Mentz, Steve, 13–14, 161n3
Merleau-Ponty, Maurice, 22
money shot, 42, 149–150
monogamy, 40, 42–43, 45, 56
monstrosity, 6, 156
Moratto, Alexandre, 3, 74–81
Mulvey, Laura, 92
Muñoz, José Esteban, 22–24, 30, 39, 57, 64, 66, 142–144, 153–154, 183n38

Nagib, Lúcia, 4, 6–66, 73, 79–80, 82, 161n4
nakedness, 1, 7, 10, 16, 22, 33, 59, 72, 78, 85, 90, 97, 109, 112–113, 116–117, 119, 127, 142
neoliberalism, 32, 66
New Argentine Cinema, 30
New Gay Sincerity, 43–44, 45–46, 57, 170n30
New Maricón Cinema, 27–28, 29, 121
New Queer Cinema, 7–8, 25–27, 28–29, 30, 37, 44–45, 50
New Queer Realism, 30, 38, 39, 40, 44–46, 51, 56, 154, 158, 168n6, 170n30

ocean, 1–2, 5–6, 8–9, 12–15, 17–18, 36–37, 64–66, 69–70, 73–74, 75, 78–81, 81–82, 83–86, 87–88, 91,

ocean *(continued)*
  97–99, 105, 106–107, 133, 140–141, 155–156, 158, 161n3, 162n25
orientation, 1, 17–18, 22, 29–30, 51, 59–60, 62, 74, 158, 181n7
Ozon, François, 9, 87

Painlevé, Jean, 5–6
parenting, same-gender, 31, 38, 40, 44–45, 57
penis, 116–117, 136–137
phenomenology, 18–20, 29, 30, 71–72, 111–112, 115–116, 121–122, 153–154
Podalsky, Laura, 71–72
pornochanchada, 67
pornography: feminist, 129–130, 131, 148–149; generic conventions, 11, 41–43, 92, 124–125, 138–140, 146, 181n9, 181n14; postpornography, 132–133, 133–138, 129–140, 146, 149–150, 158
pregnancy, 90–91
Puenzo, Lucía, 3, 16, 27, 83, 152–154, 184n2

Quebramar, 64, 74–81

race, 22, 30, 61–64, 67–68, 77–79, 79–81, 81–82, 163n38
racism, 79, 163n38. *See also* race
realism, cinematic, 25–26, 38, 43–47, 56–58, 154–155, 170n30, 184n2. *See also* New Queer Realism
Reolon, Marcio, 27, 59–61, 69–74, 83
reproductive futurity, 22–23, 44–45, 84, 89–90, 94–96
Rich, B. Ruby, 26–27, 44–45, 67
river, 1, 4, 6–7, 24–26, 140–141
road movie, 129–130
Rocha, Glauber, 65, 173n22

sand, 2, 13, 14, 15, 19, 72, 77–78, 85–87, 95–96, 103–104, 105
sauna, 8, 33, 110, 119–120, 123–124, 125–126
Schoonover, Karl, 3, 46–47, 95–96, 104, 106–107, 110–112, 115, 122–123, 126–127
scopic cinema, 11–12, 19–20, 71–72, 123, 125, 139, 144, 146, 151
script: filmic, 41, 47, 60, 71, 88, 117, 125–126; happiness, 40, 45, 50–52, 55–57; typographic, 156
sea creatures: on screen, 2, 5–6, 14–15, 140–141, 153–154; turtles, 100, 156–157; anemones, 140–141, 155–156; jellyfish, 14–15, 33, 140–141; mythical, 5–6. *See also* animals
sertão, 64–66, 173n22, 173n23
sexuality: cinematic, 1–3, 8, 9–10, 14–15, 18, 24, 28–29, 30, 34, 59–61, 61–63, 73, 94–95, 109–111, 137–138, 140–141, 146–147, 156–157; sexual intercourse, 41–43, 59–61, 71–72, 86–87, 103–104, 115–116, 133–134, 136–137, 140–141, 147–150; sex toys, 131, 133, 136–137, 140–141, 147–148
shoreline, 7, 15–16, 69, 77, 83–84, 86, 88–89, 90–91, 95–96, 97–99, 106–107, 134, 144–145
shower, 7–8, 9, 11–12, 32–33, 46, 109–110, 111, 119, 123–124
Sifuentes-Jáuregui, Ben, 103
Sobchack, Vivian, 19–20
Sócrates, 64, 74–81
Solomonoff, Julia, 110
soundtrack, 24–25, 53–54, 60–61, 105, 173n22
slowness: cinematic technique, 2, 7, 30, 38, 72–73, 109–111, 112, 116–117, 119–121, 126–127; faux-slow,

122–126; slow cinema, 110–112, 112–117, 120–121, 126–127
spectrality, 52–53, 84, 91–93
Starosielski, Nicole, 6
stereotype, 45, 49, 66–67, 68, 69, 72, 111, 156–157
structure of feeling, 40, 46–47, 50–52, 71–73, 112, 121–122
Subero, Gus, 27–30
swimming pool, 1–2, 9–12, 15, 16, 17, 19, 33, 61, 100, 109–110, 113, 117–119, 120–121, 144, 163n38

temporality, queer, 33, 39, 106
transnational: belonging, 34, 85, 97–98, 101–102, 104–106; cinema, 13, 161n4; movement, 84–85, 96–97

Urbain, Jean-Didier, 15–16, 88
utopia, 31–32, 63–64, 64–66, 74–76, 82, 95, 101, 107, 156–157

Venkatesh, Vinodh, 27–30, 121, 153–155, 158
voyeurism, 12, 32, 37, 111, 116–117, 125–126, 137–138, 18–150

waves, 7, 12–15, 23, 36, 61, 70–72, 77–78, 87, 98, 100, 133, 162n26
Webb, Jennifer, 16, 19, 79–80, 85–86, 106
Weekend, 35, 38–39, 55–56, 122
wet globalisation, 13–14
wetness, 5, 18–19, 140–141, 155–156. *See also* wet globalisation
Whishaw, Ben, 109–110
Williams, Linda, 42–43, 92, 129, 131, 139, 146–147, 148, 149, 151, 181n9, 181n14

XXY, 16, 83, 110, 153–155, 184n2

Y tu mamá también, 10

www.ingramcontent.com/pod-product-compliance
Lightning Source LLC
Chambersburg PA
CBHW070805230426
43665CB00017B/2490